FIGHTING FOR HITLER

In loving memory of

my father
Gregory Labriola
United States Air Force 1941–1945

and

my father-in-law
Alfred Schwarz
Deutsche Wehrmacht 1938–1945

FIGHTING FOR HITLER

First-hand Accounts of German Soldiers at the Frontline

Dr Patrick Labriola

Pen & Sword
MILITARY
AN IMPRINT OF PEN & SWORD BOOKS LTD.
YORKSHIRE – PHILADELPHIA

First published in Great Britain in 2025 by
PEN AND SWORD MILITARY
An imprint of
Pen & Sword Books Limited
Yorkshire – Philadelphia

ISBN 978 1 03612 457 1

A CIP catalogue record for this book is available from the British Library.

Typeset in Times New Roman 11.5/14.5 by
SJmagic DESIGN SERVICES, India.
Printed and bound in the UK by CPI Group (UK) Ltd.

The Publisher's authorised representative in the EU for product safety is Authorised Rep Compliance Ltd., Ground Floor, 71 Lower Baggot Street, Dublin D02 P593, Ireland. www.arccompliance.com

For a complete list of Pen & Sword titles please contact
PEN & SWORD BOOKS LIMITED
George House, Units 12 & 13, Beevor Street, Off Pontefract Road,
Barnsley, South Yorkshire, S71 1HN, England
E-mail: enquiries@pen-and-sword.co.uk
Website: www.pen-and-sword.co.uk

or

PEN AND SWORD BOOKS
1950 Lawrence Rd, Havertown, PA 19083, USA
E-mail: uspen-and-sword@casematepublishers.com
Website: www.penandswordbooks.com

MIX
Paper | Supporting responsible forestry
FSC® C013604

Contents

CHAPTER II – THE NAVY

CHAPTER III – WESTERN AND SOUTHERN CAMPAIGNS

CHAPTER IV – THE FALL OF THE REICH

CHAPTER V – ALLIED PRISONER-OF-WAR CAMPS

Preface

I. Idea for the book

My personal introduction to the testimonies of the Third Reich started during family gatherings at the house of my German in-laws. As we sat around the table, conversations often drifted towards recollections of the war years and the hardships endured by those who lived through them. It became increasingly clear to me that these personal narratives were fragile artefacts of history, ones that risked fading into obscurity if not captured and preserved. I began to believe that someone had to take on the responsibility of safeguarding these invaluable historical testimonies, ensuring they would not be lost to the sands of time.

My fascination with the power of oral history deepened in this period while preparing a lecture series at the University of Bonn in Germany. The topic of my course was "America in the 1920s and 30s", and as I delved into my research, I stumbled upon Studs Terkel's groundbreaking work, *Hard Times: An Oral History of the Great Depression*. Terkel's book added an entirely new dimension to my understanding of American history in this period. It showed how the narratives of ordinary people could shed valuable light on the details of historical events in a way that traditional history books often failed to do. I found myself captivated by the rich tapestry of human experiences and emotions that oral history unveiled.

Simultaneously, my curiosity led me to explore the "US Federal Writers' Project", a noble undertaking in the 1930s which included preserving the testimonies of African Americans who had endured slavery, the Civil War, and Reconstruction, as well as testimonies by Native Americans who recalled their way of life before and after the closing of the American West. While the background of these two groups was vastly different from that of Germans who found themselves on the losing side of World War II, the methodology of oral history revealed to me the universal importance of personal testimonies in understanding the intricacies of history. It became evident that, regardless of the circumstances, personal accounts offer a unique and vital perspective on the past. This insight became the driving force behind my mission to document the experiences of those who lived through the era of the Third Reich, and is the foundation upon which this book is built. The personal stories in this oral history fit together like pieces of a mosaic to create a vivid picture of the past, and they come to life through the language of ordinary Germans who experienced the tumultuous era of the Third Reich and the horrors of war.

II. Problems in finding interview partners

The difficulties in finding individuals willing to share their wartime experiences were formidable. The protests by German students in the late 1960s against the war generation had a profound impact on oral history, causing many of those who had lived through the war to close up and refuse to discuss their experiences. The accusations hurled by the youth of that era, coupled with the war generation's inability to provide satisfactory explanations or to defend themselves, further deepened the chasm of silence. In contrast with the "greatest generation" in America, England, France, and Russia, ordinary German soldiers remained a voiceless "silent generation". Consequently, I found myself at an unexpected advantage as a foreigner. As an outsider, I approached these individuals without preconceived judgments or condemnation. I was neither involved in the war nor did I have family members who had died at the hands of the Nazis. In fact, I was willing to listen objectively to their past, and this neutrality seemed to encourage many to open up to me and to share their stories, often for the first time in decades. Personal referrals from my German wife, German friends, and former interview partners also played a crucial role in convincing some individuals to talk to me. Each interview was arduous work which involved sometimes travelling great distances to witnesses' homes, having coffee and cake with them, answering personal questions about my life, and vouching for my honest intentions in conducting the project. Trust is an essential factor when dealing with such sensitive accounts, and personal connections often helped to bridge that trust gap.

The best interviews, I discovered, were those that were not overly rehearsed with a rigid set of questions. Instead, I allowed each witness to speak freely about their experiences, gently guiding the conversation through open-ended questions. This approach allowed the participants to share their memories and emotions more freely. Many of them expressed deep frustration at the disconnection between themselves and their own children. They complained that their offspring had little understanding of where they had been, what they had lived through, or the sacrifices they had made after the war. Another challenge was the fact that it often took many years for some to find the courage to speak about these deeply personal and painful experiences. Some only began to open up in their seventies, eighties, or even nineties, while many others carried their untold stories with them to the grave. The passage of time acted as both a catalyst for sharing and a pressing reminder of the need to record these accounts before they were lost forever due to advancing old age. This book, therefore, stands as a testament to those willing to break their silence, the importance of impartial listening, and the enduring significance of personal testimony in understanding the complex tapestry of history.

III. Methodology

I adopted an unconventional approach in conducting these interviews. Instead of relying on a list of preformulated questions, I engaged in open-ended conversations in German that encouraged the participants to freely recount their memories from childhood to the end of the war. This approach allowed for a more natural and unfiltered narrative, and enabled the witnesses to speak about matters that were important to them. The interviews were conducted in a comprehensive manner, often lasting anywhere from thirty minutes to three hours. The open-ended nature of the discussions permitted them to express themselves at their own pace, ensuring that no crucial details were omitted. Every interview was recorded on tape, later in digital form, and the contents were carefully examined through multiple listening sessions. This process was essential for capturing the full depth of the experiences shared.

Subsequently, I arranged individual passages from the interviews thematically according to the chapters in the book, each covering a specific topic. For example, the first chapter is on the Eastern Front, and the second chapter covers military service in the navy. The following chapters include the Western and Southern campaigns and the Fall of the Reich. Finally, the book covers POW camps, either in the German Rhineland at the end of the war, or American, French, or Russian POW camps in these respective countries. Each interview passage is accompanied by a short description of the historical witness, sometimes along with personal documents and photographs. I do not relate my personal feelings in the book, but rather present the information in a mosaic form so that the readers are able to establish their own conclusions. Supplemental or diverging information is provided in footnotes to clarify or elaborate on the testimonies. The book has taken over thirty years to compile, edit, and translate, and comprises over 100 interviews with thousands of hours of recorded documentation.

IV. Interviews, editing, and translation work

In order to create a relaxed atmosphere with each interview partner, I first questioned each person about their name, their place of birth, and their first memories of the Third Reich. From this point onwards, the interviews followed in chronological order, with me asking follow-up questions on important topics. In the initial stages of the oral history project, I sometimes attempted to direct the conversation in a certain direction, or placed emphasis on certain topics such as "the deportation of the Jews", but quickly discovered that each person had their own personal narrative that they wished to follow. This realization caused me to avoid asking too many questions, allowing them to follow their train of thought that they had been holding back for so many years. At times, certain witnesses asked me to turn off the recording device in order to reveal traumatic events that had happened during this period or because they could no longer continue with the interview out of sheer grief. In each interview, however, I tried to capture the quintessential experience that defined their experience in this period. Often, it involved one day, one event, or even a single moment.

After having recorded each interview, I was able to listen to it several times, noting down the events discussed and the time of the specific topics in the interview. These unique experiences were then placed in one of several chapters that had emerged in the course of compiling the work. The translation work that followed was the most arduous and time-consuming task. For each testimony, I often had to weigh shades of meaning between certain German terms such as "deportation", "removal", "relocation", and "transport" and also provide unified terminology for historical terms from the Third Reich such as "Reichsarbeitsdienst" or "Waffen SS". By far the greatest challenge was the identification and transcription of geographic locations and the confirmation of their validity during specific years of the war through the Internet and secondary sources. In the event of diverging or supplemental information, I offer footnotes to the reader for further explanation.

The personal photographs and documents in this work are meant to provide a face to respective interview partners. Many Germans were bombed out and lost all possessions, or their homes fell to occupied territories in the East so that they could not provide me with any personal documents. Some interview partners wished to remain anonymous and refused the use of their names or personal documents in this publication.

The question of subjectivity in compiling, editing, and translating this work also needs to be addressed. One can argue that the questions asked by me in these interviews as well as the subsequent passages chosen for the book constitute my personal narrative which steered the work in a certain direction. This is certainly valid because no book exists without any personal perspective at all. The same holds true for the translation work which compelled me to choose one word over another in describing historical accounts. I was also limited to individuals who were willing to conduct an interview with me. Although I travelled widely and interviewed a vast number of witnesses, I received only a cross-section of average Germans who had experienced the war as children, housewives, soldiers, or uninvolved parties. Although I often tried to interview a representative group from the remaining Jewish community in Germany through friends, associations, and religious groups, there was never any real willingness on their part to speak to me. The same holds true for Germans who held positions of authority in the Third Reich or were responsible for military command, the deportation of the Jews, or atrocities committed. Therefore, this work comprises interviews with average Germans who had experienced some form of the war in military campaigns or in prisoner-of-war camps. It is therefore not a book about the deportation of the Jews or the well-documented atrocities committed against the Jews. This important research has already been conducted by the Simon Wiesenthal Centre in Vienna, among many others, who are more qualified and competent in this important field.

V. Findings and conclusion

Every German experienced the reality of Nazi Germany in a different manner, depending on the respective year, geographic location, their gender, and whether they were members of the armed forces. Men who served in the German Wehrmacht on the Eastern Front certainly experienced more atrocities than their fellow soldiers who spent the war years in Paris, the Benelux countries, or Italy. In fact, life in the different branches of the military varied enormously: Many young Germans were relieved to join the navy and to avoid the hardships of the infantry, or worse yet, to be conscripted to the Armed Forces SS [Waffen SS]. Captivity under the various Allied powers differed enormously, whether in re-education camps in the UK, on farms in the USA, in French coal mines, or in camps in the Russian Caucasus. Finally, countless German soldiers held in Russian prisoner-of-war camps were first able to return to Germany in 1955, ten years after the conclusion of the war after negotiations with German Federal Chancellor Adenauer. Some former German soldiers shared their experiences as prisoners held by the Allied forces, offering a valuable perspective on what they considered fair treatment during captivity by the English, Americans, French, and Russians. Generally, the most favourable assessments were given to the British and Americans for their treatment of prisoners. There are occasional reports of less favourable conditions during captivity under the French. However, the harshest treatment is often associated with captivity under the Russians.

Many historical witnesses from this period acknowledged their mistakes in not having questioned the authority of the state and not having personally taken action. Some asserted that Germany is a country of law and order and that Germans of this generation typically followed the directives of those in power without opposing the most oppressive laws. For instance, many did not question the enforced practice of Jews wearing the Star of David armband, the prohibition of Germans from patronizing Jewish-owned businesses, or the routine house searches by the Gestapo for the removal and relocation of Jews. All of this was facilitated through the implementation of Nazi legislation, including the Nuremberg Laws, which ordinary Germans acquiesced to as mandated by the regime. This deference to authority and adherence to the law is deeply ingrained in German history, as evidenced in the literary works of numerous prominent German authors such as Heinrich von Kleist, Franz Kafka, and Heinrich Böll and warrants comprehensive research beyond the scope of this study.

As I did not personally live during the Nazi era, my understanding is derived solely from research and witness accounts. Although I have conducted hundreds of interviews, many of which were not published in this book, I did not personally experience this historical period. Consequently, it is essential to understand that our contemporary world is marked by global technology with innovations such as the Internet, mobile phones, WhatsApp, Instagram, and Facebook. In contrast, information during the Nazi era was conveyed by radio, at party rallies, and by word-of-mouth, all of which were closely monitored by the Nazi party. Entire families were sent to concentration camps or sentenced to death for dissention, or for arbitrary reasons such as race, religion, sexuality, and political conviction. This is evident through the murder of six million Jews, and hundreds of thousands of Gypsies, communists, homosexuals, and regime opponents.

My intention in compiling this oral history was not to determine guilt or to seek answers to predefined questions, but rather to preserve the testimonies of those who lived during the Third Reich, allowing readers to draw their own conclusions. The work also functions as a treasure trove of recorded interviews to facilitate further academic research on this topic while preserving the actual voices of those who lived during this distressing and horrendous period in German history.

Acknowledgements

I would like to extend my sincere gratitude to several individuals for their invaluable contributions to this book. Their support, encouragement, and expertise have been instrumental in bringing this project to fruition.

First and foremost, I extend my deepest appreciation to my wife, Elisabeth, who recommended numerous interview partners during her work as a physiotherapist and gave me the opportunity to conduct the majority of these interviews. I would also like to thank my son, Nicholas, for his critical assessment of the book and suggestions for its improvement. Many thanks to my friend and fellow translator, Jürgen Schiffer, for his endless insistence that I complete this oral history after so many decades of work. I am also thankful to numerous friends and acquaintances whose recommendations opened the door and allowed me to speak with relatives who were in the war.

Finally, I am grateful to all my interview partners who took the time to share their life stories and had enough faith in me that I would write an honest depiction of their lives.

CHAPTER I

THE EASTERN FRONT

Nuremberg Reich Party Rallies (1937/1938)

Alfred Schwarz was born in 1919 in Lindau on Lake Constance in Bavaria. He remembers marching past Hitler at the Nuremberg Reich Party Rally in 1937 during his pre-military training.

As preparation for the Nuremberg Reich Party Rally in 1937, we had to march for weeks with a sandbag in our knapsacks that weighed 20 pounds or 20 kilograms – I don't know anymore – in order to train for our stay in Nuremberg where we were supposed to march past Hitler with a knapsack on our backs. And that was so strenuous because our camp was situated on a rather steep hill, and we had to march back up the hill in the afternoon heat with the packs on our backs. That was the preparation for the Nuremberg Reich Party Rally.[1]

Can you describe the atmosphere at the Nuremberg Reich Party Rally?

Yes. I can. For the Nuremberg Reich Party Rally, we made these preparations and our uniforms had to be flawless. We practiced polishing our boots so that they would shine as much as possible. And then when we marched past, it became evident that this was completely useless. That was because so much dust was stirred up when the thousands of people marched past. Besides, we came from a camp not too far from the party rally grounds which was connected to the grounds by a dusty road so that we were completely covered in dust and the best boot polishing was entirely senseless. We marched past Hitler and naturally the scenery was managed excellently. The directors did a very good job. It certainly impressed everyone. It impressed me so much – I remember exactly – that I wrote a postcard home to my parents in which I said something like: "Whoever looks into the Führer's eyes will be inspired his entire life". I openly admit it. But, of course, I think a lot differently today. And that's not just since yesterday, but rather since 1945.

Anton Schmitz was born in Wachendorf in the Eifel in 1917. He remembers attending the Nuremberg Reich Party Rally in 1938 during his time in the Reich Labour Service.

I was in Nuremberg at the Reich Party Rally. Forty-eight thousand workers were deployed to Langwasser with shiny spades. I was there as a simple worker. They prepared us for this in the Ehrenhof building in Düsseldorf and brought us by train. We were deployed because Hitler was coming. At that time everything was for Hitler. The Nuremberg Reich Party Rally was the "Party Rally of Peace". That's what they called it. I was with guys who were working together. Naturally there was the day when we had to march – 48,000 men carrying spades. It was certainly exciting. We were in Camp Langwasser in Nuremberg for four or five days in tents. There was a rolling kitchen that prepared good food just like in the army. That was all in one camp. We were allowed to go out, but everyone had to be in bed by 10:00 pm. There were military rules. The men were from everywhere in Germany, but there weren't any difficulties. Nothing. There were isolated incidents of men drinking the whole night. That always existed. But, in general, everything was organized 100 per cent and tip top. Everything. There were no disasters. I have to say that.

How long was Hitler there?

He arrived by car and took his place on stage. We fell into formation and marched past him in rows of twelve. It didn't take long until we had marched past. But not everyone marched past. There were maybe 1,000 men who marched past of the 48,000 workers. It was supposed to be a real honour to Hitler at the "Party Rally of Peace". You also have this today. The parties all have their own party conventions. Don't they?

The Anschluss of Austria (March 1938)

Alfred Schwarz recalls the German annexation of Austria as a German soldier.

In March 1938 we were transported in cattle cars from Augsburg to an unknown destination. We had live ammunition for our rifles, but didn't know where we were going. We travelled through the night, and the train didn't stop at any of the stations – only on the outskirts – so that we didn't know where we were. On the morning of 11 March 1938, we arrived in Vienna at the freight train station where we were told to leave the train. We marched through Vienna with drums beating – the music ahead and us behind. To our disappointment, we discovered that only a few people were standing along the streets. The men had their hands in their pockets and watched us with a frown on their faces so that we had the feeling that we were very unwelcome guests. That quickly changed a few days later because Hitler came to Vienna and stated in his speech that he was proclaiming to history that he had fulfilled his task of transferring his homeland Austria to the German Reich. There was thunderous applause. People fell into each other's arms and were enthusiastic and cheered. And some of them were drenched in tears. And I don't think that these were all SS men who had come from the old Reich, but rather I believe that some Viennese or other Austrians were along who were carried away in this enthusiasm.

We spent several weeks in Vienna. It was wonderful because we had the chance to go to the theatre in the evenings. In the Viennese Opera, there was so-called "Standing Room for Officers" which cost fifty pfennigs admission. You had to stand in the back. But there weren't any officers around to be seen. I was the only one from our company who was interested in something like that. I stood in the back and listened to the Viennese Opera with great enthusiasm. Although I was far in the back, I had my binoculars along and was able to follow the performance. We were supposed to be the guard regiment in Vienna with our troops. This didn't happen for whatever reason. We were then quartered privately in a village between Vienna and the border on the Danube River – it was probably the Czechoslovakian border. While we stayed in Vienna, we were in the Rennweg barracks. It was there that we experienced the training of Austrian recruits who were in the barracks along with us. They were treated in such an unbelievably inhumane way, which we had never experienced in our training. They were chased around like rabbits and treated mercilessly which was very unpleasant for us. Another problem was that there were bugs all over the barracks so that we had problems to get rid of them. And this was during a time of peace. If something like that happened during the war, then it was natural. You had to reckon with something like that. But we couldn't believe that something like that existed in Vienna.

We were very happy to be transferred back to Augsburg after several weeks. We were welcomed like the victors of a war. We were deeply touched by this and enthusiastic that we had completed this Austrian campaign so successfully. Everyone who was along received a medal. The Austrian medal was awarded, and it was the first medal that we received as soldiers. I have to add that we became part of the German armed forces in the autumn of 1937. At this time, compulsive military service was for one year. We were hardly in the military when it was extended to two years so that we were soldiers until 1939. I believe that we were supposed to be discharged in October 1939, but the war came in between which started with the campaign in Poland on 1 September 1939.

The Invasion of Poland (September 1939)

Alfred Schwarz entered the war on 1 September 1939 in Poland as an infantryman. After a week of sporadic fighting, he was shot in the upper thigh and returned home to a military hospital in Germany.

What did the beginning of the war on 1 September 1939 mean for you?

We were immediately told to start marching in the direction of Poland from Augsburg where we were stationed after the so-called Austrian campaign. And we were deployed to Upper Silesia – and I was an infantryman – we weren't yet a motorized unit like we were later near the end of the war when the infantry was completely motorized. Unfortunately, this was not the case with us. We had to march on foot. And every day we marched ahead 20 or 25 kilometres and crossed the German-Polish border which at that time was in Upper Silesia in southwestern Poland. And we arrived in a town whose name I don't remember anymore. It was during the first days of the war. And we were quartered in a private house there. We were controlled so strictly that we had to reckon with being shot immediately for looting if we had even opened up a jar of marmalade in the private house where we were staying. The house belonged to a Pole who was no longer there. This is how strict the Germans were at that time. I don't know whether this was the case later on because I wasn't a soldier for the entire war.

We then marched on to a village, or a small town in any case, which they told us was inhabited only by Jews. And at dawn we marched into this village, and we had to make the people go outside onto the market square. They were still in bed and were totally surprised. The secret police received them – "a criminal organization" as they were later called at the Nuremberg Trials. We didn't know what happened to these people. We also didn't ask. That was the mistake that many of us made during the Nazi era. We said that if we didn't know, nothing would happen to us.

And I still remember – at that time I was a non-commissioned officer and squad leader which meant that I had approximately twelve soldiers under me – I was at the head of my squad and went into the houses. I went into one house where two incredibly beautiful young women were lying in bed – I really have to say women – and I felt so bad about making them get out of bed and go outside in their nightgowns. I had to do it because I was the head of my squad, and I would never have been able to make an exemption without getting myself into a lot of trouble. This is the way it was.

We had been marching for several days when we suddenly received orders that we were to be loaded onto trucks and transported approximately 80 kilometres, as far as I remember, through enemy territory to the Vistula River. We were supposed to establish a bridgehead there on the other side of the Vistula. We were transported there, and we wanted to take the bridge by storm. When we tried to do so, it went up in flames. It was a wooden bridge, and the Poles were ready and let the bridge go up in flames so that we couldn't cross. On the following morning, a reconnaissance patrol was supposed to cross the Vistula and the sergeant 1st class, the commander of the reconnaissance patrol, ordered me and my troops to join this reconnaissance patrol. We were brought over the Vistula in boats by assault engineers, and on the other side of the Vistula there was a steep embankment of about 10 or 12 metres. And, of course, we wanted to try to climb up this embankment and establish a bridgehead there, or at least determine which enemy troops were there, when we were attacked by machine gun fire from above. It was so severe that the commander of this reconnaissance patrol ordered us to retreat. The assault engineers had already rowed back in their boats in the meantime, and we had to swim. My machine gunner was a non-swimmer and drowned immediately without a shot. Several of my men held their heads above water and were shot. I didn't have any problems because I was able to swim underwater. Of course, I threw away my rifle, my steel helmet, my gas mask, and my belt so that I was able to survive. And I was able to safely reach the shore on this side of the Vistula.

On the previous day when we arrived in this village on the Vistula, we captured two, three, or four Poles – I don't remember anymore – young Poles who were civilians. They were searched, and it was determined that each of them had a straight razor with them. I now say, and I said it then, that they were probably on the road and wanted to shave now and then and that's why they took the straight razors along with them. That was obvious. But our company commander saw it differently. He said that they were spies, sharp shooters, who had to be shot immediately. Then he looked for volunteers who were willing to shoot them, and nobody stepped forward from the entire company. He then ordered several soldiers to do it. They had the task of shooting these three men – and they did so "successfully". It was carried out against the wall of the windmill where we were spending the night. We were so tired and so exhausted that we only realized half asleep that they had been shot. And these poor men lost their lives simply because they had straight razors along with them. By not volunteering, we showed that we disapproved of and condemned the whole matter. But that's the way it was. And that was the beginning of the war.

I'm not able to tell you in detail what happened afterwards because I was injured on 9 September in Poland. After our reconnaissance patrol wasn't successful, we were given instructions to return to our unit which was about 60 kilometres away. And then we were loaded onto trucks again and transported back. But we didn't reach our unit and instead came into the basin of a valley. And the Poles encircled it and shot at us from all sides. We received orders to attack one side – they were shooting at us from all directions – but it was completely hopeless. We were then driven back by the Poles, and during the retreat I was injured. The medics carried me onto one of the trucks, and we noticed that the Poles' artillery fire was slowly getting closer so that we had to reckon with the truck being blown up. This didn't happen because we luckily had radio equipment along. Our radio operator was able to inform our troops, who were heading in our direction, that we had fallen into this trap by the Poles. They quickly came to us and freed us just in time before the Poles shot at us with their artillery. I was brought to the military hospital and then to the replacement troops. This ended the first part of my military career.

Operation Barbarossa (1941)

H. Schmidt was sent to Romania in May 1941 in order to secure the border with Bessarabia. He remembers the start of the war against Russia on 22 June 1941.

The preparations for Russia were very strange. We were on the Prut River which borders Bessarabia. And Bessarabia was handed over to Russia at the end of 1939, or the beginning of 1940. Romania had to hand over Bessarabia to Russia.[2] We were quartered in a castle on the Prut River. And we always saw the Russians on the other side, dancing and singing around the fire in the evenings. It was a very peaceful atmosphere. And then one day, maybe one or two weeks before 22 June, a rumour circulated among us that the Russians would allow the German Army to march through because the Germans wanted to occupy the Persian oil wells. This rumour spread around. We weren't officially informed by our superiors, but people talked about it. They said: "It's strange that they're sitting over there dancing and singing, and we're supposed to get permission to march through". And then we were suddenly notified one night that we were to attack on the following day. It was something entirely unexpected for us. We had previously thought about it. But nothing had happened. And then suddenly on that night we were notified, and in the morning we started. And it became clear that it meant war with Russia. And it wasn't all that easy because we first had to cross the Prut River on the border.[3] And the Russians were prepared for what took place. You could gather that something was going on. We had been told that we would march through to the Persian oil wells, and this proved to be completely false.

But the Russians on the other side were naturally ready for battle. It was very unpleasant for us because we hardly had any tanks in the south. We didn't have any German tank units on the Bessarabia front. And we met heavy resistance from Russian tank units. We became acquainted with the infamous T-34 tanks which we didn't know until then. This tank was totally immune to our 3.7-centimetre anti-tank artillery. We were unable to seriously harm the T-34. There were some very unpleasant situations. I remember that it was very difficult for our soldiers to carry around some of the equipment. Someone had to carry around the equipment for the flash ranging station, and the heaviest thing was the radio set. It was such a large case you had to drag around. And this soldier ran into a T-34. It was in June, and he fled into a corn field. He ran around the cornfield, lying on the ground to the right and left. And they ran over the radio set that was strapped to his shoulder. He couldn't quite see what was going on. I remember when he came back, he said: "Man, they ran over the radio set".

The T-34 was a very unpleasant and rude surprise for us. It took a long time for the German Army to find an equivalent to this tank. This was our first encounter. But it improved somewhat because of course we received reinforcements and supplies. But the lack of tanks had a negative effect on us because we were all trained foot soldiers. What saved us a bit was the assault gun. It was first deployed in Greece although I didn't see it used. I only saw it on the streets. The Germans drove past with assault guns. It was a tank without the dome. It had a gun, but could only shoot straight ahead. Of course, it had a long and powerful cannon. Tanks normally have their guns mounted on a rotating dome; the assault gun was only directed forward, and the entire fully-tracked vehicle had to turn around. And that saved us a bit because even the T-34 wasn't a worthy opponent of the assault guns. But, of course, it wasn't so easy to turn the assault gun around to get the tanks in sight. And we didn't have many assault guns because their importance first became known there. We first discovered that a division with a limited number of effective assault guns was useful against tanks. That was our first impression in Russia.

The Gates of Moscow (1941/1942)

Hans Nahr was born in Aschersleben in Saxony Anhalt in 1918. He recalls the Battle of Moscow from October 1941 to January 1942.

I was in the Army Group Centre for the most part – once in a while we were brought by train to Rzhev – I remember that – but we were mainly in Yukhnov, Roslavl, Tula, and Moscow. We made it as far as Moscow – but never made it into the city. It was shortly before Christmas 1941, and it was bitter cold – I'll tell you. Bitter cold. We moved in the direction of Kaluga – it was a larger town – and there was snow and -52°C. We marched through the entire night. I don't know how we were able to withstand it. We were frozen to the bone. The horses didn't have anything to drink because the water was frozen solid. We could have gone to a river, but in Kaluga there simply wasn't any water. We took out barrels of gasoline and set fire to it and melted snow the entire day so that the horses would have water. It was horrible. We were in a barn – the kind we have at home – with a wooden frame. We had to take the horses out of there because they were devouring the wooden posts. It cost us a lot of material.

I had my normal summer clothing on. We didn't have anything else. We wore our uniforms and summer coats and cotton finger gloves. The shoe wear was so light that we easily froze. It was really horrible. We never made it into Moscow. I remember when we had to retreat. There was a horrible canyon, and we moved into the shooting – some guns slipped and took the horses with them and fell into the canyon – I still remember that. It was after 20 January [1942]. Our sergeant major took a look at the situation and said: "See how you get them out of there. I'll be in the next village. There's less traffic there". All the animals froze to death. When you arrived somewhere as a gunner or a soldier, you received your quarters and lay down and went to sleep. You couldn't do that as a driver when you had horses. You had to find a stable for them.

You had to make sure that they had something to eat. We were really worse off. Another thing that was horrible were the long marches to the East and back. We had the bad luck that we had been surrounded a few times and couldn't get out anymore. The shooting made you crazy, and you were hardly able to sleep. Replacement battalions had to come in and get you out of there. But a lot of men died.

We were quartered in private homes because we couldn't sleep in the snow. The lice started – I'll tell you – you couldn't stay clean, and everyone had lice. The lice weren't the worst thing in the private homes, but rather the bedbugs. When you got bit by a louse, you were able to catch it. But when you got bit by a bedbug, it was already gone. That's why we had to sleep with the lights on. As soon as the lights were off, they came down from the ceiling again. That was horrible.

The Crimea (1942)

H. Schmidt recalls fighting with the 11th Army for control of the Crimea in May of 1942.

We went in the direction of the Crimea which was the brunt of our attack. There are thick books about the breakthrough to the Crimea. Our superior commander was General Field Marshall von Manstein. He is well known and wrote large books about it: *Lost Victories*. You could only enter the Crimea through a single stretch of land – the Isthmus of Perekop. It was so incredibly fortified by the Russians. We were only able to gain control of the Isthmus in several stages. And when we reached Sevastopol that was the end of it. That took time. I had already left. I wasn't there anymore. Sevastopol must have been in July 1942. I wasn't on the Crimea anymore. I was there for the recapture of the Kerch Peninsula in May. The Russians landed to our backs in Kerch. That created a very difficult situation for us. The so-called Parpach position before Kerch was the most challenging. We were in a very bad situation there and were almost desperate. And we started feeling good again when Operation Bustard Hunt started in May. And we retook Kerch. The Russians had direct supply lines from the Caucasus because the distance from the Taman Peninsula to Kerch was very short. And the Russian Air Force drove us to the point of insanity from the other side. For them it was just a stroll. They came from the Caucasus, flew right across the Parpach position, and let the bombs fall.

In Germany at that time there were so-called wish concerts on the radio – television didn't exist yet. Among our soldiers we would say: "What do the soldiers of the Crimean Army want to hear? – The sound of a German airplane again". For the Russians it was so easy. The stretch of land to the Caucasus was just a stone's throw away. It was a question of a few minutes. We could see how they flung open the hatches. There's nothing so horrible as when you hear the rumbling of the bombs – they turned end over end in the air. It's so horrible. When they bombed the cities in Germany, they flew higher – but these came so low that you could see how they flung open the hatches, and the bombs spun to the ground. And we hardly had any anti-aircraft artillery, and no air defence, no fighter planes, nothing. It was a very unpleasant time back then. But before Sevastopol, the winter was the worst – we received medals – we called them "frozen meat awards" – for the hardships of the winter.[4] We shouldn't forget that it was worst for the wounded because they either froze to death or got frost in their wounds. At the first-aid stations before Sevastopol – I was there for a few months because we had our computing station next to the first-aid station – the cemetery grew from three graves to thousands of graves. The worst thing was the severe winter, and there were no villages and no lodgings. At night, we slept outside in holes. It wasn't possible to take care of these people properly. Whoever was wounded – seriously wounded – had little chance of surviving. It was a bad time – a bad time.

Stalingrad (1942)

Günter Strahl was born in Danzig in 1922. He became part of the 6th Army in July 1942 and fought in Stalingrad from August until November 1942. He recalls events from this major battle.

When I arrived [in Stalingrad] with my friend, we reported to division headquarters, to regimental headquarters, and then to battalion headquarters, and we were dispatched to the individual companies, back then they were called squadrons. They told us that we would attack early the next day, or the day after that. Then we were transported as far as possible in our armoured personnel carrier. We were dropped off and started marching. The Russians stopped our advance, and because we were held up, I had to cross areas with scattered body parts – from Germans and Russians – more from Russians than Germans. And the noise was continuous and there were shots. But what I'm telling you is not enough. I felt sick to my stomach. The older soldiers told me that it was going to get even worse – that this was nothing – we would experience other things. For example, they said that we shouldn't eat breakfast because if we got shot in the stomach then it would be over for us.

On the first day, I was buried alive under debris and was transported back to the supply lines for fourteen days. I found out that my friend had been severely injured on the same day. He died a few days later. And then I returned to the Front and stayed on the front line the entire time. My unit was in a chain-driven infantry fighting vehicle. Previously units were on horseback and weren't called companies, but rather squadrons. The captain wasn't called captain, but rather cavalry master. But that's just a side remark. After I was buried alive in August on my first day, I was on the very front line continuously until November. But not in the same area. I'd say that every ten days we were moved back and forth without knowing where we were in Stalingrad. I didn't know whether

I was in the north or the south. I first found out afterwards that we had taken over the Red October Factory. I was a private and a candidate to become an officer. First, I was a messenger. My supervisors liked me and then I became a group leader ... man oh man ... then my platoon leader was injured, and I became platoon leader ... I had two machine guns ... and ten or fifteen men under me from the whole unit of 100 men. We only advanced forward. We were never held up or pushed back – we were sometimes held up, but the Russians retreated and were able to maintain ground until Stalin said: "Stalingrad and withdraw no further". And then it became more difficult for us.

The area of Stalingrad wasn't flat. First of all, it was all shot up and bombed out. Secondly, there were canyons throughout the city so that it was really difficult for tanks. That's why we got off our vehicles and went on foot. Once I was too close to one of our tanks, and it drove over my foot – at least over my toes. It wasn't so bad. I survived. When I reported it to the medic, he said: "Private Strahl, you were buried alive on such and such a date, then you were injured by shrapnel, and now your toes have been crushed. Those are three injuries. You'll get the Wound Badge in silver." I had already received the Wound Badge in black from the first time I was buried alive. I remember another event in which a Molotov cocktail was lit and thrown. One day we were marching ahead and saw ten, twenty, or thirty such Molotov cocktails in a canyon. Everyone said stop, be careful, but one soldier was not careful and grabbed one of them when it exploded. And it was over for him.

The propaganda company came to our boss and said: "We want to make a film for the Wochenschau [news] and see how you actually storm into a house with your unit that is occupied by Russians and take it over. Volunteers should step forward." I didn't. They wanted to show it on the news. Then they actually did. One casualty and two severely injured. And they had the film. Afterwards we went into the Red October Factory very carefully – it was a munitions plant – and forced the Russians out. Suddenly there was shooting from behind us, but we couldn't imagine why because we had carefully examined the premises – the machine shop – until we noticed that the Russians had gone underground into the heating ducts and were shooting from behind. And then we were even more careful.

I know that we occupied a building on that day. The Russians were 5 metres ahead in the basement and made sure that no one was at the windows and shot immediately. One soldier was careless and went to the window. Shot to the stomach. And I saw how he died slowly for hours – fought with death for hours. Things like this really shocked me. I was twenty years old. The second time that I was buried alive was the worst. There was a building next to railway tracks. We were in the front part of the house, and the Russians in the back. And we could hear one another. If we saw one of them then we would shoot, and if they saw us then they would shoot. I was lying outside in a hole in the ground with a comrade, and a third man kept lookout. It was so cold. Every night – or almost every night – Russian planes flew overhead. They were one-motor double-decker planes that always dropped bombs. We called them "Night Witches" [Nebelkrähe]. They flew overhead and located the Front because flares were constantly fired back and forth. They dropped a bomb and made a direct hit. One man was thrown out from the explosion. A metal wall fell over our hole, and the two of us were buried inside. On the right side there was a wall, on the left there was also metal, and in the back part everything had moved. After we noticed what had happened, the man from Silesia next to me said: "I'll pull the pin on my hand grenade and then we'll both be gone". I said: "Let's wait a little while". I called to the third man through the wall and asked him to dig us out. He painstakingly dug a hole with the spade. After many hours we were able to get out again. It was a horrible matter. As I said, my comrade wanted to pull the pin on the hand grenade so that we'd blow up. It was the worst event. That's something that still haunts me today.

In November it snowed. It was terribly cold, and we didn't have any place to stay. My feet were frozen. The doctor told me that I should have my feet taken care of. I was supposed to return in a few weeks. And they sent me to the back lines on 16 November. On 17 November, my feet were washed at the aid station. They put salve on them and bandaged them. And the doctor said: "We'll have to cut a piece off. It's already black". I said: "Let's wait a little while". He said: "Alright. Go to the military hospital". I went to the military hospital after the aid station and then to Kalach near the Volga. I was transported by vehicle with my frostbite to a military hospital in Kalach.

That was on 17, 18, and 19 November [1942]. They told us to evacuate the military hospital immediately and proceed to the train station. There was a freight train waiting. We were boarded, and the train left immediately. That was the day before the Russians encircled Stalingrad. After 10, 20, or 30 kilometres we got off the train. Without exaggeration – we were moved westwards at least ten times. I never received proper treatment. My body gradually regenerated. My frozen feet slowly recovered. They weren't red-hot any longer. And suddenly I was in Dnepropetrovsk – further in the West. And there I told them that I wanted to go back to the Front. The doctor said: "Let's wait here in Dnepropetrovsk until 1 December". I said: "O.K. I'll return on 1 December". At the end of November, on the 28th or the 29th, we were transported by hospital trains to Breslau. On Christmas Eve I was in Breslau. And I was brought to a regular military hospital in Lower Silesia.

South of the Dnieper (1943)

Erich Hauer was born in Erfurt (Thuringia) in 1922. He was part of the 3rd Mountain Division which attempted to relieve the 6th Army in Stalingrad at the beginning of 1943. The division retreated south with the Front and positioned itself on the Mius River.

We were transferred from Norway to Velikiye Luki near Leningrad and were supposed to be deployed to the Caucasus. I joined them while they were marching from [Leningrad] to the Caucasus. And then Stalingrad happened. The 3rd Mountain Division was actually on its way to the Caucasus and wanted to possibly buy oil in Iran via Tbilisi. [laughs] But we turned around and marched towards Stalingrad again because it had been encircled in the meantime. General Paulus, who led the command, could have broken out. We would have pressed from the outside, and he from the inside, and they probably would have got out. But he was taken prisoner. He was forbidden by Hitler from acting otherwise. Then it was over. And we had to escape. From there we marched west in the direction of the Mius River.

Which role did you play?

I was the platoon leader in the regiment. Lieutenant and platoon leader. A platoon is the unit below a company. Companies in the Mountain Division were made up of three platoons with an SMG machine gun platoon and a grenade launcher group. These made up a company. Then there was a company that had only heavy artillery and was very different from the infantry division. The mountain divisions deployed in the mountains were more independent and didn't receive any support in serious situations. And that's why they were more effective. But we were never used in Stalingrad. We belonged to the legendary Hoth Tank Group, which was supposed to relieve Stalingrad, but didn't manage to do so. And everyone started to march west. There were battles during the retreat until spring 1943. And we were on the Mius – it was a tributary of the Donets or Dnieper – and we were totally exhausted – and the Russians were too. They couldn't continue. And we stayed on the Mius until September 1943. And then the Russians began an offensive, and we couldn't hold them back any longer. We also retreated. And then I was injured near Nikopol on the Dnieper. I was brought to a military field hospital. It was a direct hit that damaged my hearing. That's why I hear so badly today.

Battle of Kharkov (1943)

Professor Herbert Langhans was born in 1920 in Nixdorf in northern Bohemia in Czechoslovakia. During the war he served as a radio operator in an army artillery unit which was accompanied by horses. He served on the Eastern Front in Rzhev near Moscow in December 1941 and Kharkov (Army Group South) in August 1943. He describes the second tour on the Eastern Front.

I had to return to Russia a second time, and I remember something that happened. I was sitting in the last car of a transporter – we were being brought to Russia by train – and an old railroad man was sitting next to me, smoking his pipe and said: "You know, I've only escorted transporters to Russia, but never back again". That was quite a pessimistic statement, but I was young at that time, and it didn't impress me very much. Well, we were on our way to Russia a second time.

We travelled in the direction of the Southwestern Front. We were deployed there and had a very young lieutenant near Kharkov. And we had to carry out our military orders to the letter. In the meantime, we had horse-drawn wagons – those were private wagons that we seized and drove. And then the orders came that had to be carried out exactly. We had to load the radio equipment onto the horses – I was a radio operator. I remember exactly how we marched into a village one evening which was located in a valley. That's always an unpleasant situation if you're in a valley and you're being observed from above. And [the inevitable] happened. Early in the morning at sunrise the Russian Army was standing on the top of the mountain range with its tanks. And what happened? They wanted to march into this village, and we withdrew as quickly as possible. It was a sunny day in August and everything was clearly visible. We were the advanced guard of radio operators for the artillery units and were supposed to stay there to the end and provide coverage for the retreat. And we loaded the radio equipment onto our horses and left this village at the last moment. We didn't ride the horses because they had to be handled carefully. The Russians were shooting from the elevated areas behind us – it was rather far away – but you noticed the shots whistling past. And they hit one of our horses which was loaded with the radio equipment. It wasn't able to go on. We had to leave it there and unload the radio equipment. We received orders that no equipment could be left behind or thrown away. Everything had to be saved. Violations were to be severely punished. What were we supposed to do? We were standing there, and, at the last moment, an anti-tank vehicle took us along. We packed the radio equipment onto it. The soldiers looked like mice because they were all grey from the dusty streets. We were now saved, so to speak. And we drove along in the direction of Kharkov airfield.

That's where they got us – I don't know how exactly – but obviously we drove over a mine. The vehicle flew through the air. I woke up under the vehicle, which started to burn. Thank God that the heat woke me up. I was in a state of shock, stood up, and didn't know where I was. I simply ran away. Sometimes there are important people in your life, and this person was none other than the division commander. I just started running in one direction and ran into his arms, so to speak. He turned the guns around and fired directly towards the approaching Russians. When he saw me, he ordered his driver to take me to the next first-aid post. Another man drove along with us who had his arm shot off and was bleeding. Well, I owe my life to this division commander. They drove me across this immense Russian landscape to the next first-aid post in the division commander's jeep, and now and then we were fired on by low-flying planes. But all of it turned out well. But when we arrived at the first-aid post, it had already been evacuated. The German Army was retreating. Then the division commander's driver said: "I have to get back to my boss". And then we were brought to Dnepropetrovsk with the next transporter. That's what saved me. And from there the war was over for me. I received horrible burns. You can see them here on my arms and face. As I said, I woke up in time under the anti-tank vehicle and was able to get away. Thank God that I was able to walk. And I was transported back [to Germany] from one military field hospital to another. The war was over for me at this point. I was no longer fit for military service, only for the Reich

Labour Service [Reichsarbeitsdienst]. That meant that I was in the barracks and had guard duty. From there I came to northern Germany to Lingen on the Ems. The war was over for me. In retrospect, I was lucky – although I didn't see it that way at the time. If I now see reports or films about how prisoners of war were brought to Siberia, it's a sad matter. During the last part of the war, I was in barracks in Lingen on the Ems as one of the replacement troops.

Cherkasy and Tarnopil Pockets (1943/1944)

Franz Kolb was sent to the Russian Front in 1943 at the age of seventeen, where he fought with the 6th Army, 1st Tank Division. He saw action in the pockets of Cherkasy, Kamenets-Podolsky, and Tarnopil and was wounded for the first time in May 1944. Later he returned to his company as an officer in Romania and Hungary and was seriously wounded in March 1945.

A large part of our 6th Army, 1st Tank Division, was encircled in Stalingrad. But at a certain point in time, parts of this division managed to escape from the pocket in Stalingrad. Thank God that I wasn't a soldier in Russia at this time, but instead was doing my training in Erfurt. But when I went to Russia in the autumn of 1943, I joined the so-called Army Group Centre. At that time, the main line of fighting had retreated beyond the Dnieper River. It was on one line with Kiev and then down south in the direction of Romania. In practical terms, this always meant retreat because we were extremely reduced in the number of soldiers and especially in terms of equipment because of the terrible battles. When the autumn of 1943 arrived, I was a young man at the age of seventeen and a half and came to the Front. That was at a time when the bad weather started. And in Russia – you have to have experienced it – where the rural population lived in the Ukraine – Americans can hardly imagine what it looked like – there weren't any streets, but rather paths that were full of mud because of the rain. The German motorized troops couldn't get through anymore; they got stuck in the mud. That was in the autumn which was the transitional period to the winter. Besides, the supply lines didn't work anymore. This meant that we were still ready for battle, but we were greatly decimated in personnel and especially in terms of equipment. It didn't matter much to the Russians who knew these conditions, and especially the winter conditions later on, a lot better than we did. Sometimes our feet were frostbitten because we didn't have the right winter clothing. We had to leave our tanks standing because we didn't have any supplies. We were already encircled in the pocket of Cherkasy on the Dnieper River and didn't receive any supplies. Some of the tanks – not all of them – had to be left standing because we didn't have any more diesel.

The first bad weather that took us by surprise was in the autumn of 1941 – I wasn't a soldier yet – but the German troops were almost in Moscow. At that time, the Russians were already beaten. The press reported that Germany had already won the military campaign in Russia. But the Germans didn't know the Russian winter. And in 1941, German soldiers weren't equipped for all the hardships and difficulties of winter such as frostbite. Later in 1943, where I want to continue my story, we, of course, already had winter experience. I had a winter uniform – with padding and so on. But we were encircled. We didn't have any supplies from the back lines, only those things we brought into the pocket, which meant the rest of our weapons. Of course, we still had rations. And at that time the German Air Force was still intact, and we were supplied in the pocket from the air. They dropped ammunition, food, and so on by parachute. As I said, the ground conditions were so horrible in Russia because there was a great deal of mud. There were hardly any houses there; instead, there were mud huts. You can't imagine it. These mud huts housed animals, Russians, and German soldiers. It was clear that there were bugs. We all got lice and fleas and so on. I just mentioned supplies from the air – we cut the silk from the parachutes and made scarves out of them. These caught the lice that tried to move into our hair from our bodies. But that was only a small evil. When we came back from the front line and had a chance to groom ourselves a bit in a Finnish sauna, we got naked and had a shower. Today you can't call this a shower – it was simply a bucket that was hung up, and hot water was poured over us that had been heated over an open fire. And you could see the rough bodies. There were a lot of soldiers, especially those with red hair, who were infested with lice. The lice devoured their entire bodies. That was just a small evil. The battles were much worse. We had to fight day and night because the Russians naturally tried to somehow decimate us – to kill us – you could say. Of course, we defended ourselves out of deathly fear and that led to terrible battles with no mercy. Nobody wanted to be taken prisoner because they knew it meant certain death. On the part of the Germans – and I'm sure on the part of the Russians – that was not bravery because you knew that you couldn't surrender and that you had to continue until you couldn't anymore because you would have been killed anyway. So, when people say that they were especially heroic – that's not always correct; there were people who were heroic – but most of them acted out of fear because you couldn't surrender otherwise you would have been shot by the Russians. That's why they continued fighting until the last bullet, as one says.

My baptism of fire was on the Dnieper River in the city of Starokonstantinov. It was in that city that I got my Front experience at the age of seventeen and a half. I had never seen battle before. We had captured the city before, but there were counter advances by the Russians with the Joseph Stalin II tanks which we feared a great deal. Originally, the Russians had mostly T-34 battle tanks which were not equal to our Panthers and our tanks. But afterwards they developed battle tanks with extremely heavy steel armour. I don't know how thick it was or how many millimetres it had. Sometimes our shots didn't penetrate. And the Joseph Stalin tank was feared a great deal because we could hardly fight against it. You have to imagine that we were encircled and didn't even have the normal ammunition for the anti-tank guns or the 88 artillery that was normally used in air combat. We sometimes used this in close fighting to defend against Russian tank attacks. My baptism of fire was so horrible – I openly admit that I was so afraid that I was shaking with fear. And whoever says that they weren't shaking with fear is a liar. I thought that my time had come. A terribly heavy bombardment came from the Russians. They had more manpower and equipment. They had heavy weaponry – cannons, anti-tank guns, tanks – they had everything that we once had, but that we didn't have anymore because we were encircled. They fought against us, and we only had one anti-aircraft gun with 88 millimetres against the Joseph Stalin tank. Anyone who knew this anti-aircraft gun would say that it was very good. It was even able to destroy the Joseph Stalin. We only had one anti-aircraft gun at my so-called baptism of fire. And I saw that it was standing near an old decrepit wall and was probably aimed at fighting tanks, when it suddenly blew up. It was a direct hit from a Joseph Stalin tank. And then the Russians came running in such a force that you can't imagine – which meant man for man. And we were a young unit – as I said – we had just come from home – I was seventeen and a half years old. We didn't have any combat experience. And while we were lying in the ditches up front, German soldiers came back from the Front where Russian soldiers were advancing. They were ahead of our units in battle and were naturally all shot up. A few individual soldiers – old fighters – came back to our line of combat. They sat down – I'll never forget it – they sat down on top of the ditches, no matter whether they were being fired upon or not. And I said to one of them: "Friend, come on down under cover!" And he said: "Young fellow, don't worry. When you've been a soldier as long as we have, you don't care if you get shot or not". That was my baptism of fire. And that was only the beginning of the whole terror in the defensive battles. In fact, it was always pocket battles. It began with the pocket battle near Cherkasy, then Kamenets-Podolsky, and then Tarnopil. In short, from one pocket to another. And the battles were so horrible. I would like to mention just one example.

Once we attacked with an entire battalion, and at that time the fighting strength of a battalion was between 700 and 800 men. And, as I said, we didn't have a great deal of tank support. We had a few Tigers – that was a very good tank – but the Russians had a lot more material. They had anti-tank guns which we were terribly afraid of. And then they quickly destroyed our tanks – and we were driven forward – we had to attack. And then the Russians naturally riddled us with shots, as it's called. We returned with only twenty-eight men from the entire battalion. All the others were dead, seriously wounded, lying all over – that's how hard the fighting was. On the other hand, we were sometimes in control. Sometimes we were supplied with ammunition and machine guns from the air – this was still possible, but they couldn't fly heavy weaponry into the pockets – sometimes we were supplied with heavy and light machine guns and – I have to mention with praise – Germany had the MG 42 which I believe is still used today in the army. This MG 42 had an incredibly quick firing rate so that you could mow down entire companies. You couldn't do anything against tanks, but if the Russians ran towards us shouting – I experienced this personally – and we were lying under cover with our MG 42s and the Russians came in waves – we called it "mowing" – then we just mowed with our machine guns. And the Russians tumbled. I have to say that those were pocket battles, and the Russians also weren't so well equipped with heavy weaponry. I think that the Russian commissars were to blame – they forced simple Russian soldiers – who certainly didn't want to prove their bravery and didn't want to fight – to push forward. And the commissars were behind the lines. And beware if a Russian soldier wanted to turn back, then he was shot by his own men. So, these poor guys didn't have any alternative. They were being watched from both sides: either they had to charge us, and if we were well armed, we mowed them down; or if they retreated, they ran into the arms of the commissars and were mowed down there. It was a horrible battle. It's impossible to describe.

And we were lucky – or I was lucky – that the 10th SS division – and I emphasize that the SS fighting forces were something completely different than the SS security forces. Those were cowardly SS men who killed people behind the front lines. But I never experienced this myself. I was always with the SS fighting forces on the front lines. And those were brave soldiers. They fought honourably, but didn't show any mercy. We weren't able to either. In a humane war if you raised your hands, then the others didn't shoot anymore. This wasn't possible here. It was a slaughter down to the last man on both sides. That was the horrible thing. And we were lucky that the 10th SS Division was able to open up the Tarnopil pocket in battle, and I believe that 50,000 of our men who had previously been encircled – yes, I think that's the way it was – were then able to get out of the pocket and re-join the German line of fighting. And in a small skirmish with the enemy, as it's called, a piece of shrapnel got lodged in my upper arm – I think I still have it today – and I had my pass home. I was as happy as a small child. If you imagine that in those horrible times people sometimes wished – and I did as well – that someone would shoot their arm off so that they could finally get away from the fighting. I would have willingly offered an arm at that time in order to get away from the fighting and go home. I wasn't the only one. It's because the fighting and the strain were inhuman. I saw that others weren't able to bear it – especially fathers with families – who thought too much about what their families were doing at home. I have to say that I never thought about my family. My youth helped me. I never thought about them. Maybe this is the reason why I made it through the war. All the others who couldn't bear it and couldn't deal with it – shot themselves. That's how horrible it was.

Odessa (1944)

Volrad Deneke was born in Wernigerode in Saxony Anhalt in 1920. He was sent to the 9th Tank Division in the Ukraine in 1943. When his company was disbanded in 1944, he was brought to a military hospital in Odessa and evacuated to Romania.

Were you still in the Ukraine when you heard about the fall of Stalingrad?

Yes. The news came from soldiers who were replacements from home. For example, there were former paymasters who were now used as simple soldiers. While they were in Germany, they heard news from the English radio broadcasts. And they brought this information with them to the Front. We had difficulties knowing who was located next to the 9th German Tank Division which I was a part of. There was another tank division, namely from Schörner.[5] We knew that, but otherwise our level of information was that much more limited the closer we were to the Front. Most people who survived were generals because they needed to have an overview behind the lines.

Was the news a hard blow to the 9th Tank Division?

We were retreating – we had been retreating for weeks. The news from the replacements right from Germany didn't surprise us at all. There was a short period in which some of the soldiers sweeping back thought that they could build a line of defence by reaching the German border from East to West. But maybe not even the majority of soldiers believed that. We were much more worried about whether we would get something to eat on that day or not. Or whether we could find a place to stay in a warm farmhouse. Or whether we would freeze. The existential things – eating, digesting food, marching, being able to sleep, staying warm, or freezing – these primitive existential questions were of the greatest concern. It was an experience that fundamentally changed the lives of those who were in the war with a weapon. You had to fight with yourself and defend yourself in order to survive.

Our company was disbanded as a fighting force, and those who were halfway able to fight were sent to the Western Front for its protection. I myself was admitted to a military hospital in Odessa because of a very high fever. When I arrived in Odessa, I was so ill and exhausted that I first had to recover from the flu. And then I was transported in a freight train that travelled for approximately three weeks to the Transylvanian Alps in Romania because it had to continuously make stops. I was admitted to a military hospital where two floors were set up only for those with typhoid fever from our train.

During these three weeks in the train, we had a lot of deaths. Either you were too close to the oven and were sweating, or you were lying back in the corner full of snow from the cracks in the train. And once you started to become infested with lice – the outer seams of your uniform filled with lice eggs – you had to crack them. By the time you got to the bottom part of your body, the top part was filled with lice again. The last two freight cars carried the dead who were then buried in the Transylvanian Alps.

Lithuania (1944)

Lothar Härtel was born in 1925 in Hilbach near Eisenach in Thuringia. In June of 1944 he was sent to northern Lithuania as a gun layer with an artillery unit to combat the advancing Russian forces.

Later when we were in action in Lithuania and Latvia there wasn't a unified front. It was all swampland. And there were just bases everywhere – from us and the Russians. Now and then our troops tried to break through, or the Russians tried to break through. But, for the most part, we heard them when they got their vodka in the evenings and were celebrating. And on the following morning it started again. At dawn we saw them come out like ants. That wasn't the case with us where everything was somewhat concealed – with them it was like during the days of Frederick the Great when they marched in rows. We could see them approaching. It was always the same with the Russians – behind them were the Russian commissars. They were wearing stars [on their caps] about this big – commissar stars. For us, hitting one of those stars was better than getting the Iron Cross. They were targets. Yes. Yes. We were able to hit them. And when we went up to the Front, we looked around to see if there was a commissar lying there [among the bodies] with a [star on his] cap.

What was the situation in Lithuania? Did the Russians have the support of tanks or did they come on foot?

It varied. It depended on the terrain. In the swamp areas where we were, they all came on foot. They wouldn't have been able to use tanks. They would have got stuck. We would have got stuck, and they would have got stuck with their tanks. We marched on foot. For us it was less hand-to-hand fighting. But for the infantry it was more so. We kept a lookout – there was an officer, a forward observer, me, and a radio man – all communication was carried out by field telephone. There was a point here, and then 3 or 4 kilometres another point, and maybe even a Russian in between. And that's why the posts were reinforced at night. That's why we had six or eight or ten men in front at night, not just three – so that there were enough guards so that you could hear enough – because it wasn't a closed front.

[In Lithuania] hardly any people were still there. [The fighting] went back and forth. And strangely enough, we marched ahead 10 kilometres – and our fighting forces in front were able to do whatever they wanted. They took control and destroyed and so on. And when we left, the Russians came and did the same thing. But the moment in which our fighting forces were out of there – and the artillery people were 3, 4, or 5 kilometres in the back in an established position – this didn't happen anymore. Beware if someone had stolen a chicken – or a cow or anything like that – then they would have been sent to a punishment company. It was very strict. Only the fighting forces were able to do whatever they wanted. Nobody said anything about this. But in the backcountry – 5, 6, 8, or 10 kilometres behind the line – the military police were already there. They were watching out. We had our own field kitchen with us – and the munitions orders were buried a metre and half underground. All of this was taken care of by the Lithuanian helpers. Our people didn't do that – the others did. They received some artificial honey that we didn't want and bread and food and so on – they did that. And our post in the front – our forward observation post – was built by the infantry. We didn't build that ourselves – we were too dignified for that. The same is true for the dugouts so that we could observe and do all the other things. The infantry built that.

Were the Lithuanians against Stalin? Or did they have to work for the German military?

Well, people worked because they were hungry. They worked wherever they got something to eat. The locals weren't hostile towards us – they were happy when they were able to work and get something to eat. They were more against the Russians because they were radical – they carried out a policy of scorched earth. If they had to retreat, they flattened everything – flattened everything. It was autumn up there, and there was the potato harvest and so on – and they planted small anti-tank mines. Our kitchen people had to use sticks everywhere so that they wouldn't get their hands blown off. This is the way it was. But we didn't have any problems with the population itself.

We moved to the forward observation post at night in the dark – or in the early morning hours – we stayed there two or three days, and then we went back. And afterwards when the reinforcements went to this position in the evenings, they brought food from the back – a big pot of goulash. Otherwise, we had our own food along – bread, or this or that. We slept in dugouts – with a blanket on the ground. In our post in the back, we built our own bunker in the ground. You were just able to crawl into it backwards – first with your behind and then with your legs. It was wet and damp, but it was covered by a metre or a metre and a half of dirt. They shot at us – or dropped bombs by hand from so-called "sewing machines" – those were small Russian planes that came at night. And the bunkers were for shrapnel protection. This might also have been the case if the Russians had broken through our position – then we would have had a bit of protection. You have to imagine it this way – in the front there was a slope and our post was buried – with our arms and the slit inside. Everything was covered so that you couldn't see anything. And there was a hidden path that rose about one and a half metres, or 2 metres, and disappeared. And we had to take this path through the woods to get from the front of our battery to the back. We had to go up a hill and cross over it. And the Russians always waited with an anti-tank gun whenever someone came – sometimes above or below.

And I got shot. I got shot. Thank God. They shot me while I was jumping. Bang. A shot from an anti-tank gun landed behind me, and the shrapnel went through my skin. I had a thick coat on – it was cold there. It penetrated. And then the blood started to pour out. And that was the end of it. I was on my way back to the battery. And then I arrived at the battery, and they asked me what had happened. I told them, and they said that they would have a look. Someone came next to me and said: "Where are you from? I recognize your accent". "Yeah, I'm from so and so", I said. "Yeah, I'm from Dreißigacker". It was two towns away from mine. He said: "O.K. I'll take you directly to the first-aid station". In fifteen minutes, I was at the first-aid station. I was lucky. Maybe I would have had to lie there for half a day and get bandaged and so on. And then I was operated on, and they did a good job. They didn't amputate my hand. They could just as easily have cut it off.

[They did that] if there was no other choice. Or if they didn't have enough time. This wasn't so urgent. It wasn't like today when you get a mask over your face – like a fencing mask. And then you're out for three days. That's clear. They did a good job. I can't say anything else. They could just as well have cut it off. So now I can at least use my hand somewhat. But I was lucky to get out of there. And from there I went by train to Labiau – up there on the Courland Peninsula – I went to the military hospital. And all the wounded soldiers started arriving from the tank battles in East Prussia. They were all burned. It was horrible. They managed to get them out of the tanks – but they were lying in the hallway with an extremely thin silk sheet over them. It was just a question of hours before these people died. That was clear. They couldn't do anything for them. [The burns were] too extensive. If only a part of them had been burned. This was caused by the anti-tank grenades that we and the Russians used. They penetrated the tanks and exploded inside and burned everything. No one could get out. They couldn't get the lid open. That was the most horrible thing. And when I was in the military hospital, I started making some phone calls. I called up my mother at home, and she called up General Burgenstein. And four or five days later, I was on my way straight across Germany to the military sports hospital near Dresden in Altenberg. And I was able to get away from the entire bullshit up there.

Dukla Pass in the Beskids (1944)

Wolfgang Heine was born in Berlin in 1925. He spent the first part of 1944 as the personal driver of a general in France until the Allied invasion of Normandy. Afterwards, he received his marching orders for Berlin, where he was sent to a tank division on the Russian Front at the end of 1944.

I was in a training programme for reserve officers. They wanted to make an officer out of me because I was a high school graduate. But one day I refused to crawl through a puddle on the barrack grounds. I said: "You're crazy. I've just come back from the Front and I'm injured. And you want me to crawl through a puddle. I know what it's like to be under fire". They took offence at this, and I came to Bielitz in the Beskids – south of Katowice – to a stand-by unit – these were units that were gathered together and sent to the Front. And then new collecting camps were formed and they came to the Front. This is how I was sent to the Front – to the Beskids – to the Dukla Pass in the East.[6] The Russians were quickly advancing there, and we were retreating. And I was in two pockets – we were surrounded by the Russians twice – and the last time I was on an assault gun – these were open guns on top of chain-driven tanks. And there was high armour plating around them – I don't know how thick it was, but it was made of steel. The gun could be easily moved. I don't remember how large it was – 18 centimetres or something like that. And, in any case, while we were encircled, the tank commander said: "Look, we're going to try to break through – right through the Russian line. We have enough gasoline. Everything is fine with the engine. Just stay up there on top. Whoever doesn't want to come along should get down". I said: "No. No. We're coming along". We had over 100 litres of gasoline in barrels in the back tank. The engine was powerful. I think it had over 700 horse power or something like that. And he said: "We're going for maximum speed". This was about 45 to 50 kilometres per hour. He said: "Get the hand grenades, the submachine guns, and everything ready. We're going right through the front". It was on a path through the fields.

We drove full speed ahead. The Russians threw hand grenades and shot and so did we. And five minutes later we were through.

And then I came to a battalion where all the scattered troops were gathered together again. That was the worst thing because you didn't know the person next to you – your own fellow soldiers. They were strangers. And you had to make sure that you made it on your own. And we were completely exhausted because we had to march or walk continuously back in the direction of home. I had two buddies – we were together because they were also from Berlin – and we rested one at a time, but sometimes the Russians came so close that we had to defend ourselves. And when they noticed that we were shooting, they took up position. And we had a head start of a few hundred metres. Well, one day we had a really good head start, and it was at night, and we were really tired and were in a farmhouse. There were these ovens that the farmers slept on in the winter. It was terribly cold. It was in January. And it was -20°C outside. We didn't have any winter uniforms. We had normal uniforms. And we took newspapers and stuffed our clothing with it – our khaki pants. I wasn't so sensitive to the cold so it didn't affect me as much. But I remember that I was in a snow hole for ten hours because I was under fire. I couldn't get out of there. And a lot of Russians were under the influence of alcohol – intentionally – because they were given vodka before they attacked.

It was intentional?

Oh, yes. That was such a horrible thing. It was so inhuman. What were our soldiers supposed to do? They just held their finger on the trigger. Entire companies of Russians came through the snow across the fields and down the hills. And below were our machine guns. Nobody remained alive. If you think about, it's absolutely senseless and murderous. That is murder. But it was instigated by the commanders on the other side. You just can't…

And you were able to keep on going?

I went into this farmhouse with my two buddies, and we were so tired that we dropped down and fell asleep. And suddenly I heard chains rattling and looked out of the farmhouse, and on the small road there was a T-34, a Russian tank. And I said: "Hey guys, we have to get out of here!" We went out of the back of the farmhouse. The Russian tanks were coming and maybe 200 or 300 metres behind them, sometimes closer, was the Russian infantry. And they had small machine guns on sledges. In the front was an armour plate and then the sledges. And when they faced resistance, they dived down behind the armour plates and the machine guns and crouched down and shot. This also happened to us. About 50 metres ahead there was a forest, and I said: "Look, let's try to reach the edge of the forest". The Russians were 100 metres away. We were about 3 or 4 metres apart from one another, and the Russians started shooting immediately. I got a penetration wound here, but that was the only thing. And my buddy next to me was injured and hollered. And the third guy was dead immediately. I was able to make it through the forest and waved down the only car coming down the country road. It was a supply officer who had some kind of assignment – to blow up a factory.

A German?

Yes. A German. An administrative officer. And he said: "I'll take you along. In the town after the next one there is a first-aid station". That was a military hospital – a field hospital. "But I first have to give orders to my oncoming troops to blow up a schnapps factory". "A schnapps factory?" I asked. Maybe this isn't so bad I thought. I had to go along anyway. I didn't have a rifle or anything. I only had my bread bag and another bag along. And I filled them with schnapps – with small bottles so that I could barter with them. And then I came to the field hospital which was horrible. Arms and legs were lying around in barrels – it was indescribable. The poor people who had to work there, and the doctors operated to the point of exhaustion. And it was very admirable. But it was so completely senseless! How could someone cause something like this? How could someone wage war at all? In any case, I was taken care of, received a wound tag, and came onto the last train that left. That was between Hindenburg and Katowice in Silesia.

The Fall of East Prussia (1945)

Johannes Thorak was born in Dresden in 1919. He recalls the surrender of the 2nd Fortress Machine Gun Battalion 79 in East Prussia and mass executions by the Red Army in February 1945.

Our company had 218 men. By the time we crossed the German border on the return march, we had only 175 men. We continued from Warsaw to East Prussia and experienced the downfall of Königsberg, Danzig, Lodz, and Thorn. We reached the Tuchola Forest where we were encircled by the Red Army. My company – the 2nd Fortress Machine Gun Battalion 79 – surrendered on 13 February 1945 at 11:15 am. There were 128 men still alive who were then executed by Mongolians – some of whom were totally drunk – with shots to the skull of their heads. The shot that was intended for my skull landed in my upper thigh because a Soviet doctor hit the revolver out of the hand of a drunk Mongolian. But the soldier had already pulled the trigger, and the shot passed through my dispatch pouch into my upper thigh. If it hadn't been for the dispatch pouch, I would have received a bone fracture from the shot and wouldn't have survived the war. Between 2,000 and 3,000 men were executed in this way.

You have to imagine that there were enormous distilleries [in East Prussia] in Thorn and Schwetz. Alone in Thorn there was a fortress from World War I that was four floors below ground. There were millions of litres of alcohol stored there. And the Red Army got their hands on it. They were certainly drunk all the way to Berlin. The Soviet doctor said to me: "My dear friend, you were really lucky". He noticed that I was in shock since he spoke German. He told me that his grandfather had studied medicine in Heidelberg, and all of his relatives had studied in Germany and that they spoke French, German, and Russian at home. It first became clear to me how much misery this war had caused. It was absolute insanity. The Soviet doctor took me along with him. He was on horseback and said to me: “Listen, you run alongside my horse. You see that they’re all drunk. We don’t want both of us to get shot. You run on the right side next to my saddle – on the far right along the ditch in the road – so that they don’t see you. About 500 metres ahead is a barn. There are already soldiers inside”. There were Soviet soldiers there who weren’t executing soldiers. These kinds of men also existed. Not all of them were animals.

There was a huge barn with approximately 200 prisoners inside who hadn’t been bandaged yet. I had a bullet lodged in my thigh, and it now stopped bleeding. My right leg was extremely swollen, and I couldn’t get my boot off. And then I heard how two Russian lieutenants were talking to one another. Back then I was able to understand a little bit of Russian. I heard them talking about starting a fire. I became afraid – it was a community barn – and in the East these barns had huge cellars where potatoes, carrots, and vegetables were stored because there wasn’t enough room above ground. I went down into the cellar – there wasn’t anything down there except for a few carrots – and I fell asleep. I don’t know how long I slept because I hadn’t slept for at least eight days during the battles of the retreat. When I woke up, I went upstairs and the barn was no longer standing. It had been burned down. And across the road there was the administrative building for the community – I can remember it well – and there was a Red Cross flag. Older women in uniform were standing there. When they saw me coming out, they clasped their hands together over their heads. I went to them, and there was an older woman about sixty years old. She gave me a kiss. I remained there, and more Russian tanks arrived. There was a small river, and Russian tanks crossed it and stopped there. These were aggressive tank guys who also wanted to attack me. The female doctor took me into the back room. She spoke perfect German and said: “Come here, come here. Otherwise, they’ll kill you”. Two days later, two medics accompanied me by train via Schwetz to Thorn South to the prisoner-of-war camp where there were approximately 45,000 soldiers.

Seelow Heights (1945)

Friedrich Jansen was born in Leverkusen in 1927. He was drafted for military service in December 1944 and saw battle for the first time on 15 April 1945 in Letschin near Küstrin on the Oder River.

Our first deployment to the Front – and it was the only time for me – came on 15 April 1945. We were supposed to recapture a village that had been captured by the Russians a few days earlier. Our place of deployment was a village near Küstrin. The village was called Letschin. And we were supposed to recapture the village. I don't know any more whether the village that we were supposed to recapture was Letschin or another. We were driven back miserably and tried to find protection in a small ravine – a small creek. That proved to be absolutely senseless because the Russians shot down into this ravine with their grenade launchers. We had so many casualties. On the morning of 15 April 1945, we went to battle with ninety-two men in our company and in the evening only eight men were alive. All the others were dead. The night was restless. We saw burning houses – this was how the Russians marked the front line of battle. They simply burned down houses. At around four or five o'clock in the morning – I didn't have a watch along so I didn't know the time exactly – the final Russian offensive began which continued to Berlin.

It began with a huge artillery barrage – immense artillery fire. The entire Seelow Heights nearby was in a sea of flames.[7] Then the Russians used artificial fog and attacked. We were supposed to hold the 1–2 kilometre-long front line with eight men. It was useless. We tried to withdraw and during this time I somehow got separated from the other soldiers because of the fog – I don't know how. In any case, I didn't have any contact with the others. And then suddenly figures appeared before me with steel helmets which were very similar to our steel helmets. I have to say that I was a paratrooper – I had never jumped with a parachute – but our parachute helmets were different from the other branches of the military.

I thought that these guys in front of me were paratroopers and happily went towards them. But those were Russians. [laughs] Well, they took me prisoner. I couldn't understand what they were saying. There were ten or twelve soldiers under a sergeant or someone. When the German artillery started, they took cover behind the railway embankment. They were lying with me in an area where the German artillery couldn't hit them. Then after a while the artillery stopped. They wanted to advance to Berlin. They wanted to win the war. What could they do with a single soldier? So, they simply shot me. [laughs]

I didn't understand what they were talking about. In any case, the sergeant was sitting next to me and the others 10 or 12 metres away. Then someone from the group said something to the sergeant which I didn't understand. The sergeant stood up, went to the group, and one of the soldiers from the group picked up his rifle and shot me in the head. I was first unconscious. I came back to my senses when the sun was high in the sky. I had a graze wound and probably had been saved by my steel helmet because the soldier held his rifle a bit too high. Another thing was that – as far as I know – the sights of Russian rifles were set for a distance of 100 metres. This means that the ballistic trajectory had already been taken into consideration. And for that reason, the soldier was holding the rifle up too high. Well, I came to my senses again. Everything was full of blood. I took off the steel helmet. Blood was swarming out. At that moment, I was convinced that everything Nazi propaganda told us about these Russian "sub-humans" was true. I desperately tried to find the German front line again. I first climbed up the railway embankment – I was very dazed. There were no Russians around. I had to cross over the railway embankment in the direction of the West where I assumed our troops would be. On the other side of the tracks, I tripped over the signal cables and tumbled down – I was very weak – to the bottom of the embankment to the feet of two Russian soldiers. [laughs]

Well, I thought it was over. It was my good fortune that one of the Russians was wounded, and they were on the way to the first-aid station or somewhere – I don't know. They treated me well and took me along to the company or battalion command post – I'm not sure. I was interrogated. In the meantime, one or two other German prisoners joined us, among them a German classmate of mine, whom I met there by chance. And he saved my life. I'll get to that later. We were then transported to a prisoner-of-war camp. That was a march of about two days. I was wounded and weak. In the meantime, there were many other prisoners who had been brought together. It was so that if someone couldn't continue, then they were shot. The Russians believed it to be an act of mercy. I wanted to lie down several times, but my classmate forced me to continue and held me up. That's how we were brought to the first prisoner-of-war camp. My classmate and I were separated from one another. I was injured, and he wasn't. We continued on foot back over the Oder River.

Oder River (1945)

Heinz Spreer was born in Saxony in 1913. At the end of the war, he was transferred to the German-Polish border on the Oder River to fight against advancing Russian soldiers.

In 1945 I was transferred to Stettin in the East to protect a hydrogenation plant with anti-aircraft guns. Then I was sent to a bridgehead at short notice which had already been completely surrounded by the Russians. That was in January 1945, somewhat south of Stettin, but I cannot tell you the names of any towns. There was a small bridgehead there with a few German soldiers and an anti-aircraft company with four guns. We blew up the bridge and crossed over the Oder at night. And then there was utter chaos. No one knew what was going on anymore. There were seven of us – I believe – and we seized a truck. We didn't want to become Russian prisonsers of war. We wanted to surrender to the British. We drove the truck at night in the direction of the West to Travemünde. And we fell into the arms of the English. On the Front, we saw how 14- and 15-year-old boys, who had been drafted at the end of the war, had to fight against Russian tanks. It was insane. They had a few Belgian rifles, and, if they were lucky, maybe a bazooka along. Most of the time they didn't even have that. Whether they wanted to or not, they had to march in the direction of the Russian tanks. We also saw how they placed white handkerchiefs on their rifles when they were near the tanks and then surrendered. The last few days of the war were insane. You can really say that it was a crime that Hitler continued with the war. It couldn't have been worse. He said: "The Germans aren't worth it because they didn't fight the way I wanted them to".

Tank Retreat to Prague (1945)

Karl Leue was a radio man and gunner in a Hetzer tank on the Russian Front at the age of 18. He remembers his division retreating in late 1944 from Minsk to Warsaw, from Krakow to Silesia, and surrendering in Prague on 9 May 1945.

We retreated from Krakow through Silesia where I saw the worst things imaginable among the German refugees. We passed them in our tank to the right and left of the road. Those were Silesians who wanted to escape and get back to Germany. We really saw some things. I'll tell you. It was winter and cold. We saw women in horse-drawn carriages who were holding their dead children in their arms for two days because they thought that they were still alive. And when they noticed that they were dead, they stepped down from the carriages and simply placed them in the ditches on the right and left of the road. I'll never forget this flow of refugees. It was so horrible. Old men, women, and children – cows tied to the back of the wagons. Really, really, really horrible. And we also helped them with our tanks. When they got stuck in the ice and snow, we drove in front of them and pulled them out. And they were able to continue. But we weren't able to take care of all the dirty work. We had to get away from there. We had to get away. The Russians sometimes caught up with us – particularly in East Prussia. It was really bad up there. Yes, that was Silesia. And then we crossed the Giant Mountains with our Hetzers[8] into Czechoslovakia. And all hell broke loose there.

After five years of occupation, the Czechs had such a hatred of the Germans. I could tell you things. We weren't too far away from Prague, and some Germans there told us to drive up to the castle on the hill where some 100 or 200 German families had fled with their children. That was quite a climb. We drove up there with three or four tanks, some infantrymen sitting on top, and some soldiers who followed behind. When we arrived, there was deadly silence in the courtyard in front of the castle. We opened the gate and entered the castle. There were 150 families with children who were dead – all of them murdered by Czechs. Some of them had their throats cut. The women had been stripped and raped. They stuck cucumbers into their vaginas. If I had had a camera along, I would have documented it. That was the work of the Czechs. And since that time, I will never go to the Czech Republic on vacation. I can't forget it. I simply can't forget it.

And then it was the end of April or the beginning of May 1945. We took up radio contact with the Americans. Some soldiers among us knew English. And then at the end of the war on 8 May – when they were celebrating by shooting rockets into the air – we took up radio contact and told them that on 9 May we would drive into a small village near Plzeň with our tank brigade and raise the white flag. And, of course, we all cried. Five years had been utterly wasted. And, in spite of that, we had to admit that it was good. It was good that Hitler lost. And I even said so back then. And then the day arrived, and we approached the village. What was interesting about the Americans is that they were still terribly afraid. I have to say so honestly. They were terribly afraid. There was an avenue that was about a kilometre long and led to the village. And we drove along it. And in the ditches along the road to the right and left, you could see only Black soldiers. Only Blacks, not a single white soldier. We drove through, and on the outskirts of the city there were the first white soldiers. We drove into a large inner courtyard, and when I opened up the hatch to the tank, I was filmed by an American. It must be in an archive somewhere today the way that I climbed out. And they said to me: "Pistol". I took out my pistol – it was a P38 – and they took it away from me. And then they said: "Get out. Get out. Get out". "Fritz. Fritz," they said to me. "Kraut." We were the krauts to the Americans. Probably because of sauerkraut. And then I was a prisoner of war. It wasn't a glorious end. But there was a demarcation line through Czechoslovakia: the Russians to the east, the Americans to the west. And the Russians would drive past our camp and shout to us in Russian: "You'll work in Siberia!"

CHAPTER II

THE NAVY

Battleship *Admiral Graf Spee* (1939)

Kurt Diggins was born in Mohrberg near Eckernförde in 1913. He served on the battleship *Admiral Graf Spee* as adjutant to Captain Langsdorff in 1939. After the *Admiral Graf Spee* was damaged in battle with three English cruisers off the coast of Uruguay, Langsdorff entered the harbour of Montevideo to seek repairs. After negotiations with the Uruguayan government failed, he decided to scuttle the *Admiral Graf Spee* instead of surrendering it to the English fleet.

On 1 April 1939 I went to the battleship *Admiral Graf Spee*. I was the adjutant to Captain Langsdorff.[1] I experienced the events of the battleship which went to sea on 21 August 1939 – before the beginning of the war – to disrupt trade in the Atlantic. Then the war started. And there wasn't any chance for peace negotiations. The battleship *Admiral Graf Spee* was very successful under the command of Langsdorff. It suddenly approached undetected and then attacked. And that's why the battleship *Admiral Graf Spee* was in the Atlantic and then in the Indian Ocean and then in the Atlantic again. And then it met its destiny in December 1939 when Captain Langsdorff began planning the trip back to Germany with a push in the direction of Rio de la Plata. And this resulted in a battle with English naval forces that caused damage to the *Spee* which then entered the harbour of Montevideo. But the battleship didn't have the necessary amount of time to carry out the repairs.

As the adjutant to Captain Langsdorff, I was aware of all the negotiations with the Uruguayan government and with the military offices in charge in Montevideo. And I know what happened back then. In retrospect, I am also aware of some of the background information. The English envoy at that time, Sir Millington Drake, was working behind the scenes pulling strings. And the Uruguayan government was very Anglophile because England had put a lot of money into Uruguay: the railroad, the telephone, and so on were all in English hands. And the foreign minister at that time, Guani, said after the *Graf Spee* had been scuttled that the Germans still in the country could return to Germany from Uruguay. But they had to promise that they would only return to Uruguay in peace. That was an act of recognition.

Maybe I should say something about the events in Montevideo. The question was whether the battleship should leave the harbour to engage in battle with the three English ships that had assembled at the mouth of Rio de la Plata within view of Montevideo and go down with the flag flying. The captain – who was brought up in the old tradition that a commander goes down with his ship – had to fight with himself terribly to make the right decision. And he valued the lives of the 1,000 young men – which was the number of crew members – higher than his personal glory which he would certainly have gained if he had allowed the battle to take place with the cruisers. Therefore, he valued the lives of young men higher than his personal glory.

How did the battle start between the *Admiral Graf Spee* and the English cruisers?

Captain Langsdorff wanted to achieve another success before the planned trip back to Germany. Based on intelligence, we knew that convoys were travelling from the mouth of the Rio de la Plata in the direction of England. And the captain wanted to attack one of these convoys – with meat and grain – in order to disrupt the supply lines. And he made a push in the direction of the mouth of the Rio de la Plata. In the early morning hours, it was determined by the guards on the bridge that there were three ships in this part of the ocean. And at first it was assumed that there was a cruiser or auxiliary cruisers. It was at dusk that we first realized that it was the heavy cruiser, *Exeter*, and the light cruisers, *Ajax* and *Achilles*. And now it was no longer possible to sail back into the Atlantic without being detected. Instead, the captain had to accept the fight because of the situation. And he opened fire and first took aim at the *Exeter* and there were a lot of direct hits. The *Exeter* was basically put out of action.

In retrospect, I have to say that nobody actually thought that this ship would make it back to the Falkland Islands. It was a masterful accomplishment by the captain. However, this led to the English, under the command of Commodore Harwood at that time, attacking the *Spee* with the two remaining cruisers in a way normally only done by destroyers. And that was also an excellent accomplishment by the English. But they turned around when they came too close to the dangerous range of the heavy artillery. And the English then broke off the fighting. That should be said very clearly. People often say that the *Spee* broke off the fighting. That's not true. It was Commodore Harwood who broke off the fighting. He said that they would follow the battleship *Admiral Graf Spee* to see what it was going to do. And that was successful. After they came too close there was a short exchange of fire from the heavy artillery on the *Spee*. But they followed behind the ship on a course to Montevideo. And the route went to Montevideo because some damage resulted that needed to be taken care of with the help of a wharf. Langsdorff didn't want to take the chance of not having a seaworthy ship because of the severe winter storms. And that's one of the reasons why negotiations with the shipyard and the government in Montevideo always mentioned the seaworthiness of the ship. The ship then entered the harbour of Montevideo, and negotiations began on how to proceed.

Auxiliary Cruiser *Atlantis* (1941)

Wilhelm Haag was born in Bad Godesberg-Mehlem in 1917. He served aboard the auxiliary cruiser *Atlantis* from February 1940 until November 1941 during which time he journeyed to North and South America. On 21 November 1941, the *Atlantis* was sunk by the English cruiser *Exeter* and the crew was safely brought to a French harbour by the Italian ship *Calvi*.

They promised us that we would only be out at sea for one year, and it turned into practically two years. At the end of February [1940], we secretly left from the northern part of the North Sea, sailed around Jan Mayen as close to the coast of Greenland as possible, and then to the North American coast, Canada and America, and into the Atlantic. And then the operation began beyond the equator.

Which kind of operation was it?

Our assignment was to disrupt trade because they told us that we were a merchant raider. We were deployed as an auxiliary cruiser that had been converted from a Hansa liner. It was painted and camouflaged as a Russian ship. The ship had two funnels, one dummy and the other normal. And in this way, we went out to sea camouflaged as a Russian ship.[2] We were supposed to disrupt trade in general among the enemy states, whether it was England or whatever country. We had been at war with England [since September 1] when German troops marched into Poland. England started bombing us as a result of the Non-Aggression Pact with Russia. And, afterwards, we also had to view them as enemies. And, of course, we stopped and searched all ships. And if they were enemy ships, we either took away their papers or sank them. Or we seized the ship.

Can you remember a few examples of when you stopped and searched ships?

Yes, for example, there was the Egyptian steamliner *Zamzam*. It came from Australia and had a great deal of civilians on board, among them Indian merchants and Irish. And we took on so many prisoners – America wasn't in the war yet – that we had almost 1,200 people on board. And we sank the steamliner *Zamzam*. There was a medical corps from America on board with about thirty people: nurses, medics, children, and so on. We took them on board and fed them. And when they became too many, we let them out in Mogadishu. We needed to seize a ship, and then we seized a coal trimmer – it was a Greek steamliner – and we put them on board. The head engineer calculated how long they would last with their coal and if they could make it to Mogadishu.

It was normal that we stopped ships by radio communication. And if they didn't stop, then we had a 75-millimetre gun directly on the bow – on the front of the ship. We called it the "ship-stopping gun". We fired a shot from the bow, and then they had to stop. And if they didn't stop, we immediately sent a radio message that as soon as they shot, we would return fire. Out of principle – and this is very important to me – we never fired the first shot without first raising the battle flag. The battle flag was always raised first. The difference on board our ship was that the battle flag was inside a high ventilator, and it came out of the end of it. And every enemy could see it. A film was made called *Under Ten Flags* about our auxiliary cruiser. They claimed that we sailed under all the flags of the world. And that's not true. We repainted the ship. And then we sailed as Dutchmen, and we sailed as Japanese – as they described in the book. And we always camouflaged ourselves so that they didn't notice us. The English also did it. They used the same method.

During our journey to South America while we were in Jamaica [before the war], the English cruiser *Exeter* was docked in the harbour. And it was normal for foreigners, including a Polish sailing school ship, to pay a visit to one another. Among them were the crew members of the *Exeter* who came to us in the canteen and enjoyed drinking our Becks beer with delight. And, of course, we drank along with them. It was normal in the navy that beer was poured and passed around. That was camaraderie. And no one thought of war or anything like that. That was navy camaraderie and manners. And everyone enjoyed it. And, unfortunately, during the war we discovered that it was the *Exeter* that sank us. But the others didn't know it. I knew it because I had sailed on the *Schlesien* earlier. I informed only the commander of this. And I have to say that he accepted it. That's fate.

What happened to the *Atlantis*?

We were in the midst of supplying submarines with oil and some supplies that we were able to spare because we had more oil on the way home than we did when leaving harbour. We also supplied the large Italian submarines that sailed around Cape Town and came from the Red Sea. We did this so that they would be able to reach France, Saint-Nazaire, or Lorient, the next harbours in France. And that was also the case here. While we were supplying a submarine with oil, the cruiser *Achilles* spotted us via aircraft reconnaissance. And it immediately knew who we were. Of course, that had something to do with the decoding of radio messages. At that time, the English were already able to decode messages. Our commander raised the flag, the ship was in the midst of sinking, and the detonation of the ship had been set. Nevertheless, he managed to get off a few shots and that's why we lost six men. Their artillery kept its distance, and they knew that it was senseless for us to fire a shot. And since they had a direct hit, we lost six men and had injuries. Everyone jumped into the water, trying to save themselves. And we saved ourselves in the ship's boats and inflatable rafts and pieces of wood floating on the water. We got into the ship's boats. The remaining submarines that were there dived down and towed us along. At this time, we were just below the equator. More Italian submarines were ordered to come there. We got into German submarines that were there and Italian submarines that were ordered to come. And, in this way, we were brought to a French harbour. I was on the Italian submarine *Calvi* under the leadership of Captain Grossi. And this is how I reached Saint-Nazaire safely.

Joining the Navy (1943)

Wilhelm Blatzheim was born in Bonn-Bad Godesberg in 1926. At the age of 16 he was sent to Slovenia in Yugoslavia to fight partisans as part of his Reich Labour Service [Reichsarbeitsdienst]. He was forced to join the navy the following year in 1943 in order to avoid being actively recruited by the Armed SS [Waffen SS].

Why did you join the navy?

I was always interested in water and the ocean. But at that time, I was at the Vocational School in Bonn following elementary school – and my best friend is an engineer somewhere in Kerpen today – and he was my best friend [back then] and loved to build things – he lived in Beuel on Garten Street. I often did my homework with him. We built things together and talked to one another, and his older brother was in the navy. And my school friend was in the Ermekeil barracks at the Navy Radio Operator School. Boys who were interested in learning how to become radio operators could sign up at the Navy Radio Operator School. Later I was a radio operator. And he told me to go there. And I went there, liked it, and had lessons every Thursday to become a radio operator until I received certification at the speed of seventy words per minute. My lieutenant was our teacher.

I have to first mention that I was in the Hitler Youth as a squadron leader, wearing a green lanyard as part of my uniform. And one day the Hitler Youth leaders in Bad Godesberg received orders to come to the House of the German Youth on Burg Street. There was going to be a lecture by a soldier from the Front – an experienced, highly-decorated soldier from the Front. We arrived there with about thirty boys. And a man came in, but he was from the SS. I don't know his rank in the SS – but he looked like a sergeant 1st Class in the regular army. He had the Iron Cross 1st class, Iron Cross 2nd class, Infantry Assault Badge, Wound Badge, German Cross in gold – we sat there with wide-open eyes. For two hours, he told us everything that he had experienced and how he got the medals. And we were fascinated about everything that he told us. He said that it was the best unit, and they had the best troops. They had the best supplies and the widest range of weapons and so on. And we thought that it was a nice story about all the things that had happened. After about two hours, he asked who was going to sign up voluntarily for the Hitler Youth division of the SS. Nobody expected this. There were maybe five or six of the thirty who signed up. And this lecturer was now no longer as nice as before. He shouted and swore at us. And when he was finished shouting at us, he told us to form a line. We had to go to him in a line and sign our names on a piece of paper: Wilhelm Blatzheim, or Heinz Schmitz, or whoever was there. And then suddenly someone asked why we had to sign our names because we had been invited. And he said: "I just want to see which of you were here".

Fourteen days later I received a postcard at home – I lived with my parents: "To Wilhelm Blatzheim, volunteer for the Armed SS, for the purpose of registration for military service on such and such a date on Hundsgasse in Bonn". On the following morning, I went to school and showed it to Günther Grass. I said: "Günther, I never signed up voluntarily for the SS. How did they get this idea?" I told him that it probably had something to do with the list of names that we signed and that the man probably sent it to an SS unit. He probably signed up all the people as volunteers who signed their names – although only five or six signed up voluntarily. Günther then said: "Willi, don't make a big deal out of it. The Navy Radio Operator School is on Thursday in the Ermekeil barracks. Talk to the lieutenant and he'll somehow find a way so that you don't have to go". And I went there on Thursday and showed it to him. He said: "Wait until my lesson is over. Let me have the postcard". After an hour and a half, I went to his office. And he said: "Willi, it's very easy. You don't have to worry. I'll write a preliminary notice of acceptance for the navy and nothing can happen to you". At the same time, he didn't tell me that I joined voluntarily. [laughs] So, I volunteered for the navy although he didn't tell me. That's how they stole men from one another – probably.

I went to the school building at 8:00 in the morning on the day that I had to report for military service. We all had to undress, and a non-commissioned officer came and told us to strip down naked and so on. I didn't undress. He yelled at me. I said: "I'm sorry, but I have a preliminary notice of acceptance for the navy and don't have to register here for military service". He ripped that thing out of my hand and went into another room. I heard the conversation, but couldn't understand anything. And after a minute, he came back and threw the preliminary notice at my feet and said: "Get out of here before I kick you in the ass". Well, I picked it up and left and fourteen days later I was called up for the navy. That's how I went to the navy. I'm happy that I was in the navy – I'm overjoyed that I was in the navy.

Black Sea 3rd R Flotilla (1943)

Richard Kern was born in Kiel in 1920. He participated in the transport of mine sweeping boats from East Prussia to the Black Sea in 1943. These boats were dismantled, transported on the German Autobahn, and re-assembled in Regensburg before being brought down the Danube for operations on the Black Sea.

We were working in the English Channel when we received orders to travel to East Prussia in order to put together the 3rd Minesweeping Flotilla. This was a new flotilla that had just been constructed in wharfs at various harbours. When our commander heard that he was supposed to transport the first boat to the Black Sea, he said that it was unbelievable. I saw his face and asked myself whether it was April Fools. But no, it was really the truth. And we received orders on how we were supposed to carry it out. This whole matter had already been prepared before we even knew that it was going to be carried out. In fact, large trucks had been built that had about thirty-two or thirty-four wheels – the length of a boat of 40 or 44 metres. This meant that the vehicles had to be built for the entire length of the boats. The engines and everything were removed from the boats. The boats were loaded onto the trucks, and were transported as far as Regensburg. They were transported on the water. There were two motors on board, port and starboard, and one of the motors was permanently mounted and transported to Graz where it was brought to the wharf. And the boats were reconstructed into minesweeping boats. And that was a trip from East Prussia to Regensburg which was about 1,000 kilometres. And during these 1,000 kilometres, these boats were transported on semi-trailers that were about 40 metres long and had thirty-six wheels all together on the right and left – I'm not sure anymore how many wheels there were. It was the worst trip. I was along for part of it, but got out in Regensburg. I then became a petty officer 3rd class. They were on the road for fourteen days and were in Regensburg for another fourteen days.

There was horrible weather at this time. The river was flooded, and we weren't able to launch the boats because they were too light. We had to wait until the rain stopped, and then the boats were able to be transported from Regensburg to Graz on the water. In Graz the boats were rebuilt and transported down the Danube to the Black Sea. And that was the most wonderful trip for us – it was an incredibly enjoyable trip. It was 1,200 kilometres to the Black Sea. And the other boats from our 3rd R Flotilla joined us there. Fifteen other flotillas also came via the Autobahn. I have to say that the English and Americans weren't paying attention to what we were doing. An entire flotilla was transported over the Autobahn to the Black Sea. That had never been done before, and will never be done again.

Everything arrived very safely. We didn't have any casualties along the way. I wouldn't believe the story myself if I hadn't been there. It sounds like a fairy tale. There was a Russian wharf and the final touches were made on the boats in order to turn them into minesweepers. They were made of wood – and especially mahogany wood – which least attracts mines. In the end, we had boats made of metal, but it was a metal that repelled mines. In 1942 or 1943 we had boats that were made strictly out of wood. They didn't attract mines. And then a metal was introduced to the market. The old boats were sunk, and the new boats made of metal.

I was on Boat 35 which was part of the 3rd R Flotilla. It didn't have a real name. We only had boats according to numbers. There were forty-eight crew members on board, and the boat was 40 metres long and 7 metres wide. They were fully furnished with guns and mines. We had four hours of rest and four hours of duty. The cabins were such that when someone woke up, then the person who was on duty went into his room. The captain was the only one who had his own room. The food was good. The navy had the best food. We ate very well. And now I want to mention something that I personally felt to be very pleasant. The Russians were immediately very friendly to us. I had boots made for my father by a Russian bootmaker. And, in exchange, I gave him my father's suit which I stole from my father's closet during my leave home. [laughs] And while I was gone, my father found out that I gave the guy his suit. But this is all beside the point. We had a great deal of contact with the Russian people. We went on land and had to be back by dark.

One time we spent the night with our girls. The next morning, we went back on board completely drunk. Our relationship with them was good to the very end. As the petty officer 3rd class, I was the one who had to take care of the food. I had contact with farmers who had sheep. And I was assigned to get some sheep. I brought them on board, and they were prepared there. The fur was thrown overboard, and our cook always had fresh meat on board. In any case, the food was wonderful. The girls weren't allowed on board at all. After the war, the Russian Navy praised us for being so fair. We recently heard that a lieutenant from Boat 36 was an American prisoner of war after the war. While he was a prisoner, he was asked whether he wanted to join the Russian Navy. They wanted to know whether he could mobilize the kind of boats that we had on the Black Sea. He turned down the offer and said that it was a trick. But I don't think it was a trick. He said that he would go from one prisoner-of-war camp to another.

When were you there?

That was in 1943, 1944, and 1945. At the end of the war in 1945, our forty-two boats were filled with ammunition and sent out to sea and all forty-two boats were blown up. We didn't want to give the boats to the Russians. The English and the Americans would have done the same thing, wouldn't they?

Minesweepers (1944)

Dr Otto Güldenberg was born in Hochdahl near Düsseldorf in 1924. He served aboard navy minesweepers in the Netherlands and in Norway in 1944.

I had my orders to go to Norway, and I travelled by train to Travemünde – to the coast – and from there we boarded a ship to Oslo. And from Oslo we went by train to our ship in Trondheim. It was a so-called "minesweeper ship". It was a large ship as far as we were concerned – 4,000–5,000 tons. It was docked in a wharf and had been converted into a minesweeper for special use in Norway. This is because Norway is made up of numerous fjords, and some of these fjords were mined by the Norwegians. The Germans had the problem during the invasion that their destroyers went into the fjords of Oslo and suffered damage because of the Norwegian coastal artillery. The Norwegians mined some of the most important fjords. In order to find and detonate these mines, we had small boats – motor boats – like you see here on the Rhine – about eight or ten of them. They were lowered into the water and travelled in an angled formation. The first boat was in the front, and then the others staggered behind it. And they were connected by a "minesweeping device", a so-called "otter" device.

These devices were shaped like propane tanks for grills that were about 3 metres long, travelled under water, and had a cutting device in the front – a large saw. And they were connected to the ship by a long metal wire. That was in the first minesweeper I was in. The mines hung from a chain under water, and the device cut the chain that the mines were hanging on. They had to hang on a chain under water. The chain was cut and then the mine came to the surface and floated on the water. And then it was detonated with machine gun fire or carabineer fire or anti-aircraft fire. This was done from a distance because you couldn't get close to them.

In our first ship we had a mine that exploded – who knows how – maybe the metal wire came into contact with the detonator and triggered the explosion. In Norway, I didn't have to do all this work because when I arrived there in October 1944, they had other worries. The mine problem had pretty much been solved, and now we had to accompany ship convoys. They travelled through the fjords or around the rocks in the water – and it was always difficult to manoeuvre. But ammunition and supplies had to be transported to the north of Norway. And that's why we had these ship convoys. If they were heavily protected with machine guns and anti-aircraft guns or whatever, then they travelled away from the coast, practically on the open sea. And in this case, there was some contact with the enemy – with airplanes and so on – and less so with ships. Otherwise, Norway was relatively calm. Also, in terms of the population: they were reserved and not particularly hostile. There was no strong underground movement. You could go on land and into the cities. It wasn't like in France or in Russia or anything like that. It wasn't comparable.

Submarine U 1109 (1945)

Ignaz Britz was born in Bonn-Beuel in 1925. He served aboard the submarine U 1109 in 1945 as a battle station helmsman. He recalls encounters with English ships near the British Isles and the day-to-day life aboard a German submarine.

Where did you see action?

Around England. In the Irish Sea and beyond the Hebrides. The Orkney Islands and the Hebrides. The final forty or fifty submarines were deployed around England. After the invasion had taken place [D-Day], operations in the Channel were practically impossible because there was too much surveillance. Anyway, we tried to attack ship convoys between the Orkney Islands and the Hebrides or in the Irish Sea. But the area was so well monitored that we were only able to slip through, so to speak. You also have to remember that the area was heavily mined and that there were noises everywhere so that you heard banging around you the whole time.

And were you directly involved in battle?

Yes, we were directly involved in battle. One time we came across an English reconnaissance group. And by chance, those were three English destroyers. They were carrying out repairs in this area. And below in our boat we could hear the English sailors pounding on something with a hammer. I suppose that was the reason why they weren't attentive and didn't notice our approach. And we took our battle stations. The torpedoes were ready, the firing data had been calculated, and just as the commander was about to fire, our boat started to sink backwards. And it kept sinking backwards. The head engineer, who was standing next to me at the dive planes, constantly had the water trimmed towards the front in order to balance the boat. But this wasn't possible, and the boat sank backwards down to 200 metres. There was almost panic in the boat because no one knew what was going on. And, in the back of the boat, they kept asking whether everything was sealed. And the answer came back that everything was sealed. Except for one time, the electric motor was almost under water. And later they discovered that it must have been a mistake made by the torpedo mechanic in the back. I say that it must have been a mistake because it was never determined with 100 per cent certainty who flooded the bilge instead of flooding the torpedo tubes. Well, okay. We were very lucky that no one noticed us. But while we were pumping out the water and trying to establish the correct balance, our boat shot out of the water – and the entire front part of the boat together with the conning tower went back down under water again – it had to go back down. In any case, they didn't notice us, and we were able to then slip away.

Another time we had been chased for at least fifty or sixty hours. Afterwards, we were all lying in our cabins gasping for air, and we didn't know what we should do because a group of destroyers had their hooks on us from above and followed us for several hours and dropped water bombs on us, and, at some point, we had to come to the surface. And we did that. We filled all five torpedo tubes with water and got the torpedoes ready. And we came up to the surface, opened the conning tower hatch, the commander went out, the bridge crew went out, we raced to the cannons – and we were standing in a thick fog. It was unbelievable, but that's the way it was. We were standing in a thick fog. And that's why they couldn't get us, and we slipped away through an English minefield. Luckily, we didn't hit anything. We didn't go over a mine. The mines were probably a great deal deeper. And that's how we escaped once again.

You were really lucky

Yes, we were really lucky. I have to say that there was always some contact with the enemy. We tried to stay as close to the coast as possible because along the coast the radar didn't work as well. And maybe that was our protection.

Was that the last confrontation or was there another?

I had two life-threatening experiences. During the others the enemy wasn't nearby. Of course, we noticed when the enemy was approaching and always reacted accordingly. I remember another incident. When you went underwater in a submarine, you didn't come to the surface again. You have to remember that we never came to the surface. I recall the experiences of the American submarine *Nautilus* after the war which was under the ice of the North Pole. We weren't under the ice, but we did have those kinds of long trips under the water during the war without coming to the surface. Well, in a submarine you accumulate a lot of trash if you're continuously under water and you have to live from canned food. So, if you didn't want it to stink in the boat while you were under water, the cans had to be washed out with salt water, crushed, and packed into bags. But with time so many trash bags accumulated in a small submarine that we had to go to the surface at some point during the night in order to throw the bags overboard. They were passed up to the conning tower hatch and thrown overboard. We weren't on the surface for more than five minutes, when English planes were on our backs. For the surveillance of the Atlantic, the English first used radar equipment, and, just before they were over the boats, they used spotlights, and we were lit up like during the daytime. And while we were using the snorkel equipment, they often tried to shine the light on the snorkel, but the snorkel tube was difficult to locate because it had a tin covering. And it's difficult to locate the snorkel because it was so small even with the covering and because of the radar protection.

What was the atmosphere like aboard the submarine?

I would say that the atmosphere aboard submarines was good. The English, in particular, always talked about the "band of brothers". And it probably wasn't different on English and American submarines because in such a small group where you were constantly in contact with one another you were never able to spend time alone. The atmosphere had to be good for the simple reason that everyone knew that they depended on the others to the very end.

The cabins were designed in a way that only the crew that wasn't on duty could sleep in the cabin where the others had just woken up. If one person had duty, another person slept in his cabin. On a submarine there weren't many cabins – there were also a few hammocks. If the submarine was docked in a harbour, the entire crew was never able to sleep there. At least one-third or one-half of the crew went on land and slept in the submarine lodging. In terms of food, there was only a very small kitchen. There was hardly enough room for two people, and it was always a big job to cook the right things for the crew. The food was not only good – it was excellent. It was the best of the best. If you're always together in such a small area, there are naturally complaints about the toilet. One person wants to go, but can't. The other can, but doesn't want to because the toilet is occupied. We had two toilets on board: the one was a pump toilet that you could use down to 30 metres under water. It always had to be pumped out. The other was an air pressure toilet which couldn't be used often for the simple reason that when you released it with air pressure, you could see it on the surface of the water. And that was a disadvantage for the submarine because it could be detected by the enemy. It was always a difficult situation with the air pressure toilet. Our commander solved the problem by only allowing the officers to use the air pressure toilet since there were only a few officers. And after using it four, five, or seven times, it was flushed because there weren't so many officers on board. But if the entire crew had used it, then it wouldn't have worked out well. And I remember a personal story that I have to tell you: [laughs] We were at our battle stations, and I had to use the toilet urgently. And if you were at your battle station, then you couldn't use the toilet. You had to stay at your post. What else could you do than to go in your pants. And then afterwards it stunk so badly that the head engineer said: "We can't go on like this. Replacement". Since I was the battle station helmsman, I wasn't supposed to be replaced. But they somehow found a solution.

The drinking water was so scarce that it was only used to drink or brush your teeth. We were able to wash ourselves in bowls with salt water. There was a special soap. We always called it "floating soap" because it floated on the water. And then there was the German RIF soap that was made of clay, and you got even dirtier than before you used it. It was very bad. The salt water soap was okay. You had to wash with salt water and that wasn't good for your skin. You were able to shower between the two diesel engines – which means between the machine hook-ups. We built a shower made of tin cans. If you got along well with the machine room personnel, you could take a quick shower during the snorkel mode when the diesel engine was on.

The shower was rigged together. You took a tin can – there were enough on board – and you made holes on the top and connected a line leading into it from the cooling water – which was hot – and then you were able to shower. The cooling water was normally 50°C or 60°C, and you added a little cold water, and it was okay. You know, sailors weren't spoiled. That's why they all had long beards after every trip into enemy waters. You could skip shaving. But when I was in Brest in the reserves, we had to welcome home the navy guys. The first time that I saw navy guys returning home I was horrified at how pale they were. Every face was deathly pale. You can only imagine this once you've seen it. And afterwards, we got ultraviolet light on board – lamps – and you could lie down in your cabin and enjoy the ultraviolet light. But since we only had two or three lamps on board, we didn't often get a chance.

Vlasov Army in Denmark (1945)

Gerhart Kreisel was born in 1926 in Thuringia. He was a radio operator in the navy stationed on Sylt, the Faroe Islands, and in Denmark. He recalls the fate of the Vlasov Army in Denmark in 1945.

Were you at your base in western Denmark at the end of the war?

Yes. Since Germany sent its most active people to the Front, our entire base was supervised by the Vlasov Army. They were the Russians who crossed over to the German Army with General Vlasov.[3] They were from the navy and the infantry, and they brought along their own officers. They were practically integrated with us up there. These people weren't communists – they were in the most horrible situation because they were to be sent back. They received uniforms from us and were together with us at our base. One of them – Peter from Leningrad – played cards with us. They knew some German and were really nice guys. We had a small group that always met. You see, they were German soldiers, and we'd developed a certain friendship. But that all came apart at the end of the war. You've probably heard about the tragedy of the Vlasov Army.

The question was what they should do with these people who declared their loyalty to the German armed forces. The Russians demanded that they be extradited. That was the tragic thing – there were also some in Sweden back then. They were transported back by ship and many of the Russians took their own lives on the way back. In any case, I didn't have any contact with them anymore. When the war was over, the Russians – the voluntary German soldiers – gathered together and turned the entire area into their own base. And they demanded to stay with the English. But it wasn't granted to them. They were all repatriated. And the Russians put them all in penal camps when they were brought back. Stalin dictated this, and the English and the Americans couldn't prevent it. They had to be brought back to the East. Many of them took their own lives here.

Were you together with them when they found out that the war was over?

Yes, I was there. They were horrified. They were horrified. And they had their officers speak for them and said: “We won’t go along with this. We’re not going back”. But the officers were also powerless. Most of the Russian officers didn’t have anything to say when Vlasov fought for us. I have to say, this made me very depressed. We were transferred from the base one night, and I don’t know whether these men were finally handed over to the Russians.

Radio Operator in Cuxhaven (1945)

Hans Schulz was born in Kamp-Lintfort on the Lower Rhine in 1927. He volunteered for the navy in 1944 in order to avoid being sent to the Russian Front and received basic training as a radio operator.

When you were finished with your basic training you came to a so-called "replacement company". This meant that you waited until people were needed somewhere. And I was also there after my basic training. Besides our guard duty, we didn't have to do anything at all. We waited. And one evening, I was on guard duty at the main gate of the Navy Intelligence School in Aurich. I had guard duty – which meant that I had to check people coming in and out. I still remember that I was reading an interesting book at midnight by E.T.A. Hoffmann, *The Devil's Elixirs*. I was incredibly gripped by this book when the telephone rang. It was the Navy High Command in Wilhelmshaven. I answered the phone, and they gave the orders that six radio operators were to report to Nordholz in Cuxhaven the following day. They were supposed to be detached there.

When was this?

It was in March 1945. Then I asked them which names they wanted. They said that they didn't care, and that I should ask the petty officer 2nd class about who would be detached. And I knew that the petty officer 2nd class was spending the night with one of the signal communication girls. I knew where he was and knocked on the door of the room. "Who's there?" he asked. "It's Private Schulz. They need six sailors. Who should I send?" And he shouted through the door: "I don't give a damn!" [laughs] And then I picked up the phone and gave them my name first and my five roommates. And that's how we got out of there. On the next morning, we handed in our departure notices and left for Nordholz in Cuxhaven.

But nothing happened in Cuxhaven – that's the way it was when you first arrived somewhere. And we got radio sets from Phillips. I remember that they were for shortwave (40–70 watts) and longwave (40–80 watts). They weren't very powerful, but they were for radio and telephone communication. You could also speak into the microphone and send Morse code. But we still didn't know what was going on. And then we found out that they had formed a staff to cross the Elbe to take care of the transfer from Cuxhaven to Hamburg. They built these crossing points everywhere where there were ferries for the troops that came back from the East. It was rather chaotic at this time with refugees and people like that. I was then sent to the headquarters in Glückstadt up in Schleswig-Holstein. We were there with four radio operators, about two or three sailors, an administrator, a cook, and about twenty or twenty-five officers. In addition, there were 4,000 navy signal communication girls in the barracks. I never saw the head of this staff. He was an admiral – or something like that.

In any case, we didn't have to deal with him. Our boss was a reserve officer, Lieutenant Commander Westpfahl. He was the director of the Deutsche Bank and was a fine man. He had the final word. The entire staff in charge of crossing the Elbe consisted of about 2,000 people who were spread out from Hamburg to Cuxhaven. It was our job to take care of rations and things like that. We confiscated a tug boat and drove to Cuxhaven. And in Cuxhaven we picked up rations, drinks, clothing, and anything that we got our hands on and distributed these things – naturally also among ourselves. We couldn't keep the things in the barracks, and I got a room outside of the barracks with cellar storage together with another radio operator. He was two years older and cleverer than me. He knew his way around. He also had a cellar room in this same house. And, of course, we filled these rooms with everything possible: cigarettes, drinks, Steinhäger Juniper Schnapps, sweaters, binoculars, and who knows what. We also had food, corned beef, and whatever there was. Everything that we got our hands on. And then finally the end of the war drew near – the surrender was on 8 May. No one knew what was going to happen. But we were all happy that it was over. We survived the war, although not everyone had made it.

And you survived it well

Yes, if you look at it that way. And then it started – English troops marched into Glückstadt. We had to report somewhere. There were large posters in German: "All German soldiers must report to the authorities", and it added, "aside from those released before 8 May". This meant soldiers who had been released by the Germans before 8 May. And then we conferred with the lieutenant commander. We had all the official seals. And we released ourselves. You can see it here in my pay book. It's written here. Do you see it?

Could you read it aloud?

It says: "Radio operator Hans Schulz was released from military service on 28 April 1945 and must report immediately to the military command in charge and to the employment office". Lieutenant Commander Westphahl signed it and stamped it. This meant for us that we weren't soldiers, and no one could hold us as prisoners, not even the English. We had discharge papers, and they even proclaimed this themselves.

What did you do?

Yes. What did we do? The officers in our staff were gone immediately. We were only there with a senior administrator who was responsible for distributing things and for the books, etc. He was from Krefeld, and I was from Kamp-Lintfort. He immediately took all the official seals – twenty-four official seals. And then there were other people we also knew. We also released them and signed the documents ourselves. Everything was accepted. Word spread around Glückstadt in the shortest time. People from the entire area came from anti-aircraft units with suitcases full of paybooks. The girls that we knew stamped paybooks day and night and discharged people. I think that a few thousand men are indebted to me because they weren't taken as prisoners of war. I still give myself great credit for this today.

Navy and National Socialism

Gerhard Frühe was born in 1922 in Karlsruhe. He served aboard the cruiser *Köln*, the battleships *Tirpitz* and *Scharnhorst*, and the torpedo boat *T 18* in the German Navy from 1940 until 1945. He describes the ideology of the navy under the Third Reich.

During the time of Raeder,[4] who was commander-in-chief from 1928 to 1943 and was very conservative, the navy felt politically capable of carrying out anything except resistance. This is because the revolution of 1917 and 1918 in the German Imperial Navy was such an obstacle to any further resistance that no one thought that anything like that would repeat itself. And with Dönitz[5] basically nothing changed concerning this matter. In 1943 the so-called National Socialist Leadership Officer was introduced – in short, the NSLO. You had to go down to the battalion level – in the navy at that time it was called flotilla – in order to choose someone for this position. We did it this way: We looked around in the flotilla staff to find a person who had the least amount of work. Of course, this was the doctor so he became the National Socialist Leadership Officer, the Nazi commissar. This didn't turn out well because it became apparent that this person was first of all a reserve officer in an active torpedo boat, and, secondly, he had a cousin in the British Royal Navy. But both of these things weren't so bad: It was worse that he was a psychotherapist. And the regime and its leaders didn't like psychotherapists because they didn't want people looking into their souls. Therefore, he had to be replaced. But who were we going to appoint? The next unsuspicious person was an administrative officer. He participated in the Olympics and had been the high jump champion several times.

Every Sunday, the so-called church flag was raised on the battleships *Tirpitz* and *Scharnhorst*. Mass services were held. I don't know whether the pastor on the *Tirpitz* was Protestant or not – that wasn't important. I only want to give you a few examples of how the Third Reich, which in fact was so strictly organized, was never able to manipulate people – thank God that it only lasted twelve years – not the forty years of the GDR with the secret police. We didn't think about resistance or anything like that – those were thoughts far away: [We thought of] winning the war, doing our duty for the Fatherland, and sometimes we talked about a time when the Nazi party would no longer exist after the war. You could talk about this openly without feeling like resistance fighters.

If I can summarize the experience of comradeship and leadership responsibility that was established and carried out in the early years, [I can say that] you had to want to take on responsibility, you had to do your duty, and you had to be superior at least in certain areas; otherwise, you wouldn't have been believable in your leadership. And we learned these things very early on – the experiences from the German Youth were very useful.

CHAPTER III

WESTERN AND SOUTHERN CAMPAIGNS

Invasion of Belgium (1940)

Ernst Osterspey was born in 1906 in Mechernich near Cologne in North Rhine-Westphalia. He was working as a gardener in Belgium when German soldiers invaded the country on 10 May 1940.

One morning at 5:00 am, the Germans marched into town and woke me up. I looked outside to see what was going on and saw German soldiers below going past our building. That meant war. At the same time, the huge railway bridge was blown up. I believe that it was approximately 100 metres high and 1 kilometre long. It extended over the town where I was living – Moresnet. We lived somewhat out of the way and that's why we didn't notice anything – we just saw the rubble from this bridge.[1] But it meant war.

You were in Belgium in 1940?

Yes. In Belgium. Although I was German, I was on the Belgian side of the border. There were German monks who lived there. And I was asked to come there to oversee [gardening] work. We did that and were surprised at the end of this work that it was war. Well, the Germans were there. But they didn't come in like a wild horde, but rather in an orderly manner. They marched one behind the other. Below my window there was an open square, and they lined up there for roll call. They were told: "No one is allowed to enter any house in this town by force – or any store. And if you go into a store" – there were a lot of stores because it was a pilgrimage site – "no one may leave the store without paying". In the town where I lived, I never heard anything to the contrary. They were kept under strict control. And they said "Heil Hitler!" and were dismissed. They only stayed a few days and then moved on. But they raised hell in all of Belgium. When they were about 20 kilometres away, they came to a Belgian fortification. And it resulted in fighting. That was the real war with shooting.

Did you stay in Belgium during the war or were you drafted?

I stayed in Belgium. But I stopped the gardening work and went to the German railway – to the railway network that we occupied in Belgium. I went there and got work in the pay office.

The Germans wanted to conquer the world. And wherever they went, the railway had to deliver supplies. We needed them. That's why I immediately got work at the railway. I was in the pay office where I had to receive and distribute mail to every single civil servant and do other things. Later on, it was very important for my retirement. I was a railway man. And because there was a shortage of railway men, they were exempt from serving as soldiers. They were exempt from military service. It was my job to take care of the mail, and one day there was a letter addressed to me from the army. I was required to go to my boss who received the mail. But I confiscated the letter. After a few weeks my draft notice arrived. I took it to my boss and said: "A draft notice? Why that? We haven't received the first order yet. I would have known. I deliver the mail. We can't do anything about it. It must have been lost". There wasn't any registered mail – not for us on the railway. We had our own management. Well, I had to report for active duty in fourteen days.

Military Intelligence (1940)

Hans Adolf Stiehl was born in 1922 in Witzenhausen (Hesse). In 1940 he was sent to Berlin for training as an interpreter and translator for work in military intelligence.

While we were in the middle of a drill, someone came running up and said: "Private Stiehl, report to the captain". "Man, what have I done now?" I thought: "I haven't done anything". And I went there. I was completely perplexed. The captain came up to me. "Private Stiehl, congratulations. This is great. It's wonderful. My God, you are really lucky. You're being dispatched to Berlin for special training as an army interpreter and translator". I said: "Captain, I volunteered for the Front." "Oh Stiehl, be quiet, will you? You have your orders. Get ready to be sent off."

At first, I was sent to the Intelligence Interpreter Replacement Department in Meißen. They had seen my high school grades. The non-commissioned officer in his stupidity signed me up – I ordered a language magazine and it was forwarded to me. It was called *Paustians Funny Language Magazine*. It was in several languages such as English, French, Italian, and German. And it was always forwarded to me. They were looking for people who had experience in foreign languages and who had lived abroad. He didn't read everything – he only read foreign language learner. And this Private Stiehl was a terrible oaf, he did everything wrong, but he knew all the foreign languages – he was always the best in Italian, English, and French. He reported that I was a person with knowledge of foreign languages and had experience abroad – he checked all the boxes. Maybe he wanted to get rid of me. I don't know. So, I came to Meißen in the so-called Intelligence Interpreter Replacement Department. This was an intelligence unit – which was somewhat more distinguished than the normal infantry – and we were properly trained there and received our degrees as army interpreters and translators.

What was your training like?

It was typically German. And that was naturally to my greatest advantage. They simply quizzed us – grammar was very important. And there were people there who had actually spent time abroad – they had just returned from America and other places – and they couldn't answer any grammar questions. These poor idiots were sent to the Front which they didn't want – and I volunteered for the Front and was forced to do the training. But, of course, I really started to enjoy it. That's clear. And suddenly my entire ideological enthusiasm disappeared, and my love for language won over. But I wasn't happy that I didn't have to go to the Front. On the contrary, I had a bit of a bad conscience. But now I had the joy of being able to work with languages. And we had all the special privileges imaginable. We were able to watch foreign films in closed presentations in order to improve our language skills. Most of the men in the intelligence unit were sent to the Front, but somewhat back from the front line in order to interrogate prisoners and so on. And, at that time in Berlin, they were looking for people who could break the encoded "enemy messages" as they called them back then – in French and English. And for this work they needed foreign language learners who also had mathematics skills in order to be trained in cryptology.

After we had our basic training and were put to work in Berlin, everything was decentralized – which means that we were assigned to individual radio companies which recorded the radio messages. They discovered that it took too much time to break down the big codes, so they went to work on the smaller codes which were no longer valid after two or three days but were easier to crack. But if they were broken down on time, they provided the officers on the Front with information about troop concentrations and so on. This means that we were actually able to crack these day codes, and it made more sense to do so right at the radio company. There was a special enciphering department. I was first assigned to a radio company in Norway – in Bergen and Trondheim – and then near Oslo.

What did the day codes look like?

There was one that was called Rommel I believe. There are basically two kinds of enciphering: the one is a substitution process, and the other is a transposition process. The substitution process consists of a simple

Caesar cipher that is used. I simply shift two letters of the alphabet. The simplest form is when I say one – Caesar cipher one – which can be broken down immediately: A = B, B = C, C = D. That is the simple Caesar cipher. Of course, you make it more difficult if you say Caesar cipher five or seven – this is a larger shift in which A is not just equal to B. And this is the simplest form of the substitution process. You substitute one letter for another. The other is a transposition process. It was used very seldom by the enemy, but sometimes it was used as well. The letters are mixed according to a certain pattern. This means that A remains A, and B remains B, and C remains C, but they are scrambled according to a certain secret pattern. If I have this basic schema, then I can put it back together again. And the simple Caesar cipher was naturally hardly used anymore. The main problem is that the system has to be as secure as possible so that the enemy doesn't solve it immediately. On the other hand, it can't be too complicated because otherwise it causes too many mistakes for the people receiving the message on your own side. And then there are duplicate messages which are a stroke of luck for any enemy decipherer – or code breaker. If radio operator A sends the enciphered message to radio operator B and makes a mistake in one spot, and the other tries to decipher it and can't and sends a message back and says: "Something is wrong. Send it through again correctly" – when he enciphers it, I have the spot where I can break into the code. Then I have the correct code and the incorrect code. These are so-called duplicate messages. That's why it was strictly forbidden on both sides during the war to make any corrections. I could tell you about this for hours.

In Norway we observed the Americans on Iceland. Every day they sent relatively uninteresting reports about the weather. And we were able to orientate ourselves according to which day codes they were using. If they had been using ground troops, then this would have been useful. The theory states that I can break into any system if I have sufficient material. I need 100 elements for a simple Caesar cipher, and then I'll break in. For a more complicated system, I need more and so on. And the more complicated the system is, the more material I need. And these simple codes – the day codes – are easy, but you can't get enough material together. And on the next day they're not valid anymore. We had a few geniuses with us who were able to break into important systems, but of course not into the really big ones.

North Africa (1943)

Walter Düsseldorf was born in Monschau near Cologne in 1923. He flew with the German Air Force to Tunisia at the beginning of 1943 and was assigned to the 6th Tank Division near Gabès, Tunesia. During the fighting against Allied forces in the mountains of Gafsa, he was severely wounded on 1 April 1943 and lost his leg.

At the beginning of January 1943, we flew from Reggio di Calabria [in southern Italy] to Bizerte in Tunisia. On the way, there was a great deal of contact with enemy fighter planes, and it was a very turbulent flight because our plane, a U52, flew approximately 30–35 metres above the sea in order to avoid enemy fighter planes from attacking. We arrived in Bizerte at the airport, and enemy fighter planes were also reported there. This meant that we had to throw our equipment and bags out of the airplane while it was still rolling and carefully leave the airplane while running. The airplane started again immediately and flew back to Italy.

Describe your uniform and the equipment that you had along with you.

We had the normal khaki uniform for the southern theatre which we were wearing in southern Italy, Sicily, and Crete. We had a pair of shorts – there was also a pair of long pants – but we were wearing the shorts. There was a khaki shirt and a cap, and, of course, a steel helmet. The equipment included a tent, a machine gun, and everyone had his own carbine, and a bayonet. We gathered all these things together [on the runway], and had to report to headquarters in Bizerte. This headquarters was next to a soldiers' dormitory where we were able to spend the night. The next day we were supposed to find our troops in Sfax, about 350 kilometres away in the eastern part of Tunisia. This meant that we drove in this direction with different vehicles and met them somewhere near Gabès. We were then transported further because in the meantime we had received orders about where we had to go exactly. And that was near Gabès, but I don't remember the exact name of the town anymore.

It was there that we were assigned to the 6th Tank Division – we were responsible for the weapons. And I was supposed to do my training on the Front for three months before being sent to pilot school in Moravská Ostrava [in Czechoslovakia]. And I was injured during these three months of training. This happened in the mountains around Gafsa – that's not far from the saltwater lakes. We were camped in a mountain range across from American troops. Before we were sent to Gafsa, we were in the desert and dug fox holes and experienced thirty air raids on one day. A lot of our fellow soldiers died there. Then we were moved to the area near Gafsa – in the mountains – and were located across from a North American unit. We were supposed to carry out so-called "observations". This meant that we set up an observation post in this mountain range. We had to crawl on our bellies from our camp to this observation post because each of our movements was being watched by the other side and answered with shrapnel. We had two soldiers at the post and had to remain lying on the ground for two hours. After the first hour, one soldier left and was supposed to wake up the replacement. At 6:00 am, I crawled to this observation post on my belly. At 7:00 am, the other soldier, who was lying there with me, went back and was supposed to arrange the changing of the guards. And the new guard never showed up. A tech sergeant came and examined the observation post and said that it should be made bigger. I said that we couldn't do that because they were watching our every move. He told me that we shouldn't be overly afraid, and then he removed some of the stones so that we had a better view. And then he went back. As soon as he left, they started shooting with shrapnel, and I noticed that they had observed everything before they started shooting. And then I was hit with shrapnel. First, I only felt a pain in my right leg, but then I looked down and saw that I couldn't move my left foot. Three centimetres were torn from my calf muscle and 2 centimetres from my shin. I first bandaged it together myself – and I also screamed – and my fellow soldiers came to me crawling on their bellies and got me out of this post and bandaged it up. Because of the military activity and the superiority of the Allies, we had problems reaching the casualty clearing station. It took a long time until we reached one, and they attended to me, but they didn't amputate the leg. I think that after seven days I arrived in Sfax. The ambulance was only allowed to drive at night because it was much too dangerous during the day due to the air raids by the Allies. And then I arrived in Sfax in the evening and was supposed to be brought to Naples by hospital ship. During the night that I spent in Sfax – three of us were in one room – the military hospital was hit by a bomb and the two men who were lying next to me in the room were killed, and I was thrown out of my bed and received other injuries.

Early the next morning, I was brought to a hospital ship that was underway for six days: first in the direction of Naples, and then shortly before Naples they said that the port had been bombed so badly that we had to be detoured to Bari. We were detoured to Bari, but underway we often experienced so-called "water bombs" which rocked the ship and caused a lot of anxiety. It's a horrible feeling and situation to lie there in the ship helpless with an injury. We docked in Bari, and the soldiers who were able to be transported were brought to Munich by train. I was no longer able to be transported and had to stay in Bari. And then I met an extremely humane doctor, a major from Austria, who arranged for my leg to be amputated just below the knee. He said that I was so young that we had to do everything to save as much of it as possible. And then he determined that I had gangrene deep in my upper thigh, and he treated this gangrene with a grape-sugar solution. I first stayed in Bari for a few weeks. The leg was amputated, and, as I said, there was the treatment with the grape sugar.

And from there I travelled to Munich by hospital train. I was in a military hospital in München-Schwabing where they continued to treat the injury. And after a few weeks in July, I went from there to Altötting. Did I mention that I was injured on 1 April 1943? No, I didn't mention that. It was on 1 April 1943 when I was at the observation post and was injured. Yes, then I went to Altötting and put in a request to be brought to my home hospital [in St Vitt]. I was moved [to St Vitt], and I was able to make this trip home alone on crutches. I tied a belt around my luggage and went. I was in the hospital there for a few weeks, but I had real problems with the master sergeant. He was such a crazy military fanatic who demanded that the soldiers salute him no matter how severely injured they were. And I found this unbearable and walked past him with my crutches. I thought to myself: "Don't salute him."

And then I thought to myself: “Oh, you’re going to regret it.” And then I thought: “I don’t care.” I walked past him in the courtyard on cobble stones and looked down at the ground, at my crutches, the whole time. And then I heard steps and knew it was him. But I just kept on walking. After I was 2 or 3 metres past him, he shouted at me: “What do you think you’re doing? Don’t you know that you have to salute a superior officer?” And, at that time, I was in the right mood to answer him. And then I turned around with an ironic smile on my lips and said: “O.K., but if I’m walking on cobble stones with crutches and the cobble stones are wet, then I’m going to concentrate on walking and not on what’s going on around me.” And then life was no longer pleasant with him. Shortly afterwards, I asked to be moved to Euskirchen.

And they took very good care of me there.

Before the Normandy Invasion (June 1944)

Heinz Kendziora was born in Lauterberg in Lusatia (Brandenburg) in 1923. He was part of a navy artillery unit in Lorient, France (Brittany), where he suffered from an appendicitis shortly before the Normandy invasion on 6 June 1944.

You were lucky that you were in a military hospital during the invasion

Very. Very. I spoke with people afterwards who were in my company, and they said that they were attacked and a lot of soldiers died. I was first in a military hospital in Sainte-Anne – that's a small town not far away from Lorient – and then I came to Angers for my second operation. I was lying in the military hospital, and, when the invasion came closer, I was supposed to be transported to Germany. I can remember that there were railway cars – the normal cars that they used for cattle with a little bit of straw in them – and this was the transport for the military hospital. I don't know where it was anymore – either in Le Mans or Angers – where we were all gathered and the transport started. But the tracks had been so destroyed in the meantime – the French resistance was very active. They interrupted most of the important railway lines – blew them up – so that we had to travel in a zigzag. We had to first travel here and then there. And while we were travelling for several days via Le Mans as far as Orleans, we came under fire from three English airplanes. These were so-called fighter bombers. They attacked the train although it was clearly marked with the Red Cross. You had to mark them back then.

Was it on the top of the train?

Yes. It was on the top. You could see it. In the meantime, we found out that the Germans weren't obeying the rules and disregarded the Red

Cross. They shot at English ambulances that were marked with the Red Cross – where people were being transported. And naturally the English also shot at our trains. Our train immediately came to a stop, we took cover, and my foot was injured. A bomb fell right in front of me – although they were only able to drop small bombs, but the effect of the shrapnel was incredible. I was sitting in a railway car, the doors were open, and we heard the fighter bombers coming. We heard the roaring of the bombs, and I wanted to lie further back in the railway car and lifted my leg, and while I had my foot in the air, a piece of shrapnel hit it. It wasn't so bad.

It could have been worse

Yes. Yes. When I went back to the train after it was over, people who had been lying next to me were dead. They weren't lucky at all. Luckily, I only had a piece of shrapnel in my foot. That worked out well. They shot at us with 2-centimetre guns – they had everything on board. The fighter bombers were very well equipped and could cause a lot of damage. And the French cared for us. The injured soldiers were taken to the hospital or a kind of clinic. I still remember the name. It was called Château-Renault. It was an old castle that they converted into a military hospital. And that's where we received first-aid treatment.

CHAPTER IV

THE FALL OF THE REICH

D-Day (June 1944)

Paul Golz was born in Waldow/Rummelsburg in Pomerania (present-day Poland) in 1925. He was transferred to Normandy in mid-May 1944 as part of an SMG group [Schweres Maschinengewehr], or heavy machine gun group prior to the Allied landing on D-Day. He describes his experiences in the invasion.

At the beginning of May, we made our way to Saint-Nazaire on foot. We went there with Panjewagen [two-wheeled carts used for transporting heavy guns] that were pulled by mules and led by Ukrainians carrying carbines. The Ukrainians had been taken prisoner of war and were told that if they worked in the German military, they would be released. We walked behind these wagons from Baumholder [in Rhineland-Palatinate, Germany] to Saint-Nazaire. You can only imagine what it was like with the guns on these wagons and all the mules and soldiers. It all took up an incredible amount of space. We walked on foot behind the animals the entire time. In Saint-Nazaire they made aerial observations. Suddenly they discovered that the Allies were looking for a harbour – Saint-Nazaire – and would land in Normandy. I'm not sure whether Rommel said that – or if I read it years later.

In any case, we went to the Cherbourg Heights in Normandy. We dug ourselves in and had tents on the Heights. In the following weeks, we set up so-called "Rommel asparagus" in the swamps: logs about 4 metres long that were buried in the ground and then connected with barbed wire. We had very little to eat because water was part of our rations. There was a farmhouse with a large room and a cooking pot – like in the Middle Ages. Next to the pot was a bed where the farmer and his family slept – they were very simple people. They knew me because I always went for milk to keep up my strength. On the morning of the invasion, we didn't get bombed because we were well camouflaged. I could see how the bombs fell on the other Heights. You could actually see the bombs coming down. While I was standing guard, I saw flares dropping down. They crackled in the air and lit up everything up so that the paratroopers could see the area. That was the idea behind it. That was in the area of Carentan though. I first thought that it was further away. On the following morning, I went to get a litre of milk and the French told me: “Get out, the Allies have landed”.

We marched in the direction of Sainte-Mère-Église and spent more time in ditches than on the road. The planes flew so low that you could see the pilots. We never made it as far as Sainte-Mère-Église. The heavy fighting had already taken place on 6 and 7 June, and we didn’t have to attack. On the way there, I saw something white that was moving. I went to it and saw that a black-faced paratrooper had put a white sock on his gun. I cocked my gun and walked toward him. He was trembling all over with fright. I couldn’t speak English, but I said to him in German: “I won’t harm you”. Because of my calm tone, he realized that nothing would happen to him. I hadn’t eaten anything for a few days and was terribly thirsty. I made it clear to him that I needed something to drink. He offered me his canteen with the words “good water”. He drank first, and then I drank, too. He had cigarettes along, but I didn’t take them away from him because I didn’t smoke. What was I supposed to do with them? He was then transported to the holding area for prisoners.

During the next few days, I searched for paratroopers together with a comrade from Saxony by the name of Schneider. The two of us looked for hidden paratroopers. In another meadow, we found a paratrooper lying there with his eyes open. He was the first corpse I had ever seen in my life. He was lying there very calmly, and I thought to myself: “Is he still alive?” The two of us went to him, but I couldn’t see if he had been injured. Schneider then searched him. I didn’t like that. My father told me that once you took a weapon away from a soldier, he was no longer your enemy. Schneider took the man’s wallet and opened it up. There was a picture of a blond woman from New York. I told him: “Leave it there. It doesn’t belong to you. It is probably his wife.” He said: “No. I like it,” and put it into his pocket. I got really angry. The man had a beautiful gold ring – probably his wedding band – and Schneider couldn’t get it off. He then said: “I’ll cut his finger off.” Suddenly I got really angry. I pointed my carbine at him and said: “If you cut off his finger, I’ll blow you away.” He got afraid and left it alone.

A few days later when we were leaving this meadow, Americans started shooting at us. We steered clear of them and hid behind a pile of wood. Schneider started shooting at the tanks. We were the only ones on the right side in an open area of 1,000 metres who could shoot. The other soldiers couldn't shoot that far. It wasn't possible. I told him that we had to leave the area because they had spotted us, and there would be an enormous barrage of gunfire. We left the spot immediately and crossed the road. We couldn't continue on the road and went into the woods where we found holes in the ground from past German soldiers. When we jumped into the holes, we found a bazooka. There was a German officer there who probably also did not want to fight. Schneider wanted to shoot at the tank with his pistol. The lieutenant shouted at him: "Throw the pistol away! Are you crazy? You can't shoot at a tank with a pistol". He then threw the pistol away. The tank was positioned there – an American tank – a Sherman – the big one. The American soldiers accompanying the tank said: "Hey boy, come on. Let's go. Hands up". Thank God the war was over for me. I was lucky that I didn't have to go through the major battles. That's how I stayed alive. I later saw that the cemetery in Normandy was lined with soldiers who were my age. I was really lucky.

We were brought to the holding camp for prisoners in Cauquigny and searched. They discovered the dead American's wallet with my comrade from Saxony. I said to him: "You should have left that with the dead man". A guard struck him in the behind with the butt of his rifle. I said to him: "See, that's what you get. If they had found the ring with you, they would have killed you immediately". We marched to the coast for three hours. I didn't see any bunkers along the way. It was the flat area on the coast. We waited on the beach in the sand for a few hours. I was really hungry and discovered a can of lard. I somehow opened it and ate some of the pure lard. We then boarded the landing boats – thirteen or fourteen men fit on board. The water wasn't so deep that you needed to swim – it came up to your knees. We didn't want to get our clothes wet and took off our boots and rolled up our pants and boarded the landing boats. The Americans watched us and thought: "The Germans aren't so stupid". When we were in the boat, we rolled down our pants, put on our boots again, and were dry. There was drinking water on board, and we all had something to drink. There wasn't any shooting at that time. From the landing boats we were boarded onto ships. There were thousands of ships there. I thought to myself: "We should really stop fighting with the Americans and the English. What is the sense of it? Young men are being sacrificed unnecessarily. We should end the war here and fight the Russians". Those were my thoughts as a 19-year-old.

We boarded the English ship and hadn't had anything to eat for a few days. We were enormously hungry. On the first floor there was a mess hall. They had mashed potatoes, Frankfurt sausage, coffee, and white bread – which I didn't like too much – you could squeeze it together. We stood in the line to eat and then lined up one more time. Some guys ate two or three times. The mess officer shouted out: "What the hell is going on here? We only have 800 German prisoners and 3,000 have eaten." [laughs] After we had been taken to England, an old English colonel came and wanted to order us around. He said in German: "Stood at attention!" Everyone started to laugh. It's called "stand at attention" in German. He was insulted. We were then marched through a small town in England to the train station. We wanted to show them that we hadn't been demoralized and sang: "We're marching against England". Civilians were standing along the side of the road, but didn't say anything negative to us. They probably thought that the Germans weren't so demoralized. We were brought to the train and guarded by Scots. We were curious whether they wore anything under their kilts. Of course, they did. We were then lodged for fourteen days and boarded the ship *Queen Mary I* for America.

Heinz Rosenthal was born in Treptow an der Rega in present-day Poland in 1926. In April 1944 he was deployed to Normandy as part of the 3rd Parachute Division, Reconnaissance Unit 12 under General Meindl at the age of seventeen. He recalls his experiences on D-Day.

I had guard duty from July 5 to 6 in a large bunker with a huge artillery gun pointed in the direction of England. At 2:00 am, I went into the bunker where my fellow soldiers were lying down and sleeping. In the corner was a buddy of mine who had a radio. He was able to receive the British Broadcasting Station which always started with the sound "BOOM, BOOM, BOOM, BOOM.... BOOM, BOOM, BOOM, BOOM". [imitates the sound] "This is the station of the English soldiers – we are speaking to the German soldiers. Last evening our planes bombed the cities of Hamburg and Bremen. And we would like to announce that it's Berlin tomorrow." We sat there and wondered. At 2:00 am I placed my submachine gun on the bench and wanted to lie down. Suddenly, shelling began across the English Channel – all of us jumped up and ran outside. The sky was red, and there was enormous shelling in a crossfire – 42-centimetre calibre guns. They whistled across the sky [imitates the sound] and landed far behind us and exploded. Even our bunker was shaking. That was the trick they used. During the night, they dropped at least 1,000 paratroopers and gliders from the sky so that we wouldn't notice anything because of the shelling. That was really a shrewd way of conducting war.

In the morning at sunrise, we were suddenly told: "Paratroopers fall in". We walked down the village road until we reached the woods. They didn't know what to do with us. We had been trained in ground combat, but we were basically paratroopers. We were a special unit. We went into the woods, and our squad leader said: "There's a farmhouse over there. Let's go to it and quench our thirst". In Normandy, there is cider and calvados. We filled our canteens and our mess kits and sat in a corner. The shelling and the shooting were all around us. We thought that we would never get out of there. I took my mess kit and drank calvados – we were only seventeen and a half at that time – we didn't have any experience with alcohol. We were immediately buzzed. And then we thought: "Okay, go ahead and shoot us. Eventually the planes will come and hit us".

This went on day and night in a state between sleeping and being awake. The detonations of the bombs and the shelling were a part of it just as much as the alcohol. If we hadn't been so young, we would certainly have died without having even been hit by a single bullet. My luck didn't last very long as I was injured on my right hip by a piece of shrapnel from a shell fired by American combat troops. Our medic hung a yellow and red tag around my chest. With this I was able to leave the Front. I ran to the first best truck that was driving back to the next first-aid station. It was just behind the Front.

Due to this injury, I was able to stay several kilometres behind the Front with the supply lines. We dug ourselves into the ground and set up our tarps like tents. My company commander, Lieutenant Terjung, told me to go to the field kitchen to get something to eat because it was already lunchtime. I received a large plate of freshly fried liver from the cook and walked back to my lieutenant. On the way back on the village road, our company doctor suddenly drove up next to me and asked me where I was going with the plate of food. We discovered that we were going to the same place. So, I hopped inside the vehicle. He asked: "What do you have on your plate?" He took a piece of freshly fried liver and ate it. Then he said to me: "The war will be over soon". I thought that I hadn't heard him correctly. In the meantime, we arrived at the lieutenant's tent. I reported back to duty, placed my plate on the table and eavesdropped to what they were saying in the next room. "The Führer is dead! A bomb went off in the Führer's headquarters." There was great silence. I immediately ran to my fellow soldiers who were cleaning their weapons and reported what I had heard.

The guys immediately dropped everything. There was suddenly another mood in the room. Plans were now being made about which trucks would drive us in the direction of home. The entire group was excited, but they first wanted to understand what would happen. But there was a news blackout. Our radio operator was no longer allowed to use his radio equipment from this moment on. We were perplexed and cut off from the world. We stood over the maps we had along and tried to find the fastest route home. In the meantime, it was early evening when a motorcycle drove to our camp, and a soldier went into the company commander's tent. We were all excited about the news he brought. It didn't take long before all the platoon leaders were told to receive their orders in the company tent. They returned and ordered us to get ready for deployment immediately. We climbed onto trucks, drove for three hours on bumpy country roads, and were told repeatedly to "get off" – this time directly behind a bridge.

We jumped into ditches on the right and left of the road. It was pitch-black. Our trucks drove back. Tanks suddenly appeared before us on the dark road. We thought that they were German tanks! They drove so close to us that we were almost able to touch them. Apparently, they didn't see us in the ditches. Suddenly, there were detonations and shooting. I ran up the embankment onto a field. The tanks drove up to the bridge. I ran through a field in the direction of the canal. A tank exploded on the bridge. Our guys blew up this tank with a bazooka. At once several guys from my platoon appeared around me, and we started to cross a river. In the next village, we were stopped by the "watchdogs" – the SS military police. Everyone who arrived had to go to a barn. When everyone had assembled, we were told that the Führer was still alive.

The Americans were still held up on the other side of the river when we took up our positions in the early morning hours. During the day, they crossed the river at some point and were involved in heavy fighting. In the afternoon, my friend Hans-Walter called out to me and told me to come. A few metres away Lieutenant Terjung lay on the ground with his eyes open and a hole in his forehead. Before the invasion, he had received special leave to get married in Berlin. We then went to the foremost part of the Front. Many of my fellow soldiers had died in battle or were injured. Thank God that my friend Hans-Walter from Sonneberg in Thuringia was still there. We had been deployed as company messengers from the very beginning.

Again and again, there was terrible fighting. We were waiting for our lives to come to an end. In the early morning hours of 12 August 1944, there was a horrible tank attack by the Allies. From the air, American fighter bombers shot at us. On the previous evening, our company sergeant major arrived with rations and mail. I was just about to open a letter from my mother when a fellow soldier started to scream horribly. In spite of the heavy shooting, I ran to him and saw that his right foot was attached only by the Achilles tendon. The first tanks and troops of the Allies were already so close. I couldn't help the poor guy anymore and only had the chance to escape.

We tried to find cover in an area of the woods, but the tanks kept shooting at us. Suddenly, I felt a sharp pain on my right bottom rib. I unbuttoned my uniform and felt inside with my hand and had blood on my fingers. We crossed a large field in the direction of a farmhouse to find cover. On my way, a dead SS soldier lay on the ground still holding a pistol in his right hand. I jumped over him and ran across the field in the direction of some trees under which I looked for cover. I jumped down into a ravine and glanced in the direction of the farmhouse as an American tank approached from the field and shot at me. In the ravine there were several soldiers from other units. The shelling from the tank hit a tree trunk 3 metres away from me. In front of me, a soldier jumped up screaming terribly and then collapsed. At that moment, I felt a terrible pain on my right shoulder. I wanted to reach for my submachine gun with my right hand, but I couldn't move it. I first noticed what had happened when I touched my right shoulder with my left hand. Suddenly a fellow soldier appeared from my group. He took a look at my injury and said: "You won't make it." I asked him to bandage it, and he immediately tried. "I need ten bandage packs for it," he said, but only had two.

He bandaged it as well as possible and suddenly disappeared. I crawled out of the ravine with all my strength. In front of me, there was a large field of wheat that I wanted to cross. When I finally reached the woods, I noticed the terrible confusion. An entire unit of motorized vehicles had been bombed and shot up. Even the huge trees had been cut in half. I noticed how my strength was slowly leaving me. Blood was dripping down my entire body into my right shoe. Suddenly, I saw a street in front of me. I looked to the left and saw a tank in the distance, hoping that it was a German tank. Unfortunately, I was mistaken.

I ran across the street as fast as I could and dived into a deep ditch. I must have been asleep – unconscious for a while. I noticed that I was lying with my face in water. I heard a voice up on the street. I stood up with great effort and struggled to climb up the embankment. An amphibious vehicle with a doctor and a medic were there who had been gathering up injured soldiers. I approached the doctor who said to me: "If you can still walk, I'll take you directly to the next first-aid station". In the background, a stretcher with a severely injured soldier was being carried off.

After a short trip, I was taken to a barn that was full of injured soldiers. I received an injection and a drink from a canteen and fell asleep. At midnight, all hell broke loose when suddenly a shell hit the barn. They pulled me out by my legs because the barn was burning, tossed me onto a truck, and drove off. Many wounded soldiers lay on the truck. We drove over the bombed roads of Normandy for several hours while the sun was coming up. The truck stopped, and we were unloaded. A first-aid station had been set up in a large country house. A few minutes later, I lay on an operating table, and they removed shrapnel from my body. Of course, again with injections. A new bandage was applied. I was placed onto a stretcher and brought to a tent. Afterwards, I fell into a deep sleep. I dreamt of home: I saw my mother and my little brother Klaus. I saw the chickens on the farmyard, and everything was the way it used to be. But I woke up suddenly because the stretcher was being carried away. I was brought to a medical vehicle and the trip continued. After five hours we reached the city of Évreux. Here we were unloaded onto a large schoolyard. There were drinks and medication for the pain.

On the next morning on 15 August 1944, I was carried out and placed in the schoolyard as if they were bringing out the rubbish bins. The schoolyard was full of wounded soldiers. The sun was beating down on us unbearably. Suddenly there was the sound of alarms in the city. The sky was cloudless, and I saw numerous planes flying towards the city. Bombs, bombs, and the earth shook. Luckily, I was able to sit and was carried onto the truck. Nobody knew where to.

Suddenly, a fellow soldier next to me said: "Isn't that the Eiffel Tower?" We couldn't believe it when we drove under the Eiffel Tower in Paris. There were again medics, and again operations. The nurses asked for my paybook. Although it was soaked in blood, the nurses were able to read my date of birth. Then someone said: "It's the boy's birthday today". It was on 15 August, my eighteenth birthday, that my injury was taken care of properly for the first time. The doctors, the medics, and the nurses drank to my health. Apparently, everyone thought that I wouldn't make it long. Afterwards, I didn't notice anything anymore and first woke up during the night when I felt sick. Everything around me was dark in the room. The window was open, and I could see the Eiffel Tower in front of me. I felt so sick that I threw up out of the tenth floor window of a building. I wasn't able to find the bathroom.

A medic woke me the next morning on 16 August 1944. Another trip to an unknown place. After we had been on the road an entire day, we were transported to a hospital on the Belgian border. I was operated on there and finally came into a bed with white sheets. On the third day the Allies bombed the train station, and we heard the news that the Allies were no longer far away. My roommate who had lost both legs pushed his pillow to the side and showed me his pistol. He said: "When they come, that'll be my last act".

A medic came running into the room and asked: "Who can walk?" The next trip to an unknown place. Nothing to eat, nothing to drink. Two days long. Finally, the train stopped at a large supply station. All the medics, nurses, and wounded soldiers who could walk, stormed into the entrance to get something to eat and drink. From our compartment, four soldiers left in order to get something to eat. They brought back four cardboard boxes. We opened them immediately. To our great disappointment, there was only chocolate inside. The soldiers in the next compartment had canned meat in their cardboard boxes. Others managed to find warm bread. Others had a case of wine. Then we started to barter among ourselves. We were full and satisfied when the journey continued.

A day later we were transported to Mönchengladbach. From the train station we were brought by tram to a large gym. There was something to eat, and our bandages were changed. On the following day, our journey continued on the same hospital train. A railway bridge had just received makeshift repairs, and we couldn't continue. On the tracks to the right and left, hospital trains were being fired on by low-flying planes. What I saw there I'll never be able to forget my entire life.

Assassination Attempt on Hitler (July 1944)

Kunrat von Hammerstein was born in Berlin in 1918. As the son of General von Hammerstein who opposed Hitler, he joined the resistance movement together with his elder brother Ludwig. After the assassination attempt on Hitler failed on 20 July 1944, von Hammerstein was forced to flee from the Gestapo. His mother, sister, and younger brother were arrested and sent to Dachau as political prisoners and later freed by Allied forces in 1945.

On the morning of 20 July, I phoned my brother from Steinhorst in the Lüneburg Heath on my way to Berlin. He said: "Watch attention today!" And I knew exactly what he meant. He meant that another assassination attempt would be made on Hitler that day.

What did he say?

"Watch attention today!" He didn't say what every idiot says: "Watch out today!" He said it in a special way, not the way people normally say it. "Watch attention today!" I was supposed to notice that another assassination attempt was being made that day. And I understood it that way. And, on the radio, I heard that the attempt had failed. But I knew my brother had been there because he said the strange words: "Watch attention today!" So, the next morning I hitch-hiked from the Lüneburg Heath to Berlin and carefully went to our family home at night in the dark during the air raid alarms in the city. I asked where my brother was – and he was where I knew he would be – where I imagined he would be – he wasn't at home because the Gestapo would have found him immediately. But some people knew where he was. And it wasn't very far away from our home. So, I cautiously went there at night so that nobody would shoot me thinking that I was a Gestapo man in the dark. I carefully met him and made plans to find a better place for him to stay.

And then on 22 July I cautiously went to the address where Goerdeler would have been if he had come to Berlin. I knew that he wouldn't come because otherwise he would have been caught as he later was.[1] I looked for this address and people thought that I was a Gestapo man myself, and I carefully asked about Goerdeler. Of course, if you asked people that you didn't know about someone like Goerdeler, who was certainly a great enemy of Hitler, they thought that you were from the Gestapo. But I was still able to ease their suspicions. And I didn't try to get a better place for my brother to stay from them, but rather from colleagues in the military. And then I arranged for two women I knew – whom I really knew to be anti-Nazi women which was unusual – to pick him up at night from the temporary place where he was staying. I didn't have adequate papers for Berlin and wasn't travelling to Leipzig as an official friend of Goerdeler, but rather in order to help him. And I knew that he wouldn't be there and also wasn't able to be there.

But I secretly travelled back to Leipzig, hitch-hiking on the Autobahn, travelling for a while with a regimental commander from the Hitler Youth, who had become even more Nazi since 20 July. He thought that it was strange that I was hitch-hiking on the Autobahn. And I thought that he was taking me along so that he could bring me to the police for questioning. I would have shot him dead with my pistol while we were still on the Autobahn. But I was able to leave him. I told him that I had to take a different route. I thought that he would come back with a commando and arrest me on the spot where he let me out of his car. But he didn't come back, and I was able to find another car and continue my journey. So, I was actually able to travel to Leipzig. And then I tried to get papers there so that I would be able to travel to Breslau. And I managed to get these papers and carefully travelled to Breslau and visited relatives. I told them that the Gestapo would certainly be looking for me very soon because I knew that they had already been looking for my brother. And I knew that it wasn't far from one brother to another. And, in fact, on the second night when I was no longer staying with my relatives because it was too dangerous, three Gestapo men came to arrest me at 12 o'clock midnight. I wisely told my aunt that I wouldn't meet her in her flat, but rather on the square in front of her house near the tram. And, in fact, I met my aunt there near the tram. I snuck into the tram when she got in because I knew that she'd seen me. She then told me in the tram that the three Gestapo men had been there and what she had told them about me – where I went and why. I had my aunt tell the Gestapo that I was continuing my trip from Breslau to Bonn.

During this time, I was still secretly in Silesia for one or two weeks, and then I went back to the Autobahn and took a ride from an SS senior group leader. I couldn't see who I was waving down – I waved him down – and then wham – he stopped on command because I was wearing a uniform. I was a severely disabled soldier, so to speak, but I had a uniform. And then he stopped. By chance he was a non-commissioned officer in my regiment – not in the SS – in the regular army. We got along well and he even changed his route so that I would be able to travel better. And then, from a telephone booth in Lübben, I phoned with the department in the evacuated Ministry of War that dealt with severely disabled soldiers. And I found out on the phone that they didn't even know that the Gestapo was looking for my brother – which I knew precisely because the Gestapo had been at our home on 21 July and wanted to arrest Ludwig. I knew that exactly. And now I noticed on the phone that the Military Disability Office didn't know what was going on with my brother – because my brother had been wounded twice and was no longer fit for active service just like me – and if they didn't know what was going on with my brother, then they certainly didn't know what was going on with me. And that's the reason I went there in order to get a new travel document to Bonn. I thought that since I had informed the Gestapo through my relatives in Breslau that I was travelling to Bonn, and that was now fourteen days ago, they would have already looked for me there and determined that I wasn't there. That's why I thought that in the autumn – Goerdeler argued that the war would be over by then – I would go directly to the British and the Americans because I had spent a year in America and spoke English well. I thought that I would rather surrender to them and not to the Russians. My father had good contacts with the Russian Army, but I didn't know any Russian and my father had died in the meantime. And so, I thought that I would rather cross over to the English and the Americans. I had a new travel document for Bonn and hitch-hiked and travelled a bit by train.

And before I got onto the train, I looked around to see if a Gestapo patrol had gone past or onto the train. And I even tried to get into the first car which was always closed for all passengers because it was often fired upon from the air, and you could easily die that way. So, nobody was supposed to get into the first passenger car. But I tried to because I thought that the Gestapo men were so afraid that they wouldn't be there and then I'd be alone in the first car. And then a man was there who was very friendly and said to me that I wasn't allowed to get into the car although I wanted to. I wasn't allowed to get in, and I wondered why he had stopped me from doing so. You might have thought that if I wanted to die alone in that car then it was my business. And he said to me in a friendly way: "That's not allowed. That's not allowed." And then I noticed that he had the key to the next passenger car. He was friendly, but he had some sort of official function; otherwise, he wouldn't have had the key to the next car. And then I went into the next car and the car after that and looked to see if this friendly man was following me. I thought that he might be a friendly Gestapo man – that was also possible. And then I noticed that he wasn't following me. Each time when the train stopped, I tried to see if he had walked outside to the back of the train in order to check the tickets. I didn't think that he went by outside – in any case, I didn't see him although I was paying close attention.

And then I gradually went to a compartment and sat down with a few women who were anti-aircraft helpers or something like that. They were allowed to travel along as part of their job, and there were also a few elderly people. So, I sat down in the corner near the window, and then I noticed that the conductor was coming. He went into each of the compartments, and in this express train you could hear the doors opening and closing regularly – opening and closing. The conductor came, and the papers I had were fine. I got them from the authority which didn't know that they were looking for us. So, the conductor went through. But right after that it started again – bang – bang – on a regular basis – one door would open and then the next one – as if another conductor was coming. But I knew that the conductor had already gone through. And then I felt it getting dangerous. And, in fact, the door opened and the civilian, whom I met in the first passenger car who threw me out, came into our compartment and said: "Identification. Gestapo check." And I had my pistol in my pocket directed at him like this. And when he saw my papers and looked into my face, he was friendly to me. He was friendlier to me than to the others. But then I thought to myself that maybe he was just being friendly in order to get reinforcements because he knew that

I would shoot him and he would return with two others. And then they would catch me. And that's why I stood up and thought to myself that if I noticed that they were coming back, and if the train slowed down, I would jump down from the train into the countryside. But the man was genuinely friendly to me and didn't come back so I didn't have to jump off the train. Instead, I stayed on the train as far as Cologne where I wanted to make myself scarce because the Gestapo knew through my relatives in Breslau that I had travelled there fourteen days ago, and if I wasn't there, they wouldn't look for me now after these fourteen days.

I had known a few people in and around Cologne since 1940, and so I tried to find a place to stay with them until the autumn. And I was able to do so. But sometimes it was too dangerous so I changed places to stay right in the middle of the bombings on the outskirts of the city where I thought that they wouldn't look for me. I got in contact with a Jesuit priest through the people where I was staying on the outskirts of the city. And, as a Jesuit priest, he also had to be very careful because Jesuit priests were often arrested by the Nazis. Through this Jesuit priest I was able to change places to stay during the bombings, and we were both able to survive until the Americans arrived on 5 March 1945. I always thought that the war would be over by the autumn at the latest, as Goerdeler had claimed, but this didn't happen. I didn't try to travel in the direction of the Front and cross over to the enemy, but rather I thought that I had a place to stay in Cologne through the Jesuit priest and it was less dangerous to stay in Cologne in spite of the bombings. But, of course, there were also bombs on the Front and you could also get killed. So, I survived until the Americans finally reached us on 5 March 1945.

Home Guard in the Rhineland (October 1944)

Hans Henseler was born in 1921 in Friesdorf near Bonn. In 1944 he became the company leader of the Volkssturm near Bonn to protect Germany from the advance of the Allies on the Western Front.

The Western Front started in 1944. There was the so-called "Volkssturm" who were older men who weren't in the military, but dug trenches and did things like this.[2] I became the company leader of approximately eighty men. This company was under the authority of the party leadership, not the military. Every morning – or every evening – I had to go to headquarters and let them know which trenches had been dug during the day and which positions had been established. And I received instructions for the next day about what still had to be done. It was somewhat dangerous back then because low-flying English planes came and many men were killed.

Which practical work did you do?

We dug trenches. By 1944 the Allies were already in Aachen and in other cities. They had observers posted on high piles of coal. By the end of 1944 it became really serious. The general attitude among these older men was not good. They had to be kept in a good mood by giving them brandy. Every evening, I had to go to the neighbouring town with two large buckets and fill them with brandy. [laughs] It's really true. It was really cheap rotgut brandy. I had my room at an inn, and the men slept together in one large room. When I entered the room in the morning, I felt sick to my stomach from the smell. It stunk so badly. It wasn't an easy situation. On 27 October [1944] there was an air strike on Bonn, and when I came into the room the next morning no one was there. I didn't notice, but they all had left – they all went home. Then I had to travel to Bonn and round them up again. That wasn't so easy because everything in Bonn had been destroyed. I had difficulty finding them because they no longer lived where they used to.

Did they come back with you?

They had to. I was accompanied by the military. They wouldn't have sent me alone. [laughs] We continued our work until November or December. Until then it was relatively calm on the Front. The Americans were in Alsdorf, Aachen, and Geilenkirchen. When I went to the neighbouring town in the mornings to get the brandy, I always had to be very careful. It was a country road with ditches on both sides – the way it used to be with simple roads – with a few plume trees – and the Allies were waiting in Alsdorf and Geilenkirchen on the coal piles and observed the area and shot with artillery when they saw any movement. There were times when my bucket was half empty when I returned because I had to jump into the ditches several times. [laughs] The men didn't want to work without brandy, but they didn't have any choice. If they had refused – it would have been desertion – and they would have been shot. They would have gone before the party court and been shot. They were under the authority of the party, not the military. And it was worse than military court. The military understood that these old men didn't want to do the work – especially since they had served in World War I.

How long were you able to hold your position?

Well. When was that? I believe it was in November [1944]. The Allies continued their advance – but until then it was relatively calm. At night we sometimes had contact with American soldiers because some of the animals settled in one area. And we somehow had to find something to eat – the food supply was bad at that time. We went to this no-man's land and drove the animals together and slaughtered them. And the Americans did the same. And we met there. We didn't talk with one another, and no acts of war were carried out. Nobody shot – it was practically a ceasefire. It was a little difficult. Most of us didn't speak English, and the Americans didn't speak German. It was difficult to have a conversation. But you had to be careful – you didn't know if someone would shoot or not. Directly behind us was the German Front. We were practically ahead of the Front when we were working. If we weren't working – then this wasn't the case. In this area there were only Americans.

How did you move back towards the Rhine?

At that time, I had an elderly man who helped me as the company leader. He took care of me, cooked for me, and so on. He woke me up during the night and said that the Americans were coming and that we had to leave. We slaughtered a pig and loaded it onto a wheelbarrow and retreated to Linnich – near Düren. We spent the night there and then an accident happened to me. A cow stepped on my foot, and I couldn't walk anymore. The man pushed me in the wheelbarrow together with the slaughtered pig, and a coal truck approached. I was loaded on top and brought back to Bad Godesberg. I was really afraid because low-flying planes came and shot at this truck. I couldn't get down – I couldn't even move. I was lying on top of the briquettes. [laughs]

Freedom Action of Bavaria (April 1945)

Hans-Walter Stark was born in Trier in 1922. Near the end of the war, he participated in the Freedom Action of Bavaria on 27 and 28 April 1945 which attempted to overthrow the Nazi regime.

In 1945 I reached Lake Starnberg. I contacted Lieutenant Colonel von Finck and was supposed to serve as his adjutant. I arrived there and he said: "Leave. I don't need you anymore. You see what we're doing here." He was busy burning documents, sorting out papers, packing civilian items, and saying his goodbyes. "I don't need you anymore. Go to Freimann near Munich."

I arrived there at the Air Force Intelligence Division. I was supposed to make myself useful as an anti-tank gunner. They said: "Leave here and go to Freising near Munich". There was an anti-tank gunner division there. And the major of this division had good connections to the Americans. We discovered this a short time after we arrived. He called his officers together and said that he wanted to do this and that. "The Americans have promised to stop bombing southern Germany, especially Munich. And, therefore, destruction and deaths in the civil population will be prevented." This was possible if we were able to take over military control. The administrative district leader was to be arrested. We all said that we would participate. Everyone knew that soldiers were retreating on all fronts. And we could imagine what would have happened to us. We said that we would take part. The worst that could happen to us was that we could have got injured. And if we died, then at least we had tried. The orders were carried out and were successful.

The administrative district leader, who also received his military authority from Adolf Hitler, was arrested. Reichsstatthalter [Reich Governor] Ritter von Epp was arrested.[3] The Munich radio station was occupied. Participating on the German side in the Freedom Action of Bavaria[4] were the infantry, engineers, we as anti-tank gunners, and a military intelligence broadcasting station. Dr Gerngroß was the person under whose name the entire action took place. The SS from the regions of Rosenheim and Dachau – in the concentration camps – received orders from Hitler, Göring, and Goebbels to quell the action because those responsible were all miserable traitors. The officers were supposed to be liquidated. The troops were supposed to be left alone. After three days everything was back to normal from their perspective. I was with Reichsstatthalter Ritter von Epp on a farm near Freising when he read his speech to the German people on the radio while guarded by our officers. He told them to put down their weapons and to remain calm because of promises made by the Americans. They also kept their promises. But the SS thought and acted differently.

I wasn't able to listen to the speech by Reichsstatthalter Ritter von Epp in which he had talked about everything that went wrong. I couldn't listen to this because at the beginning of the speech my commander said to me: "Stark, go to the room behind you and rest for a while. You'll have enough time to do your part later." I had a good conscience, but not a good feeling. We didn't know that it had failed and discovered this out during the speech by Reichsstatthalter Ritter von Epp. I was terribly tired and fell asleep and suddenly woke up. When I awoke, no one was there and the vehicles had gone. No light was burning on the farm. It was completely dark and quiet. I tried to travel to Freising to the barracks in the neighbouring village. I travelled there and saw that the division – which was made up of four companies – had already left with their vehicles for action. But I didn't see any officers anymore. I had to obey another officer who wasn't from my division.

In Freising, I stole a bicycle on the side of the road – there weren't any cars on the street – and rode the bike in the direction of Rosenheim, in a southerly direction, in the direction of Tyrol along the Autobahn through woods and country lanes. After a short time, I reached some woods where German troops were camped out and resting. A captain asked: "Where are you coming from?" "From Freising from the anti-tank gunners." "What!" he said. "Didn't you hear what was going on in Munich and the area?" "No. I didn't hear," I told him. He said: "Give me you pistol. You're my prisoner." In this part of the woods where he had stopped me, there were soldiers hiding everywhere. And those were my anti-tank gunners from Freising. Without a commanding officer they had either disappeared or were murdered by special SS units. I didn't see them in the following weeks or months or hear anything about them.

On the following morning the captain said: "I know what you will do. You'll get your marching orders from me for Czechoslovakia for Field Marshall Schörner." I thought I didn't hear him correctly. He gave me marching orders. In this way, he got rid of me and the anti-tank gunners in the woods under our own reconnaissance. He was able to keep fleeing or do whatever he wanted. It was a real advantage with the marching orders. I was allowed to travel with my anti-tank gunners in vehicles over the Inn Valley bridges where SS officers were standing guard waiting for anyone wanting to flee south in the direction of Tyrol into the mountains. The troops gradually dispersed.

Torgau Prison (May 1945)

Josef de Bache was sentenced to Torgau Prison near Berlin for defamatory remarks after having served on the Russian Front, in Italy, and in East Prussia. Once freed by Russian soldiers in 1945, de Bache was again incarcerated by American troops.

I was sentenced to one year in a military prison because of defamatory remarks. A fellow soldier turned me in and said that I had my doubts about the final [Nazi] victory and so on. And I had to serve one year in military prison. I came from there to Torgau – it was an infamous military prison.[5] I was really lucky. I'm a barber by profession. First, we were in a large dormitory room with thirty or forty prisoners. And then I had to go to the sick room. And I had to shave the heads of the new arrivals. And then I got my own small barber shop – it was in a barracks building – and I shaved and cut the hair of the officers. And afterwards, I went to another barracks building with four other prisoners who worked in the office. This was a unit – no you can't call it a unit – they had to work in a battery workshop – old batteries were taken apart and new ones were made. I don't know. In any case, I had my small barber shop on the premises. I was the orderly for the officer of our company. And later units were put together in prison as penal companies and were sent to the Front somewhere. I stayed in my barber shop in Torgau.

The Russians and the Americans met in Torgau. The German prisoners were there when the Russians and the Americans came closer. I had a middle ear infection and came into the sick room of the prison. The guards and the prisoners left who were able to march – I don't know where to – and the prisoners who weren't able to march stayed in the sick room. And the shooting came closer and closer, and one of the ill prisoners said: "I'm an officer and belong to the committee of General Seidlitz." That was a German general who had been taken prisoner in Stalingrad and later worked together with the Russians. "When the

Russians come, stay calm. The Russians generally give the prisoners a meal." In any case, we stayed calm and then the Russians came. There was a female doctor with them. She attended to those prisoners in need of medical help. She injected something into my ear that buzzed and rang. The Russians marched on, and we were left on our own. We were left on our own as the ill prisoners from the prison.

I went to the City Hospital of Torgau along with the other prisoners. That was also deserted – the entire population had gone. And, in the prison, there was a Yugoslavian who was acting as a kind of doctor. He wrote a pass for us. And a fellow soldier and I took a hand cart from the supply room. My mother and sister had been evacuated to Düben near Torgau. And this fellow soldier had a leg amputated. He was from Mainz. I don't remember his name. In any case, the two of us went in the direction of Düben. I tried to make a phone call to Düben on the way. There was no connection. We were told that there were still German soldiers in Düben. There was no way we could go there. [laughs] We weren't able to go there at all. In Nerchau we stayed at an inn together with other refugees from the West – civilians – who had been evacuated there. They were waiting to cross the – I don't know the name of the river – the Mulde or something like that. In any case, it was a river near Nerchau. They wanted to cross the river, and then suddenly an American soldier called out with a trumpet signal: "All German soldiers who have not been properly discharged from the military should report to the town hall." We went there, were registered, and were able to come back again. On the next day there was the same signal again; we went to the town hall again; and then they said that we had to line up as American prisoners of war.

I wasn't doing well physically. The food in prison wasn't very good. I was skinny and weak. And the first American prisoner-of-war camp was in Eisleben. And in this prisoner-of-war camp, they suddenly said that all the prisoners who had been in the military prison in Torgau should come to the gate. I was unsure whether I should go. We had problems getting food in the camp – it didn't go well. There were Germans there who had cooked in the field kitchens – and when the food was finished, the strongest and the quickest got something to eat and the others didn't get anything. And, after some time, the prisoners who had been in Torgau came back and brought along with them an army chaplain from

Torgau. And then the American guards asked: "What's going on with him?" They said: "SS. SS. He was involved in executions." And then the American soldiers gave the German soldiers cigarettes and cookies. And they started to mistreat the chaplain. They hit him, stripped him of his uniform, and beat him with iron rods. He was bleeding all over. And then the chaplain said: "My poor old mother". The American soldiers gave cigarettes and cookies to the men who had hit him. The German soldiers beat the man to death – and threw him into the latrine.

War Crimes (May 1945)

Werner Schönemann was born in 1911 in East Prussia. In 1931 he began his career with the criminal police in Berlin working on cases of treason and crimes committed by Nazi party members. From 1938 to 1941 he worked for the Security Police in Cologne as a police detective.[6] In 1942 he was transferred to Vienna, Austria to work for the Security Police as the senior officer in counter-intelligence.

I was in Vienna from 1942 until the end of the war. But during that time, I suppressed the Slovak uprising.[7]

How did you do that?

There was a coup by the Slovakian-Czech Hussite military – the Slovakians weren't paying attention after independence – the Slovakian people were devoutly Catholic – nice people – I love them – and we pulled together everything that we had – there was a shortage of staff – so, I was sent over there and came as the police chief directly in the middle of the uprising in Žilina in the north. It was a bloody uprising. They committed murder. I have to tell you that all the men were taken out of the ethnic German villages and were killed with a shot through the base of the skull and buried in mass graves. The German soldiers who were being transported to the Front were taken from the express trains and shot. In Kremnica, where there were German settlements, the wives of functionaries, who had fled, were locked in prisons, and before we were able to take control of the prisons with the help of the 183rd Division, were all killed in their cells with shots to the base of the skull. And I was very radical. We were helpers according to the international treaty with the Slovakian government. I made sure that all those involved were stood up against the wall and shot. But, there was not one case among them that would not have been dealt with in

Alfred Schwarz: Reich Labour Service 1937.

Alfred Schwarz: Wehrmacht uniform.

Above: Günter Strahl: As the squad leader. Attack on the Red October Factory on foot.

Below: Günter Strahl: Day of rest in front of a military vehicle in 1942.

Right: Erich Hauer: Lieutenant Hauer after the War School Vienna-Neustadt in the summer of 1942.

Below: Erich Hauer: Lieutenant Hauer, 3rd Mountain Division, high mountain military exercise.

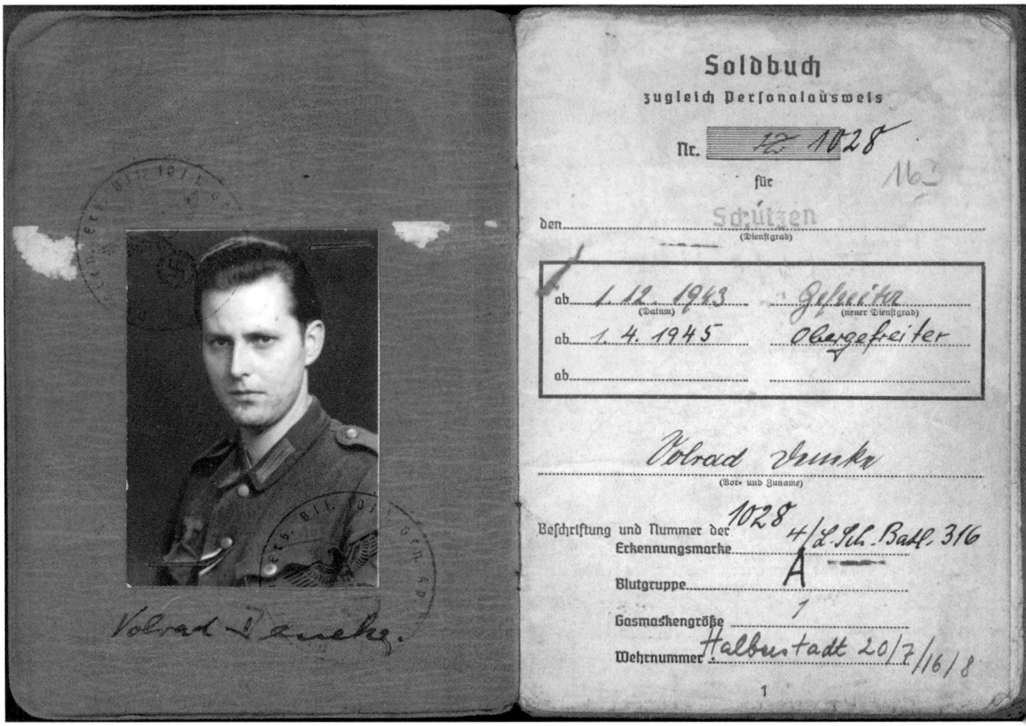

Soldbuch
zugleich Personalausweis

Nr. 1028

für

den Schützen
(Dienstgrad)

ab 1.12.1943 Gefreiter
(Datum) (neuer Dienstgrad)

ab 1.4.1945 Obergefreiter

ab

Volrad Deneke
(Vor- und Zuname)

Beschriftung und Nummer der Erkennungsmarke 1028 4/L.Sch.Batl. 316

Blutgruppe A

Gasmaskengröße 1

Wehrnummer Halberstadt 20/7/16/8

1

Above: Volrad Deneke: Pay Book: Promoted to Corporal on 1 April 1945.

Left: Friedrich Jansen: Air-raid shelter helper. 12 March 1944.

Right: Wilhelm Haag: Artillery training in Cuxhaven 1937.

Below: Wilhelm Haag: Second from right, Gotenhafen Maritime School 1942.

Wilhelm Blatzheim: Three days of front leave in Pillau, East Prussia (near Königsberg) in January 1945.

Richard Kern: 1940 before promotion to seaman.

Above: Richard Kern: R 35 in tow on the Upper Danube River still without superstructures in the summer of 1942.

Below: Ignaz Britz: Pay Book: Promoted to Sailor Apprentice on 1 May 1944.

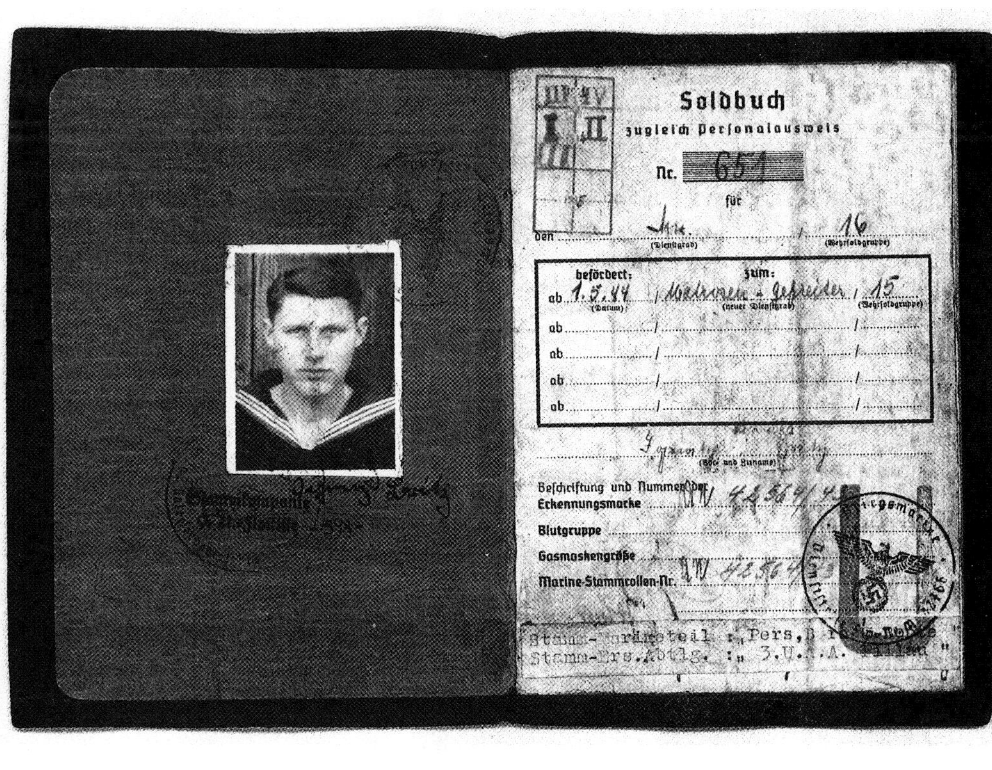

Soldbuch
zugleich Personalausweis
Nr. 651
für
den Mtr. / 16
(Dienstgrad) (Wehrsoldgruppe)

befördert: zum:
ab 1.5.44 / Matrosen - Gefreiter / 15
(Datum) (neuer Dienstgrad) (Wehrsoldgruppe)
ab / /
ab / /
ab / /
ab / /

(Vor- und Zuname)

Beschriftung und Nummer der Erkennungsmarke
Blutgruppe
Gasmaskengröße
Marine-Stammrollen-Nr.

Stamm-Marineteil : Pers.
Stamm-Ers.Abtlg. : 3.U. A.

Left: Hans Schulz: 1944.

Below: Hans Schulz: Hand-written note in the Pay Book by Lieutenant Commander Westphahl that Hans Schulz had been released from military service on 28 April 1945.

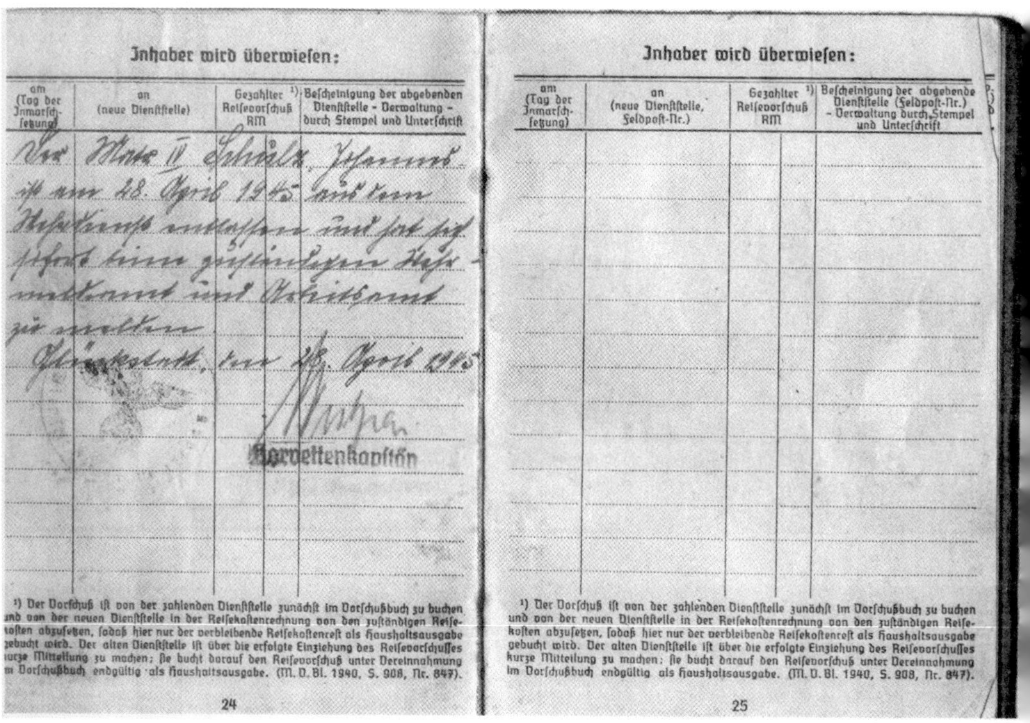

Inhaber wird überwiesen:

am (Tag der Inmarschsetzung)	an (neue Dienststelle)	Gezahlter [1] Reisevorschuß RM	Bescheinigung der abgebenden Dienststelle - Verwaltung - durch Stempel und Unterschrift

Der Maat II Schulz, Johannes ist am 28. April 1945 aus dem Wehrdienst entlassen und hat sich sofort beim zuständigen Wehrmeldeamt und Arbeitsamt zu melden.

Glückstadt, den 28. April 1945

Korvettenkapitän

[1] Der Vorschuß ist von der zahlenden Dienststelle zunächst im Vorschußbuch zu buchen und von der neuen Dienststelle in der Reisekostenrechnung von den zuständigen Reisekosten abzusetzen, sodaß hier nur der verbleibende Reisekostenrest als Haushaltsausgabe gebucht wird. Der alten Dienststelle ist über die erfolgte Einziehung des Reisevorschusses kurze Mitteilung zu machen; sie bucht darauf den Reisevorschuß unter Vereinnahmung im Vorschußbuch endgültig als Haushaltsausgabe. (M.V.Bl. 1940, S. 908, Nr. 847).

24

Inhaber wird überwiesen:

am (Tag der Inmarschsetzung)	an (neue Dienststelle, Feldpost-Nr.)	Gezahlter [1] Reisevorschuß RM	Bescheinigung der abgebende Dienststelle (Feldpost-Nr.) - Verwaltung durch Stempel und Unterschrift

[1] Der Vorschuß ist von der zahlenden Dienststelle zunächst im Vorschußbuch zu buchen und von der neuen Dienststelle in der Reisekostenrechnung von den zuständigen Reisekosten abzusetzen, sodaß hier nur der verbleibende Reisekostenrest als Haushaltsausgabe gebucht wird. Der alten Dienststelle ist über die erfolgte Einziehung des Reisevorschusses kurze Mitteilung zu machen; sie bucht darauf den Reisevorschuß unter Vereinnahmung im Vorschußbuch endgültig als Haushaltsausgabe. (M.V.Bl. 1940, S. 908, Nr. 847).

25

Hans Adolf Stiehl: Norway 1943.

Walter Düsseldorf: Tropical training in Foggia, Italy shortly before deployment in 1942.

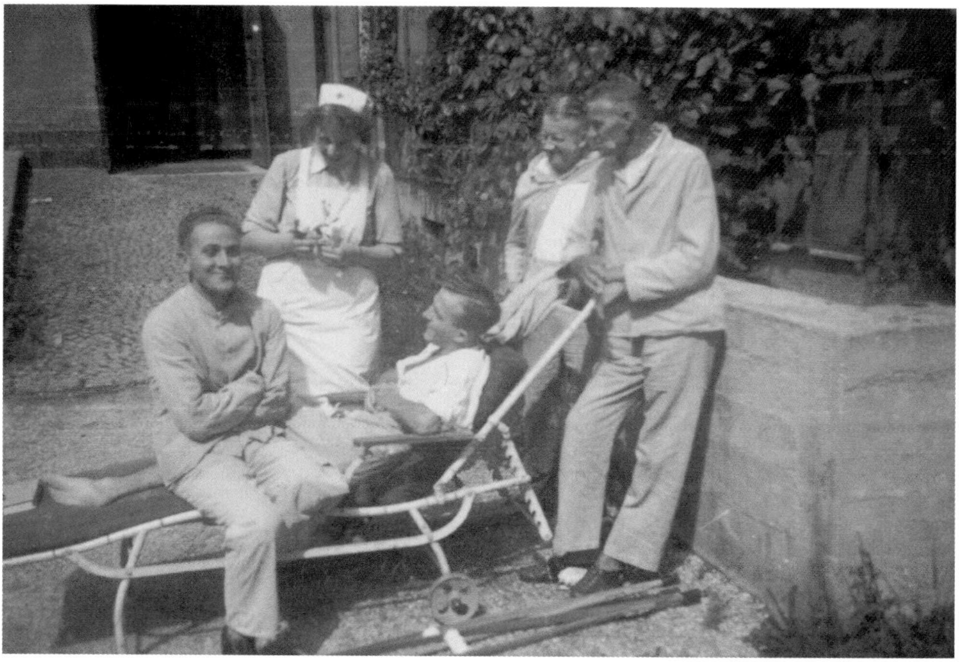

Above: Walter Düsseldorf: Lying down during his hospital stay in München-Schwabing in 1943 after leg amputation.

Below left: Heinz Kenzjiora.

Below right: Kunrat von Hammerstein.

Zuteilung von Taschenlampenbatterien für die Kriegsfahndung

Nach Mitteilung des Hauptamtes Ordnungspolizei vom 14. 12. 44 — Kdo. Gn. W G 2 a 14 Nr. 74/44 — sind die Polizeiverwaltungen nach erfolgter Zuteilung **zusätzlicher** Mengen von Taschenlampenbatterien nunmehr in der Lage, auch dem **durch die Kriegsfahndung erhöhten Bedarf der Kriminalpolizei Rechnung zu tragen.**

Alle Dienststellen der Kriminalpolizei haben ihre Anträge auf Zuteilung von Taschenlampenbatterien im Hinblick auf die eingetretene Besserung in der Versorgungslage **erneut** an die zuständigen Polizeiverwaltungen zu richten.

Etwa eintretende Schwierigkeiten sind sofort der Kriegsfahndungszentrale zu melden.

Zusatz für die Kommandeure der Sicherheitspolizei — Abt. 1 —:

Die Kommandeure der Sicherheitspolizei — Abt. 1 — fordern den Bedarf ihrer Abteilung V bei der für diese zuständigen Polizeiverwaltung an.

Verteiler:
Alle Dienststellen der Kriminalpolizei.

1400/44 — C 1 b. 21. 12. 44. **Reichskriminalpolizeiamt, Kriegsfahndungszentrale**

A. Neuausschreibungen

I. Raubmord durch ϟϟ-Angehörigen in Chynorany (Slowakei)

In der Nacht zum 9. 12. 44 wurde in Chynorany (Slowakei) 76jähr. Landwirtin und deren 40jähr. Tochter in ihrer Wohnung mit Beil ermordet. Hinzukommenden Sohn fesselte unbek. Täter auf Stuhl. Geraubt wurden: 3 Anzüge (schwa., gra., bla.); slow. Gendarmerie-Reithose; bla. Wintermantel; hellgra. Ballonseidenmantel; 2 P. schwa. Damenstiefel; 2 P. schwa. Herrenstiefel; 830 Kronen; Herrenfahrrad „Pelikan", Nr. 424449; Koffer. Als Täter kommt der Schütze der ϟϟ-Einheit „Dirlewanger" in Frage, der sich bei der Familie 3 Tage lang einquartiert hatte. Er war im Besitze eines Marschbefehls, auf dem der Ort Dvormik verzeichnet war. Offenbar ist richtige Ortsbezeichnung Dvorrec bei Banovce (Slow.), da dort bezeichnete Einheit gelegen hat. Beschr.: Etwa 19 Jahre, etwa 1,68 m, ov. voll. Gesicht, bra. gewellte Haare, dklbra. Augen, ausgebogene kl. Nase; Wehrmachtschiffchenmütze mit schwa.-weiß-rot. Kokarde, Tarnjacke mit weiß. Futter, Feldbluse ohne Spiegel, rot. eingefaßte Schulterklappen, lg. gra. Militärhose, schwa. Stiefel, Aermelstreifen der Einheit „Dirlewanger".

Energische Fahndung! Festnahme!

C 2 a Nr. 76/44. 20. 12. 44. **Reichskriminalpolizeiamt**

II. Fahnenflüchtige Wehrmachtangehörige

Wegen Fahnenflucht sind festzunehmen: Ludwig **von Hammerstein,** Stud. des Bergbaues, 17. 11. 19 Berlin, zul. Berlin-Zehlendorf, Breisacher Str. 19, bis Anfang September in Berlin illegal aufhältlich gewesen, will ins Ausland. Beschr.: 1,88 m, fast schwa. Haare, schlank; Narbe über r. Auge.

Kunrat **von Hammerstein,** stud. jur., 14. 6. 18 Berlin, zul. aufhältl. in Leipzig, jetzt möglicherweise im Rheinland (Köln, Bonn, Koblenz). Beschr.: 1,92 m, dklblo. Haare, schlank, kurzsichtig. Es handelt sich um Brüder. **Sie sind hierunter abgebildet.**

Festnehmen!

IV 1 b (S K IV) 422/44 g. 29. 11. 44. **StapoLSt Berlin**

Ludwig von Hammerstein

Kunrat von Hammerstein

sind festzunehmen.

Kunrat von Hammerstein: Search for Kunrat and Ludwig Hammerstein by the Nazi Criminal Police.

Left: Hans Stark: Shortly before his deployment to the Russian front in February 1944.

Below: Dr Heinrich Rödder: Medical course at the Wainwright Alberta camp. Lecturers on the right, students on the left. Dr Rödder is in the foreground in the centre of the picture with his hands folded.

Dr Heinrich Rödder: “Request Concert”: The large prisoner symphony orchestra in Bowmanville, Ontario.

Walter Scharnagl: Third from the right in the back row as a prisoner of war in Hertfordshire; Uncle Theo is directly next to him to his right.

Left: Aloysius Rohfleisch in his desert khaki uniform.

Below: Aloysius Rohfleisch: German prisoners of war in the Abu Sultan harbour camp in 1947; he is second from the right in the bottom row.

Bernd Steinlein: The picture shows him in the garden of his parents' house in the clothes that he received upon being discharged in the Caucasus: quilted jacket, quilted trousers, and tent shoes.

Heinz Poll in Wehrmacht uniform.

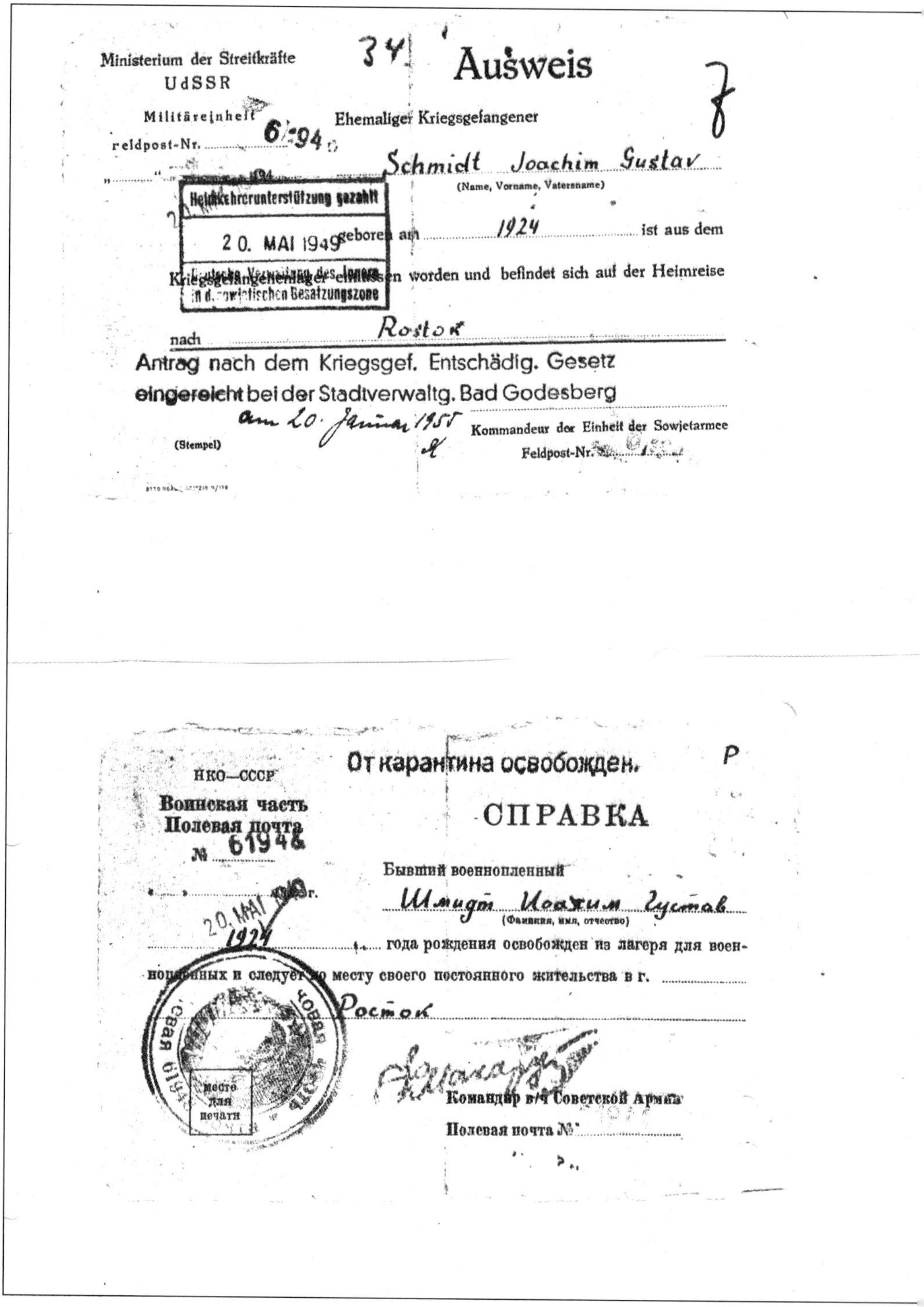

Ministerium der Streitkräfte
UdSSR

34

Ausweis

7

Militäreinheit
Feldpost-Nr. 61:94

Ehemaliger Kriegsgefangener

Schmidt Joachim Gustav
(Name, Vorname, Vatersname)

Heimkehrerunterstützung gezahlt
20. MAI 1949
Deutsche Verwaltung des Innern
in d. sowjetischen Besatzungszone

geboren am 1924 ist aus dem Kriegsgefangenenlager entlassen worden und befindet sich auf der Heimreise

nach Rostok

Antrag nach dem Kriegsgef. Entschädig. Gesetz
eingereicht bei der Stadtverwaltg. Bad Godesberg
am 20. Januar 1955

(Stempel)

Kommandeur der Einheit der Sowjetarmee
Feldpost-Nr.

От карантина освобожден.

P

НКО—СССР
Воинская часть
Полевая почта
№ 61946

20. MAI 1949 г.

СПРАВКА

Бывший военнопленный

Шмидт Иоахим Густав
(Фамилия, имя, отчество)

1924 года рождения освобожден из лагеря для военнопленных и следует по месту своего постоянного жительства в г. Росток

место для печати

Командир в/ч Советской Армии
Полевая почта №

Joachim Schmidt: Request submitted to the town of Bad Godesberg for financial assistance in accordance with the German Prisoner-of-War Compensation Law.

exactly the same way in international law. And the decision was made by the Slovakians. But I was too smart for that. And after the war I was sentenced to death three times in absentia because of this. In Slovakia. The Czechs demanded my extradition.

And did they get your extradition?

The Austrians sabotaged it. In Austria I had the best reputation. And then General Clay became involved in the matter. The Allied Council overturned the extradition order – and by the way, the French did as well. I also had French contacts – they turned down the extradition – the Czechs had to hand over all the documents – the Austrians carried out the proceedings – they didn't even charge me with murder – nothing became of it – it took a long time and went back and forth. I was in custody from 1945 to the end of 1951 in Vienna. Then the head of the legal department at the U.S. Embassy, Mr Levy, an emigrant Viennese Jew, brought me through the Russian zone to an airfield in Tulln and flew me back to Germany with a military aircraft. Top secret!

And why did they do that?

Apparently, they were somehow in my debt. I was also well liked among the French. From Vienna we carried out very good espionage work – we had five radio contacts with the Russians from agents who had jumped as paratroopers. We knew about all of them. I had a colleague, Hans Sarnitzer, and he did that – he radioed every night – he had such bad rheumatism – rheumatism of the bones – that he couldn't sleep anyway. And that was very interesting because we played tricks on the Russians. We also had two radio contacts with the Americans in North Africa and Italy. They treated us very fairly.

What happened during these six years in custody in Vienna?

I was fine. I was in the library and could move about freely in the court prison.

You were in custody under all three Allies?

Under all four of them. The Russians wanted me. The Western powers – the Americans, the French, and the English – were fighting with the Russians over me. That's remarkable, isn't it? The Western powers turned down the extradition request. And in Vienna they didn't have anything to charge me with. And I was flown back to Germany. And the matter wasn't finished! The Czechs sent the last ten files of incriminating evidence in 1975. But all the charges were dropped.

CHAPTER V

ALLIED PRISONER-OF-WAR CAMPS

The Queen Elisabeth

Anton Schmitz was born in Wachendorf in the Eifel in 1917. He was taken prison of war with the Africa Corps near Tobruk, Libya in 1941 and was transported via Egypt to South Africa where he boarded the *Queen Elisabeth* and travelled to Rio de Janeiro and New York. He recalls the journey on the luxury liner.

We were docked in Cape Town for four or five days and were able to see Table Mountain and everything. The South Africans from the English Army came on board and were supposed to travel with us to America and would therefore complete their military service. Travel there and back. And then people started to talk: "Which ship are we taking? Which ship are we taking?" And the South Africans were strict. They held their fingers on the trigger of their rifles – always on the trigger. And once it happened. They shot a few soldiers. These men wanted to come inside because there was food. It turned out all right in the end because they weren't dead. In any case, we travelled on small boats to a big ship. It was the *Queen Elisabeth*. We were astonished. We knew that it was the largest ship in the world. And we looked up high! We travelled with it to Rio de Janeiro across the South Atlantic. And I can tell you: There were such high waves that the bolts became loose in the back. That's how stormy it was in the South Atlantic. It was well known that it was stormy. So, we travelled to Rio de Janeiro. We couldn't believe our eyes.

And we filled our bellies on the *Queen Elisabeth*. We received food coupons and were able to get food for six men. And then we went back and got food without coupons. The last guy didn't get anything anymore. I think there were 600 or 800 prisoners on board – I don't remember exactly anymore. And there were a lot of civilians! A lot of them! And I – and others – was lucky because I slept on the B deck. We had a cabin with three or four men. And many others slept in rooms on the E deck or F deck with 200 men. And every morning and every afternoon we were allowed on deck for two hours – separated from the others with barbed wire. The *Queen Elisabeth* is a city in itself. A city in itself. There were shops on board, cinemas, four or five swimming pools, and who knows what else. It was great! It was great! It was great! Afterwards, I received newspapers in the prisoner-of-war camp where all of that was described.

Were you allowed to move around freely?

No. We were led up on deck and back down again. Always. With a rifle pointed towards us. Always. Always. Always. They were all afraid of Germans and quickly discovered that Germans were completely different from what the propaganda made them out to be. And there were many, many civilians. They were apparently travelling to New York just like us. First to Rio, and then up to New York. There was real excitement after Rio. You can't imagine. Every hour all the portholes were controlled. And before Rio they said that no one should try to jump out of the portholes because the harbour of Rio was filled with so many sharks that no one would survive. And this was on their minds. We had a large number of men who had families in Brazil because Germany companies such as Mercedes had branches there. The children who were in Germany were drafted to become soldiers. And there were a lot of them there – very many – and they wanted to jump overboard, but didn't dare. It was so tense that on the A deck or the B deck a South African guard shot one of his comrades who was leaning over the side. He thought that it was a German because the guard was so nervous. That's the attitude they had.

And I'll tell you. We had a wonderful view of Rio with the beach below and Sugarloaf Mountain with the statue of Jesus. And when we left Rio, we were accompanied by a convoy. The region was like a painting. Like a painting. Great. Really great. We travelled up the coast past Mexico – or whatever it's called. The German submarines were horrible at that time, you know? They tried to go into the St. Lawrence River and everywhere but couldn't. And near Mexico they were able to sink some ships. And it was always really dangerous. At night it was horrible. Luckily, we were able to make it to New York harbour. We sailed past the Statue of Liberty. You know it, don't you? For us it was an incomparable experience, except with an empty stomach and in a strange situation. It was a strange situation, wasn't it? But I enjoyed it, and I still remember all of it today.

Were you able to get off the ship in New York?

Yes, wait and see. We weren't able to dock with the *Queen Elisabeth.* It wasn't deep enough. We had to get off earlier and take smaller boats. The trains drove right to the harbour. And the Canadian Pacific Railroad drove there. You probably know it. And we thought to ourselves: What's that? We got off the ship with twenty or thirty men. And there were Americans, not Englishmen there. I don't know exactly. We were English prisoners of war and were brought to the Canadian train because Canada belonged to England at that time.

The Queen Mary

Paul Golz was born in Waldow/Rummelsburg in Pomerania (present-day Poland) in 1925. After being captured by American soldiers in Normandy in 1944, he was transported aboard the *Queen Mary I* across the Atlantic to New York and from there to a prisoner-of-war camp at Fort Henry in West Virginia. In 1946 he was shipped to Scotland and held as a prisoner of war until 1947.

On the *Queen Mary* there were 2,000 German prisoners of war. It was announced in advance so that German submarines wouldn't attack. It was well known. There were also wounded soldiers on the trip to America as well as civilians. We saw them. Once a day we were allowed to go on deck and smoke cigarettes. The *Queen Mary* travelled alone to America and was in New York in five and a half days. You have to imagine that. It travelled alone and was accompanied by air surveillance from England for two days – and from the coast of America for two days. In the meantime – for the two days on the Atlantic – there wasn't any surveillance. It travelled in a zigzag route. We were on deck and could see how it travelled in a zigzag. I didn't get seasick at all on this huge ship. Everything was just fine.

We arrived in New York and many civilians were standing there. After we had disembarked, we undressed and were deloused with DDT under our arms although we didn't have any lice. Horrible stuff. Our clothing was heated, and we got it back again all wrinkled. We then entered a Pullman train and travelled in the direction of West Virginia for two days. We travelled past Washington, D.C., and I saw traffic lanes with seven and eight cars driving next to one another. I had never seen anything like that before. I wasn't homesick at all because I knew the situation at home, and in America everyone was living in peace. There was work and good food in the camp. It turned me into a man. My good health is due to the fact that I had such good Californian fruit.

After Washington, D.C., we continued in the direction of West Virginia to Camp Patrick Henry. It took two days to get there.

Then we arrived at Camp Patrick Henry. It was an American military camp that had been built in the woods. A part of the camp was reserved for German prisoners of war. One hundred men from the German Africa Corps welcomed us. They had made up our beds in white sheets. I remember that we were in barracks with forty beds that were not on top of one another, but rather next to one another. In the front of the camp were American soldiers. At the head of the bed there was a shelf for clothing. The German soldiers made up the beds for us in white sheets, and, on each bed, there was a bar of chocolate and a carton of cigarettes. American military rations were waiting for us in the cafeteria. And I drank my first Coca Cola. It tasted great! We were really thirsty. In the mess hall, we got things that I had never known before – such as melons. Every morning, we had American-style breakfast: bacon – which I had never eaten before, a bottle of milk, and cereal. Those were things that I didn't know. We had the same rations as the American soldiers.

We went to work at 5:00 am., at 10:00 am roll call, ate, and then we were able to do sports. In the German armed forces, we were also locked up and couldn't do what we wanted. There was no difference. I really wasn't homesick at all. So many new things were happening. I first worked in the kitchen – it was a little hot – but the Americans were happy that we cooked for them. The Germans were proper and clean. We cooked and also served them. The Americans walked past in line and if they made a stupid comment, then they got a small piece of meat the next time. And they noticed that. But that generally didn't happen. I then had another job in the activity centre where the soldiers played badminton – I hadn't known that sport before. They also had bowling – the soldiers came and we cleaned up. They came at 10:00 pm and told me: "Come on boy, have a game with me." I said that I couldn't because they were officers, but they insisted. A lot of actors and actresses also came there – among them Ingrid Bergman. I had a poster of her above my bed. She looked good. And Red Skelton – a comedian – a tall guy over 2 metres tall came there. The soldiers all sat around and listened to him. In the mornings, the Americans sat in the military kitchen and ate cake and drank coffee. We served them. At 10:00 am the actors came – Red Skelton, too – and they ate breakfast together in this room. Red Skelton said: "You know what? I'll give you a special performance," and then he stood up to perform. He showed us how women dress in the morning and rolled up his stockings. It was great what he showed us. It was a special performance. That's the way it was. It was a nice job. The entertainers came at 10:00 am and practiced. At that time, I was finished for the most part and was able to watch for a while. The young actors and actresses performed for the soldiers. It was an enjoyable place to work.

At the officers' club we planted vegetables. Four of us had a tractor and planted corn and 1,000 tomato plants and melons and vegetables on 10 acres of land. We found the tomato plants that the Americans threw away and transported them in a small wagon. We had a shed and a table with a bench. One American soldier once told us: "Boys, watch out for my camera. I'm going to lie down for a while." We said: "Don't worry. We'll make sure that nothing happens." That's the way it was there. We mowed the lawn for them so that they could play football. There was also a WAC [Women's Army Corps] company. They came to us and said: "Hey boys, we'll show you how to eat corn on the cob." They told us that we had to boil it and spread butter on it and eat it with white bread. It tasted really good. They showed us how to do it.

I didn't have any unpleasant jobs. The kitchen job was a little hot. I also had malaria and was sent to the military hospital. There was a nurse there who gave me medication. She remained standing there and told me that I had to drink two glasses of ice water. I said: "One is enough." "No, no". She remained standing until I drank everything. I was quickly back on my feet again. I had a job on a farm and there were two engineers who checked the sewage. One of them played golf, and I shagged balls for him 200 metres away on the farm. I told him that I couldn't return home [to Pomerania] because it was now Poland. He said to me: "You know what Paul? I'll take you home with me". "Where to?" I asked. "North Carolina"; he said. I would have gone along, but the American authorities wouldn't allow it. All of us had to return home. He wanted to take me along. "You'll get a job", he said. That was the good relationship we had with them. Across the road there was a black farmer with a small farm. He showed us his harvest, and the leaves on the plants were full of potato beetles. It was horrible because they destroyed the harvest. He showed us. That was my introduction to the potato beetle. I rode in a jeep to Norfolk. That was the next port. They said: "Hey boy, we have work there, and we'll take you along". In Normandy, I also rode in a jeep. It was a hard ride because it wasn't cushioned. My feet hung out over the side on the way there. [laughs] That's the way it was. I always took everything with a sense of humour and that served me well.

My stay in America was over in May 1946. The American authorities discharged all of us and sent us home. I got really seasick on the Liberty ship and threw up. The captain told us that he had to take us to Scotland. Why didn't they tell us that earlier? If he had said so, then I would have stayed in America. We had a good life in America. What could we do about it? It had been decided, and we were sent to Scotland.

American Camps in the USA

Hans Henseler was born in Friesdorf near Bonn in 1921. He was a radio operator in a Tiger Tank and was taken prisoner in Remagen on 30 April 1945. Henseler was then transported in a Liberty ship to the Isle of Man and across the Atlantic to New York and Boston. He describes his experiences as a prisoner of war in the USA.

We arrived in New York, but didn't leave the ship. We basically travelled from the Hudson to Boston. It was really an experience to see the city of New York, especially the civilian airplanes. Every minute practically an airplane started. The well-lit streets were something that we didn't know from Germany anymore because everything was dark due to the war. We didn't know traffic lights. We hadn't seen them until that time. It was really very impressive. We remained on board and travelled up the Hudson to Boston where we disembarked and were deloused. We went into a large barracks. As far as I know, they still do that in America with immigrants today. They are sent to the showers and get covered with powder – at least that's the way it was with us. We were sprinkled with DDT powder – there were a lot of lice I have to say because of the journey on the ship. Of course, the hygiene wasn't that great on board. We lay on the floor and there were remnants from the troops that were transported before us. The water below in the keel was somewhat foul. And that's why it was a feast for the pests. As I said, we were deloused and got the "PW" on our backs – "Prisoner of War" – and then we were brought to the railway cars. And we travelled straight through America for five days and five nights as far as Iowa. There were more than 600 of us aboard ship. As far as I know, it was the last prisoner-of-war transporter to travel to America. The war was over. And it was foreseeable that American soldiers would gradually start to return home. And they didn't want to bring over any more prisoners of war.

How many people left from Boston?

I guess about 500. There were 100 that were sick or injured and sent to various hospitals. We never found out where they were sent. No one died aboard ship. There were several along who were seasick – very seasick – guys who couldn't eat anything while crossing the ocean – who vomited bile – and they really had to be treated. There were at least fifty or sixty of these guys, and fifty or sixty were wounded. There were really a great number who were seasick. Luckily, I was spared this – at least on the way over. We were then transported in railway cars. The journey wasn't that pleasant. In the front and back of the railway cars was an American soldier as a guard. Depending on the mood they were in – and if you had to go to the bathroom – they sometimes refused to let you stand up – and you went to the bathroom right on the cushioned seats. That wasn't very pleasant. These were normal railway cars with cushioned seats. You basically had a seat for two people – the way it normally is in trains. You were able to lie down. Once a day there were military rations – not twice a day like on the ship, but rather once a day. We travelled mostly during the day, and the train remained standing at night.

What were your impressions of the country?

The farther we travelled west, the fewer cities there were and more countryside. We didn't know that from Germany – these large farmlands. Of course, it was very impressive for us. I imagine that they transported us to Iowa because there was room in the camps. The prisoner-of-war camps were divided into main camps and secondary camps. You were first brought to the main camp. The camp in Iowa was somewhere near St. Paul. The name of the town was [tries to remember the name] … it wasn't directly in a town, but rather near a large national park. There were small wooden cabins which were rented to American families in the summer who spent their holiday there. And we kept the park clean during the time we were at the main camp. There were many rattle snakes there. We caught them and did work like that. We mainly kept the park clean. There were already German prisoners of war who had come from Africa and had been there for years. In the first camp where I was – the name of the town was Algona – it was a very small town that I never found on a map – there were over 4,000 prisoners of war.[1] Prisoners were able to work in the park if they wanted – but they didn't have to – they could play sports or read, and sometimes there was also a university course of study. It was organized by the Germans with permission from the U.S. military authority.

They held real lectures because there was a large number of professors and university lecturers among the prisoners of war. They practically organized a university and held lectures for the German prisoners who interrupted their studies because of the war or never got a chance to study after high school. It was very well organized. And they made small gardens and planted flowers around the barracks. You weren't ordered to do anything except to appear at roll call in the morning and again in the evening. They made sure that you were there and then you could do whatever you wanted. This meant that the German prisoners were self-governing. They also set up an orchestra. There were all kinds of possibilities: singing clubs and so on. I didn't have an advanced high school diploma for university study and therefore couldn't participate in the courses. But from what I heard from the others who studied there, soldiers finished their PhDs in Germany based on the lectures they heard in the U.S. They had to prove that they had attended the courses, and credit hours were counted towards their studies. I assume that the professors sent the information to the respective universities in Germany. In the U.S., the lecturers didn't have the authority to award credit hours. It always depended on the leadership in the camp which was under the authority of the Americans. The guards were also Americans. But this self-government was established by the Germans: clubs and so on. Now and then, there were lessons on politics: movies were shown on the concentration camps and the atrocities and similar things. They called it "re-education".

Was it a surprise for you that the atrocities had taken place?

It certainly was for us. I knew it from my grandfather: not in terms of the Jews, but rather about the communists and the socialists after 1933 before the war. These were people in the political movement. In the villages, there were hardly any people who knew anything about the concentration camps, for example Buchenwald or Auschwitz. The first time that I had heard about these camps was when I was in America.

Before that I had never heard the names of these cities. That was also true for most of the soldiers. In America it was the same story in the small towns. People were cut off from the world and lived in their own small-town communities. And some never went beyond their own horizons. And that was the same case in Germany.

Where did you work afterwards?

They asked us whether we wanted to work. We were sent to a so-called "work camp" or a "secondary camp". These were small camps with thirty or forty or fifty men which were under American military authority with American guards who were in charge of this camp. We went outside in the morning, and the farmers came and picked up a certain number of men – or they came from factories or something like that. And you spent the day in the factory or in the fields or somewhere. And, in the evenings, you were brought back. You experienced different things. I'll never forget that we worked for a Jewish guy who gave us water to drink from dirty buckets. On the other hand, I have to tell you that I got to know the American military authorities from a very positive side. If we complained, then they came out – it was normally the captain – and he examined the situation. And if it was true, then the farmers normally didn't get any more prisoners of war. They were very fair. And I acknowledged that. The farmers had to pay money to the military authorities for our services. We also received money. But it was so-called "camp money". It amounted to eighty cents per day, but a certain work quota had to be fulfilled: for example, 4 tons of corn had to be harvested, or 4 tons of sugar beets, or eighty bags of potatoes per day. These were the guidelines that had to be followed. Or a bag of cotton in New Mexico.

I got around quite a bit. It was always too boring for me in the main camp, and I thought: "At least you'll get around and meet people and see something of the area". I went from Iowa to Minnesota, from there to New Mexico, to California, and up to Maine. Those are the camps where I spent time. It was standard that we received eighty cents per day. In the main camps and sometimes in the secondary camps, there were so-called "drugstores" where you could buy shoe polish, toothpaste, and things that you wanted for your daily needs. Of course, eighty cents was gone very quickly. It wasn't real money; it was so-called "camp money" which were small pieces of paper. I was over there for a good year and saved $10 in camp money. I was mostly with farmers – I seldom worked in factories – only once actually – I was once on a farm for a long period of time because the farm was too far away from the camp – it was almost 150 kilometres away. I spent a whole week there, and the farmer drove me to the camp on Saturdays and checked me in, and I was able to drive back to the farm with him. That was a farmer who had emigrated from Schleswig-Holstein and spoke German at home. As I said, I was over there from Easter 1945 until March 1946.

During that time, I learned a bit of English because I had to make myself understood. I met an elderly man who took a liking to me – he was in charge of the farms. In America, the farmers received the seeds from factories. They planted the seeds in their fields, harvested the crops, and brought them back to the factories for processing. No matter whether peas, corn, or sugar beets, or anything similar. And there was a so-called "farm overseer" who was in charge of the fields where the crops grew. And this elderly man, who was the "farm overseer" for a canning factory, liked me. In the morning when he came to pick us up, he always wanted to have me alone. First, we went to the drugstore and drank coffee and ate breakfast, and then he drove onto the fields with me. We had long pointed sticks along to remove the thistles and weeds where the peas came up or later the beets. And we removed them. That was our work. So, you had to learn a bit of English. He didn't speak any German. But it worked out well.

Paul Hoffmann was born in Saxony in 1924. He served in the Africa Corps and was captured by English troops on 17 April 1943. After being transported by train across Algeria to Casablanca (Morocco), he was brought by ship to the USA. There he worked as a prisoner of war in Adamsville, Alabama; Clarksdale, Mississippi; and in Camp Blanding, Florida.

In Casablanca we were handed over to the Americans and placed on an accompanying ship to New York. We were on a ship with a Red

Cross flag because a very large number of injured American soldiers were on board. We were separate from the Americans and were below the waterline of the ship. We arrived over there and were treated like human beings. We travelled by Pullman train to Adamsville, Alabama – there was a large camp there – and we didn't have to work. Every day we received ten cents. There was a coupon card for one month with twenty-eight or twenty-nine or thirty coupons. And with ten cents we could buy something in the mess hall. And we didn't have to work. Since I didn't care for sitting around and being lazy, I reported to the German doctor in the large hospital that we had there. I told him that I had been a medic in Africa, but didn't want any money for my services. And then he gave me a job, and I received an additional eighty cents per day. And then I was in hospital unit A6 which was a ward for skin disorders and sexually transmitted diseases. There were a lot of German soldiers there from Africa who had venereal disease. I did the bookkeeping and prepared the food, and so on. The Germans had slept with Arabs and others. In any case, it had been arranged by the International Red Cross that many of them would be sent back to Germany during the war.

The camp was then closed, and we were brought to Clarksdale, Mississippi – to pick cotton. In Clarksdale, the farmer always came out onto the fields with ice water. And I asked him whether he could get me a belt – mine was broken. He spoke with the guard who took me to town and bought me a belt – and bought himself a pair of shoes – and we got along just fine. We had to pick 100 pounds of cotton every day. That was quite a bit for us. The Blacks started picking cotton at 3:00 or 4:00 am and picked 250 to 300 pounds of cotton every day in contrast with us. I personally had very good experiences especially with the Blacks who to a certain extent were under the farmers. They didn't have any money and lived in small shacks on the fields. They bought groceries and things from the farmers during the whole year and had to pay back their debt during the harvest. They were bound to the farmers, so to speak. That's why the relationship between the German prisoners and the Blacks was so good. I learned English at school, but I'm not very talented at foreign languages. Of course, we spoke with them and also with the white Americans. That was not a big problem. I have to say that these three and a half years that I spent in America were 50 per cent very good, 25 per cent good, and 25 per cent bad.

How would you describe the relationship between the farmers and the Blacks?

Not very good. Not very good. I can tell you the following story: A white officer from the U.S. Army was eating there, and a black American officer came towards him, and the white officer moved 2 metres away from him. And the black officer said to the white: "Listen, I'm also a GI". I didn't understand everything, but that is what I saw.

At the end of the harvest, I was brought to Camp Blanding in Florida. It was a huge training area with forty-two warehouses, so you can imagine how large it was. And I had the great fortune of being assigned to an American who was a plumbing and heating technician. He was responsible for repairs in the hospital and the refrigerated warehouse at the camp. He was a family man and his name was Mr Gross. We worked on repairs together, and, after the war, he wrote letters to me in Germany. [weeps] He wrote about everyday things such as how tall his son was, and so on. It was a good relationship. And through Mr Gross, I met the chief civil engineer at Camp Blanding, Mr Bennett. I got along with him really well. The American civil population allegedly – allegedly – didn't have enough sugar. And then Mr Bennett said to me as the boss: "Hoffmann, find me 100 pounds of sugar." [laughs] The reason was that the maximum sentence for prisoners was thirty days in confinement. That was the maximum sentence. And because I had a good relationship with him, I did it for him. I borrowed a truck and got the sugar. Through these people and connections, I really had it good. You know?

On 20 April 1945, which was Hitler's birthday in Germany, everything became very strict in America. In the kitchen, Ms Henderson, a Swedish-American woman, said: "Paul, it's D-Day. The war is over." And, and … how should I explain this to you. We were no longer allowed to work as prisoners of war since we were taking jobs away from American civilians. Many people had been discharged from the army – also in Germany – and they were unemployed. And we as prisoners had jobs.

So, they discontinued it. I went to Mr Bennett and asked him: "What's going to happen to me?" And he asked: "What do you want to do?" And I said: "I want to go to the officers' mess hall". There were prisoners of war there. I was in the officers' mess hall, and there was an American captain. He was an Italian American with a hotel in New York. And instead of the officers' mess hall, we put up a sign: "Tony's Spaghetti House". And so, we had a little bit of status. And I was in the kitchen, and an American general came inside who had fought against our troops in the Ardennes in Belgium in 1945. He was a guest at the restaurant and inspected the kitchen. I stood at the stove, and he asked me whether the burners were clean. "Yes", I said, "the stove is clean". He asked me to turn over the burners and underneath there was some soot from the coal. And he said to me: "When I say that the burner should be clean, I mean completely clean". And then I said: "Yes, General". The general was there at lunch, and Tony, with whom I got along well, wanted to tease me a little bit and told me to serve him. And they were serving fried chicken. I brought the general his plate, and he stood up from his chair and said to me: "Since when don't chickens have legs?" In the kitchen, they didn't put any drum sticks on his plate. [laughs] Everyone in the kitchen was laughing. You know? My face turned red, and I had to bring him another plate of food. What I want to say is that I always had a good relationship with those guys. That was not necessarily the case with other prisoners. It was because I assimilated more. You know? And, in this way, I got on well. You have to imagine that I was 19 years old. And you learn faster than when you're older. Really. This is my opinion at least.

And when we were discharged, we were brought by ship to Antwerp in Belgium – no more than 1,500 prisoners of war were allowed to be transported at one time – and we were handed over to the English. We arrived with two duffel bags, and, of course, the English took them away from us. I still have a dictionary today that the Americans certified as mine. The English brought us from Antwerp to a camp near Brussels – to La Hulpe near Waterloo. And from there everyone was brought to England to work for an entire year. And I met Major Hicks, the discharge officer, who arranged for my discharge to Cologne. In 1946 I was a free man again.

Willi Schneider was born in 1924 in Klostergrab (present-day Hrob in the Czech Republic) in the Sudetenland. In 1943 he was taken prisoner in Morocco and brought to the USA on a transport ship. He describes his experiences in camps in the USA from 1943 until 1946.

We were transported to Casablanca and slept in small tents. And then we were brought aboard ship in Rabat. It was a large American Red Cross ship. It was a passenger ship that was converted into a Red Cross ship and transported wounded American soldiers to America. And we were also along as prisoners. As Germans, we were the service personnel for the wounded. We set the tables in the dining room and served the injured soldiers. We brought them whatever they wanted. The Italians weren't allowed to do this work. We were also supposed to serve the Italians. So, we did. Of course, we aggravated them a bit. Instead of sugar we put salt into the dispensers. We travelled for several weeks. It was a large convoy with several ships. These were battleships that were used in the convoy. There was always the danger of submarines. German submarines were in the area and sometimes sank ships. That's the reason why it took so long. They had to travel in a zigzag.

We arrived in New York and were deloused. We had to pass through a delousing line. On board ship we made our uniforms look nice and washed them. And then we were brought directly to the train station with a small ship after the delousing. And there was a crowd of people there. The Americans all wanted to know what Germans looked like – many of them probably had relatives in Germany. They most likely had never had seen a German before. The propaganda told them that Germans had a club foot and horns and were Nazis. And the Americans came to the train cars. These weren't cattle cars, but rather normal cars used for second-class passengers. And there was always an American MP in the front and back. We travelled in the train for three days and three nights as far as Texas. We always got our food on paper plates. The rations were very good. When we drove into the train stations, a lot of people were there waving – they thought that we were their soldiers who came back from Africa. [laughs] So we took the paper plates and drew swastikas on them – really big – and held them against the windows. Every time we drove into the train stations, we showed them. [laughs] First they cheered, and then looked baffled.

In Texas we arrived at a camp. We had to walk several kilometres from the train station to the camp. But on the way to the camp – which was several kilometres away – one American was standing next to the other on the right and left of the street with MPs. That's how afraid they were. And then a number of us – I don't know how many – went to the wooden barracks that were built on stilts. And for months, we didn't do anything – only played sports. According to the Geneva Convention we were allowed to play sports. From the Argentinians, we got soccer balls and equipment and everything. We also received money every month from Germany – in dollars – about three dollars per month. And we were able to go shopping with the money. A carton of cigarettes was cheap in dollars. Then we built a stadium for ourselves. They allowed us to use the equipment to build. And we built a football stadium with everything that we needed and had championships – one company against the other. The Americans – the commanders of each company – were also interested in the games. They made bets and thought that their teams would win. That was the incentive.

And we had food there! We had never seen anything like it. We lived in the lap of luxury. We had roasts and…breakfast with cold cuts and cheese…cornflakes with milk…and marmalade…and at lunch more food and the same in the evenings. After dinner the company had to fall in for roll call. And then they counted to see if anyone was missing. And we had a commander for the German camp and an interpreter. And somehow, we had connections to the men who picked up the garbage. These were always Blacks. They went from one company to the other and collected the garbage from the mess hall. We somehow had contact with them and smuggled in a radio. And so, we always listened to German radio stations to find out what was happening on the Front. We had roll call in the evenings, and then someone always reported the latest news. We had some Austrians along who naturally told on us. And so, everything was taken away from us. These guys were killed once they were discovered. They were beaten so long until they died from the injuries. And then they were buried, and we were supposed to attend. But the Germans didn't go along. They said that they were traitors. There was a three-gun salute even if someone died this way. They were officially buried.

I then went from Texas to Fort Knox. That was a large garrison. The gold from the entire world was there below sea level at that time. We were supposed to work there. And we did. We received eighty cents per day for the work. Forty cents was paid to us. And forty cents was credited to us. I first worked in agriculture laying bricks. The fields were so large that you could hardly see to the other side. And from there I went to the kitchen – no, first to a storage building with a few others. We had to travel to the freight train station and pick up new goods that had arrived there and brought them to the individual warehouses. Entire bales of socks arrived for the army – and uniforms, pants, shirts, and so on. Sometimes we took a pair of pants, or a shirt, or socks when ours were torn. Nobody noticed it. And then I came to a women's company. All of them were in uniform. I was in a room with three men and worked two shifts – the morning shift and the afternoon shift. We alternated. And then we went to the kitchen as helpers. The mess hall was cleaned, the tables set, and the women were served. The food was prepared, and the silverware washed. And the men in the kitchen had girlfriends. We got along well with them. I remember that I was with the female butcher and another was with the female baker – and we were under the table at that moment. I don't remember what we were doing. And the American camp commander came in and all hell broke loose. The entire company had to fall in for roll call. Nothing happened to us because we were working in the kitchen. But they had to fall in and were told that they shouldn't fraternize with the prisoners of war. They were supposed to keep more distance to us.

And did you stick to it?

Yes, we stuck to it. At Christmas time the women collected money for us. They had a piggy bank, and the women from the entire company were able to put some money inside. And we received the money and divided it among ourselves. And we were able to buy various things such as cigarettes or schnapps. A bottle of whisky cost five dollars. Certain people always brought us that. We had contact with the people who picked up the garbage and gave them a certain amount of dollars to get us things. And they did. They liked us better than the white Americans. I remember that we were once in Indiana for the tobacco harvest. In the mornings, a farmer always came with his truck and said that he needed ten men for the tobacco harvest on that day. And we received a rations package for the road. It was made up of canned goods with cookies and meat, etc. But we normally drove with the farmer through various villages and threw away the cans. We wanted sensible food from the farmers for our work; otherwise, we wouldn't do anything. One time we went to one farmer. We always said: "We'll work normally until breakfast, and we'll see what we get for breakfast". Most of them introduced us to their wives and children before we even started and showed us their houses and fields. And they said that there were cucumbers that we could eat. And then we thought: "O.K., we'll wait and see". At breakfast we got milk and buttered bread. And we said: "Good, we'll finish harvesting this man's field today". And then we finished the harvest. And one time we were with another farmer who gave us those canned goods that were rusted. He gave them to us. And a milk jug with only water inside. Nothing to eat. And then we said: "We'll show him". We destroyed his tobacco harvest. We didn't spear the whole stalk onto sticks to be hung up, but rather cut off the leaves. He was so angry that he drove us to his brother at lunchtime. "You fucking Nazis", he said. [laughs] He brought us right to his brother. He was a poor guy, but he immediately introduced us to his wife. He showed us how much work we had to do. And we said: "You know what, we're going to finish his harvest today. When the other brother comes to pick us up and sees it, he'll have a heart attack". [laughs] And we really went to work. And in the afternoon at 3:00 pm, the housewife came to us and brought us coffee and cake. He was a poor guy in comparison to his brother who had a mansion. And in the evening at around 5:00 or 6:00 pm, the other farmer came back and was astonished at the way the field looked. "Fucking Nazis", he said. That's the way it was sometimes.

Hans Broschinski was born in 1916 in Prenzlau Uckermark in Brandenburg. In June 1944 his ship was attacked by American fighter planes en route from St Helena to Cape Town. An American destroyer rescued the remaining German crew members and brought them to an aircraft carrier. In the USA, he was transported to Camp Elders in Mississippi to pick cotton, a branch camp of Camp McCain.

We came to Camp McCain. It was a large camp, and many people came together there. I think there were also some men from the army there. They asked us unimportant questions about how it was in Germany at that time. But we couldn't answer them because we had been away from home for so long. We also had lessons in English. We were able to make up our high school diploma. There were doctors from submarines and other ships who were prisoners and gave lessons in biology, languages, mathematics, and law. That was going well until shortly before the end of the war.

All the submarine guys had to march several kilometres to a small camp in the afternoon sun. And, at this camp, we had to pick cotton. It was normally the work of the Blacks. The Blacks that we met there weren't very happy with us because they couldn't earn any money. We did all the picking, of course for a lot less money – and the Americans also saved. We never had any real contact with the Blacks. In the mornings, we were picked up by the farmers and driven to the fields. And in the evenings, we were brought back again. And we hardly saw them. But there was one Black man who was a leader in my group. He was very sensible and allowed us to get off early in the evenings. We also had lessons in this camp, but many of the soldiers weren't used to it. Afterwards it got better. We worked the whole day and had to pick 150 pounds of cotton per day. The good thing was that the work of the entire group was counted together. Some of the men picked 160 pounds of cotton. I only managed 130 pounds. And that's how the amount for the group was achieved. However, when I returned to the camp in the evenings, the guards noticed this, and I had to shovel one pile of coal onto another. That was Camp Elders.

We stayed in Mississippi the entire time and received money to buy small things in the mess hall – milk and cookies and extras. Work was obligatory, but there were sick days. You had to stay at the camp and do work – take care of the lawn, clean the path, and sweep. We had to get up at 6:00 am. Breakfast was in the barracks, and there were three cooks from submarines there. All the men in this camp were from the navy and had been sent intentionally to Mississippi. After breakfast, five, six, or even eight farmers came in their trucks and took small groups of men with them – some took ten men, others took twelve, and others took only three prisoners. These men were assigned by the German camp leadership. Sometimes the same groups were created for certain farmers. But sometimes men were substituted if a farmer needed only eight men and not ten, so two had to go to another group. The farms were various distances from the camp: some were fifteen or twenty minutes away, and others half an hour.

Matthias Henseler was born in Geislar near Bonn in 1921. He served in the Africa Corps in a supply unit until 1943. Captured in Tunis and brought by ship to the USA from Casablanca, he worked on cotton and sugar cane plantations in Louisiana and Kentucky and in a military depot in New Jersey.

We were at sea for nine days with a convoy of twenty-seven ships. We had radio contact the whole time. There were some cruisers around us which weren't allowed to be attacked because they were registered with the Red Cross. As I said, it took nine days. During the day we were allowed on deck for a certain period of time. Below deck we had three beds on top of one another. It was a troop transporter. Then we sailed to New York. I saw the Statue of Liberty for the first time. We were taken off board, deloused, and given suitable clothing. Our things were thrown away. And then we continued from there.

Some men went into one train, others into another, and still others into another train. I went into a train that went to Louisiana near New Orleans. That's in the south of North America – in the southernmost state. From there I was brought more inland. I was in Kentucky. I was also in Fort Knox. I saw it from the outside. You can't go inside. You know? There were ruins there from when Al Capone blew it up. And we continued from there. In Kentucky I was in an army depot. We had to clean things up there. We were allowed to drive and do everything. Afterwards, I was together with farmers and picked sugar cane. There was a cotton and sugar cane harvest. I liked the sugar cane harvest better. You had to pick the cotton in a special way. Sugar cane was better. We were allowed to drive to the factory. [with emphasis] We were allowed to drive! Where could we have gone? Right? The first farmer rode along with us. But those guys were easy-going. When we were with the farmers, they went to bed and said to wake them if an officer came. They took the ammunition out of the weapons. But what could we possibly have done there? We lived well with the farmers. We got food from the farmers and food from the camps – eggs and sausage. I always say that with the farmers we lived off the fat of the land. We were young in America and weren't fathers yet. When we got older, we had more understanding for them. They had families with children, and it wasn't so easy for them.

And that's how we lived. Afterwards, I was in New Jersey. It's near New York. And I worked in a depot again. I was in America for exactly three years. First, I worked in the sugar cane fields in Louisiana and then in military depots, and, near Fort Knox, we were in the tobacco fields in Kentucky. Otherwise, as I said, I can't complain about America. But that's me. There were others in the camp who had problems, but that was their own fault. Some of them went on strike. They were just sent to a tent for a few days. There was water and bread there. It also wasn't a problem. They didn't starve. [laughs] Well, we thought that they would send us home. But no way. We were sent to England.

American Rhine Camps

Herbert Kneip was born in Cologne in 1928. He finished high school in 1944 while living in barracks and performing anti-aircraft work. At the end of the war, he was held as an American prisoner of war in the Rhine camp in Sinzig.

In 1944 we could see how the Front was coming closer. We could already hear it. For example, when there were air raids by the Americans and the English in Düren, you could see it from Cologne – day and night. There were clouds of smoke and trails of smoke. That continued until we suddenly had to retreat. We couldn't hold these positions any longer. What were we supposed to do on our own? We would have been overrun, and we left as far as the Rhine. And we tried to cross the Rhine with the artillery guns, but it wasn't possible because there wasn't any transport. We crossed the Rhine without our artillery guns – just with our backpacks – I think in a boat or in a ship. Everything was in the process of being disbanded. You could hear skirmishes and rifle shots in the outskirts of Cologne. We crossed the Rhine as a unit until everything fell apart afterwards in Bergisches Land. And we were told: "Please go to Lüdenscheid. There are barracks there, and you'll receive further instructions". We went there, and men from different units were arriving from all over the place. I even met acquaintances from Cologne there. And then we were simply told: "You'll have to manage on your own".

We had our IDs, but we didn't have orders to move out or anything. And then I thought to myself that I would march in the direction of the Americans instead of trying to do great things. I took out a white undershirt and found a stick and went in the direction of the Americans. Of course, they were distrustful. That's clear. But they rounded us up. We sat down. I had my arms extended over my knee while I was sitting. And the first thing they said was: "Please give us the watch". [laughs] I had to give it to them. It was stupid of me. I should have hidden it. But, otherwise, everything was done correctly. Of course, it wasn't friendly. But it was correct. We had to spend a night there.

And then on the next day we were brought to Sinzig on the Rhine. I had two unpleasant experiences concerning the German population: We were thirsty and it was hot, but nobody came and brought us water or anything. Maybe they weren't allowed to. I don't know exactly. In any case, they kept to themselves. And in Sinzig on the first night there were thousands of people in the Rhine camps. And when I woke up the next morning – the most important piece of equipment you needed for this entire time was a so-called mess kit that you could use for food and drink – and this was stolen from me by a fellow soldier while I was asleep during the first night.

You received small cans from the Americans as daily rations. Inside were beans with tomato sauce and bacon and things like that. And afterwards we put six cans next to one another and held it together with a wire, and it was our water basin. We had to stand in long lines to get water. There were huge tarpaulin containers that were filled from the top, and you could get water from them. Of course, everything had to go quickly. I can still hear them saying [in English]: "Let's go. Let's go. Let's go". And then we were left on our own, and we had to see how we could live there. The unpleasant thing was the change from heat during the day to cold at night. This was very awkward. And you were exposed to all kinds of weather – unless you had a coat or a piece of canvas. But with time you dug holes in the ground where you could exist – with a bench and all possible things. It was all right. You got your daily food – a small amount of food – and you were able to survive.

Were there only soldiers in the large Rhine camps?

Yes. Yes. Yes. Yes. Yes. I was a young guy at the age of 15 or 16 at that time, but I don't know whether the young people were first separated. I remember that there were a lot of young people there. And one of them – by chance – had contact with an American – with one of the guards, and he was picked up every day to help out in the kitchen. And, of course, that was THE job. And he always came back with things and would start frying and cooking in his cave. He also gave us things. And whatever we had – leather goods or wallets – we would swap them for something to eat. Everything returned to normal – the hygienic situation was also somehow okay – as good as it could be. People always asked for the doctor and the medical tent. If you had any problems, you could go there. And there were apparently German chaplains who had organized a kind of church service with the Americans on Sundays and on other days. But they had to do everything themselves. They celebrated Mass in a hole about four times as big as this table here, with an old wooden crate as the altar, and a blanket or something as a cloth over it. That was really impressive, I have to say.

How did the Americans treat the prisoners in general?

I didn't notice or hear anything that you could complain about. They were objective and fair. After all, we weren't friends, right? But it was on a basis that you could deal with. At least that was my impression.

How long did you have to stay in that Rhine camp?

I can't tell you exact dates, but I would say that it must have been two, or two and a half months.

Were you then suddenly released?

The country was divided into zones: the French, British, American, and Russian zones. The Americans withdrew and went further south, while the area that is Rhineland-Palatinate today was taken over by the French because it almost bordered France. And they were also really fair in my opinion.

Willi Müller was born in Mönchengladbach in 1923. He joined the air force in 1942 and was trained as an aircraft radio operator. He flew reconnaissance flights over Hungary and the Adriatic before his flight crew was grounded at the end of 1943. He came into the American prisoner-of-war camp in Andernach in March 1945.

We were taken as American prisoners of war in Olpe in Sauerland. The Americans were very angry with the Germans and didn't treat us well. They took away everything from us – not only wallets and rings and watches – but also our coats, wool blankets, and bicycles. All of these things were thrown onto a pile and burned. We were then loaded onto a truck with others and brought across the Rhine to Andernach in several stages. That was in March – it was cold and rainy. It was raining and the weather was bad when we arrived in the camps in Andernach. These were swampy fields that were damp and wet with puddles. We didn't have any blankets, coats, or anything at all. And we didn't have anything to eat or drink for three days. We had to camp out in the rain – in this swamp area.

In the morning, the men who had died during the night – I don't know whether it was because of hunger or thirst or the cold – were gathered together, loaded onto a wheelbarrow, and wheeled out. That was in Andernach. I was there for three days, and I realized that if I had stayed there one or two days longer, I would have been among the dead. I was there as a young man – 20 or 21 years old – relatively strong, but worn out from the war and the hardships that we had gone through. And I asked a fellow soldier if he wanted to try to escape. He refused, and then I looked for and found another person. On a rainy night – it was the third night – we went from our full camp into a neighbouring camp that had already been evacuated. That was relatively easy. And from there we had to go through the outside fence. There was a roll of wire that you could pull apart, but it would spring back together again. The spotlights from the towers crossed the camp the entire night. And two guards constantly walked around the camp. We wondered what we should do. And once the guards went past, we tried to get through the wire in this rainy weather. It was horrible. As I said, the wire sprang back together when you pulled it apart. Our uniforms were torn and bloody all over. And I made it through, but my companion didn't. He was shot in the wire. I realized this once I was through. And then they looked for me, but they didn't know whether another person was along. I went into the woods, and during the night I walked to Andernach to get free. The war was still going on.

Ernst Isenlar was born in Cologne in 1921. After being declared unfit for military service at the start of the war, he was later sent to an engineering unit for river crossings and explosives at the end of the war. In April 1945, he was transported to the American prisoner-of-war camp in Sinzig.

We were sent home at the end of the war when the fighting was over. And I was also at home and didn't have a uniform on or anything anymore. And then there was an announcement from the occupying forces at that time – I suppose it was from the Americans or the English, I don't know anymore, but I think that it was from the Americans. Whoever was no longer a soldier and wasn't a prisoner of war was supposed to report to a certain location on the next day or the next following days. Well, we had the impression that we could go there the next day with our toothbrushes and so on. I went there because I was afraid that whoever did not show up would be picked up by force. So, I went to the area of Cologne called Wahn or Porz-Wahn where I was supposed to report. It was a small storage building next to a church. There was horse feed stored there and others things. All the men from this part of the city and from neighbouring areas gathered there. These were predominantly older men who were not regular soldiers, but rather belonged to the so-called "Home Guard". They were older men. We were then brought inside and the door was closed. Well, now we were inside. Then we were brought to another storage building on the following day – there was another storage area where the Cologne Airport is today – and we had to wait there, too. We asked and they said that something would soon happen.

And then one day – two or three days later – soldiers came there – men with dark skin and steel helmets and so on – and they said: "Go. Get out. Get onto the trucks". We were loaded onto the trucks, penned up closely together on them. We didn't sit, but rather stood on them. And off they drove. We didn't know where they were going, but we soon found out when we arrived in Sinzig in a large area of land where there was nothing at all. Only fields. On the Rhine, there was a huge area that was fenced in. We drove inside and were unloaded. Everything that we had in our pockets – scissors, nail clippers, everything that we were supposed to bring along – was confiscated so that nothing would happen and so that these things could not be used as weapons. They took away these things and then off we went. We had to form a few small groups and then there we were and we had to wait. There weren't any tents or anything, just the ground. And the men who were already there before us dug holes in the ground, with tin cans and so on, and lived down there because the wind came blowing right across.

And then we waited to see what would happen. Nothing happened. And at first there was nothing to eat. Also, nothing to drink. It was later that we got something – I don't know any more how long it took – I only remember that the food we got wasn't cooked at all. It was dried vegetables. These dried vegetables were dry. We would have been able to eat the food if it had been cooked first. What were we supposed to do with it? There were several fellow prisoners who turned tin cans into small stoves. They tried to find water and then were able to cook the vegetables a bit. But it wasn't good at all. It all took time. Every morning, they counted how many people were there, and you had to fall in. We were in this huge camp. And after 10:00 pm, we could see how they drove around the fence in their jeeps so that they could see from their headlights that nothing was going on. One jeep went around this way, and the other the other way. And then they passed one another and could see what was going on. In spite of that, we tried to escape. But it was hardly possible. However, one or two of my prison mates were able to escape over the fence.

And then Pentecost arrived. And it rained and rained! It rained so much that I was almost pulled to the ground because I was wearing civilian clothing that was soaking wet and heavy. I hooked my coat onto the barbed wire fence so that I had some traction. [laughs] And then we waited to see what would happen. Several men tried to barter for a few cigarettes. Some of them traded their wedding rings, and the dark-skinned soldiers threw a few cigarettes over the fence. Well, it was a difficult time. All of this took about four weeks. They started to organize the camp a little bit and to count the prisoners. And then the first prisoners were released. After eight or ten days, we were asked to come to a tent in the camp. And then we went there and told them our names and everything. And, one or two days later, we got our release papers and were loaded back onto the trucks and were brought back home. And altogether it lasted four weeks. Four or five weeks, I guess. But I don't know exactly.

We were hungry and looked horrible. One fellow prisoner had canned meat in his backpack – I'm not sure where he got it from. He was a playwright by profession. I still remember that. And he was released before me and said: "Go ahead, take a can of meat". I took a can of meat and opened it immediately because I was starving and ate it. It was pork – greasy pork. And a few days later when I arrived home, I was sick! That was clear. That greasy pork in my empty stomach. Right? And I ate a whole can of it. Well, that was the consequence. And I didn't have shoes anymore. They gave me a pair of boots at the camp because the ground was so muddy from the rain. I didn't have any heels on my shoes anymore. I was wearing my private shoes because I had just come from home. And then I managed to get a pair of boots. And they took those back.

In general, I can't say that they beat us up. If someone was standing near the fence, he was pushed away with the butt of the rifle. But nothing other than that. And sometimes we had short conversations with the soldiers. They saw how we were living and didn't care for it either. But we had the impression that they gathered all the men together so that there would be no resistance in the country and then put everybody into the camp. And then they weren't able to deal with the large number of men so quickly. It was a matter of organization. A lot of the American soldiers who worked there spoke German because those were men who went over to America from the Third Reich because of relatives. They came back as soldiers or camp guards or supervisors so that we were able to speak with them. But as I said, I had the feeling – or we had the feeling – that the organization didn't work and that it was too much for them. In such a short period of time, hundreds and almost thousands of people were thrown together. And they had to be taken care of, and it didn't work. That was my time there.

Did people die while you were there?

A man who was older than me at that time didn't die directly, but he was in such bad shape because he was starving. And he was extremely old. Every morning when we woke up, we had to kick him in the pants so that he woke up. Otherwise, he would have died on us. I personally didn't see any dead people there. I can't say that. No one was shot or beaten or anything else either. That didn't happen.

Josef Dregger was born in Cologne in 1920. He first saw military action in Yugoslavia in 1940/41. Afterwards, he was sent to the Ukraine to lay communication cables for an intelligence unit and then accompanied his unit to Caucasus. After becoming ill, he was transferred to a military hospital in the West. In 1941/42, he was reunited with his military unit near Kiev and in 1943 returned to the West because of illness. In May 1945, he was brought to the American prisoner-of-war camp in Rheinbach.

After having marched through the Ebbe Mountains for three days, I finally arrived in Sauerland. That's where my parents were after they had been completely bombed out in Cologne. That happened in October. They had been evacuated there. I was lucky to arrive there in my civilian clothing. My mother was sitting in front of the house and was knitting. She saw a complete stranger approaching her in civilian clothing and did not recognize me. And she ran into the house very quickly almost screaming as if I were a foreign worker who wanted to harm her. And then I called out: "Mother, mother, it's me!" And then, slowly she came out again and recognized me. That was our reunion. It was at the end of April. I had some nice days there and was spoiled by life in the village.

But everyone had officially been discharged as soldiers. I told everyone – my mother and my father – that my military service record stated that I had been discharged because of illness. However, I knew that there were discharge papers by the Allies which were abbreviated LA 2. My father urged me – because he didn't want to get into trouble either – to report to the military authorities right across the road. He said that I was certain to get my discharge papers because of my military service record. It was the morning of 2 May – I remember exactly – we had just started eating breakfast and my father said: "Go over there now.

No one else is there. They'll wait on you immediately. And afterwards you can finish breakfast". I gave in and went over. The American officer in charge shook his head contemplatively and said: "I can't do it. In this case, the next office in charge is in Attendorn. I'll have to have you brought there". He waved over a jeep, and my father was just able to throw me a civilian coat in spite of objections by the soldiers. I was dressed in civilian clothing. And they brought me to Attendorn, and here's what happened.

They brought me into a basement, and more and more German soldiered were gathered there during the course of the day. Some were in military uniforms, others were not. All of them didn't have any discharge papers. By the evening, the basement was filled with about 100 soldiers. And then an American truck drove to the front of the building and picked us up and brought us to Klettenberg. We were brought to a factory building, and I was in the middle of the room with about 300 or 400 German soldiers. The room was so full that we were only able to spend the night standing up. And we didn't get anything to eat. The first time that we got something to eat was after four days. The next day they asked who wanted to be transported. I raised my hand because I didn't want to stay, and I was transported with others on the back of a truck in very bad cold weather. On 2 May, there were snow flurries. And this was 3 May. We were driven very far away and arrived in Wesel at the Rhine crossing. We drove over the bridge, and near Wesel there's a town called Rheinbach. We didn't know what would happen to us. We were all brought to a large piece of land – a field – every hour new people joined us. In the end, there were 50,000 or 100,000 soldiers. And there we were. Left on our own.

Every day we only got enough food to fill the palm of our hand. We were actually suffering from hunger. But worse was the fact that we didn't have a roof, a blanket, or anything over our heads. We dug holes in the ground with the things that we had along with us. One person dug with a spoon, and the other person with his bare hands in order to protect ourselves from the wind and weather. Nobody told us what would happen to us. We only heard that the Americans, the English, and all the Allies were terribly afraid of what Joseph Goebbels once stated: "The German soldier will never give up, even when he's beaten. He'll still offer resistance". This was called "Operation Werewolf". But in reality, it didn't even exist. Well, in mid-July – in the middle of the summer – I was finally released in Cologne. In the meantime, we had been handed over to the English, but the rations weren't much better. And then life continued in Cologne. We had to make sure that we found a flat and so on. I managed to find one. We found a rather run-down apartment. We fixed it up and repaired the windows. I went and got my parents, and my brother also later returned from a prisoner-of-war camp. And my sister was there anyway. And that was the story. There's nothing more to say.

In your opinion, how did the Americans treat you?

They didn't tell us anything. Even our officers tried to find out what would happen to us. There is the Hague Convention. But we didn't get an answer. They told us: "You have to wait. We are also waiting for orders". The Americans were better with the rations for their own people and let us suffer. They handed us six beans and a little chocolate powder and practically nothing to drink. We didn't even have the chance to get water. The only well was muddy and marshy. If we wanted water, then we had to stand in line for three hours. There was no water for all the men. And there also weren't any toilets. So, it was really degrading. I remember exactly that people were desperate and went close to the fence – which was strictly forbidden – and were then shot. And some people simply collapsed because they were hungry and didn't have anything to eat. I myself had the experience that I stood up quickly from the ground – I was also feeble – and they told me afterwards that I had turned around three times and fell down. I was dizzy. That was life in the camp.

I heard that the actions by the Americans triggered great criticism in their own country. And there are books on the topic. By the way, I have a book at home which is a reminder of this time in the camp,[2] which means between May and July. If you see it correctly – other men were prisoners of war much longer – with the Russians. We were spared this. But one still cannot forget this time. We weren't treated like human beings. Not really. Not even the sick – not even the sick received medical treatment. There was only one building there, and the extremely ill, who were suffering from a high fever, were sheltered there. But without any medical care. There was no one there to look after them. That is the story, and I'll never forget it. I think that the American military command should have thought about what to do with so many prisoners and how to treat them with dignity. Even enemies in war deserve that. And as far as I know, the Germans stuck to that. And in other countries it was also the case. Others told great stories about their time as prisoners of war where they worked as masons in America or in France. They were always well accepted and well taken care of.

Werner Blumenthal was born in Bad Godesberg near Bonn in 1927. He served as an air force support helper in 1943 and was taken prisoner of war by American forces in April 1945 in Sinzig.

What was it like to be taken prisoner?

It was a strange feeling. The Americans had creased pants and creased shirts and looked very neat. The soldiers that took us prisoner weren't troops from the Front. Those men had already passed through. These were men who came from behind. They didn't do anything bad to us. Absolutely normal. You know? They asked us: "Do you have a watch? Do you have a watch?" I didn't have a watch, so I couldn't give them one. Some of the American soldiers had a whole arm full of watches. What could you do, you know? [laughs] We were in a few camps, but only for one night at a time. We crossed the Rhine near Koblenz over a pontoon bridge and were brought to a camp in Andernach near Koblenz. I don't remember the exact name anymore. We didn't see any towns, and then we left. It was very difficult. Once we didn't get anything to drink for three days. No rations.

I was lucky because I had 1,200 cigarettes along with me. We were able to go to a German supply vehicle that had been blown up. I didn't smoke, but I was able to barter. One person had a potato, another had a piece of chocolate, and another person had something else. That's how it worked. And the Americans didn't take the cigarettes away from me. They had their own cigarettes. [laughs] Then we were brought a few kilometres by train from Andernach to Sinzig. The railway cars were open on the top – not closed. Other men were brought to France and spent years in France. I was brought there, not far from home, you know? I didn't think about trying to escape because it was too well guarded, and I didn't have any money in my pockets.

What were your first impressions of Sinzig?

Not good. [laughs] I spent a month and a half sleeping on the bare ground. I didn't have a roof over my head. But one night I got a German Army camouflage coat. One guy had a whole pile of them and didn't need two or five of them, and I was able to use one myself. I won't say that it saved my life, but it was fantastic. It was in field-grey with all the colours on the outside the way they are today in the German Army. And white on the inside. You could turn it inside out and then it was white. It was waterproof and had a hood, and you could lie down on the ground and sleep. It was great. One time they brought us down to the Rhine. Each of us got a piece of curd soap. We had just got into the water, and the soap slipped out of our hands and was gone. [laughs] First, the rations were very mediocre. A water line was set up, but you had to stand in line for twelve hours. You were always together in a group. It wasn't possible to live on your own. So, we formed a small group. One person stood in line at first, and then another person relieved him. I had the feeling that the Americans were overwhelmed at this moment with this enormous number of prisoners – an enormous number of prisoners. A six-wheeler once drove into the camp, and we went to the driver in the front and asked him whether he had anything to eat. He had a can of C-ration[3] and gave it to me. I knew a bit of English from school.

And then suddenly they called for the prisoners from the city of Bonn and vicinity. We had to gather at the gate and give them our paybooks. A few days later, they called for us. We were examined by a doctor and then released. It was Sunday, 10 June 1945. I can't complain because I was released one month after having surrendered. They took us on a six-wheeler through Bad Godesberg to Bonn to the employment office. And then they said to us in the back: "Get out! Schnell. Schnell. Get out!" [laughs] I was a prisoner of war from 11 April 1945 until 10 June

1945. Two months. Nobody did anything bad to me. I can't complain. Time was kind to me. And my eldest brother, who had been injured, was at home ten days before me. Ten days before me. The Americans drove him right to Mehlem train station. "You're there now. Get down from the truck", they told him. And my other brother from Wickrath came home about four or five weeks later. It was lucky for our family. Three young soldiers came home safely, although the oldest brother was not completely healthy. Our neighbour who lived two houses away lost two sons and the father, and the mother was alone with the youngest son. It was awful.

Canadian Camps

Dr Heinrich Rödder was born in Siegburg near Bonn in 1910. He volunteered for the air force in 1937 and was shot down over England as a bombardier in 1940. He then spent seven years as a prisoner of war in England and Canada. In the prisoner-of-war camp in Canada, he attended several lectures on medicine and completed the first part of his medical studies.

How did the English treat you?

Correctly. Very correctly. I can't say anything else. The English treated us correctly, and the Canadians even better. The English were correct. They didn't yell at us or anything. The rations came from the English Army. They were very modest. They didn't have anything themselves. That was also the main reason why they sent us to Canada. Before I was sent to Canada, there was a transporter that left for Canada – it was the first one – and was mainly made up of prisoners from Holland and Norway. The English also captured them. There is a rumour: An acquaintance of mine saw how the English left their own men on the beach in Dunkirk and took along German prisoners of war. This is what people said who were there.

As I said, we soon left for Canada. And it was very good there. The Veterans Guard – that was the equivalent of the Home Guard in Germany – was our guard detail that more or less had paternal feelings for us. They were in World War I and after World War I were the occupying forces in Germany. They had been active soldiers. They were now Veteran Guards and guarded us. We worked well together, and sometimes we could even bribe them. My stay in Canada lasted five and a half years. You can say that it was a time of recuperation. After I was shot down, my promotion to lieutenant was submitted, and I received the news in the camp on the Great Lakes in Canada that I had been promoted to lieutenant. I was immediately moved from the regular soldiers' camp to the officers' camp. And, in the officers' camp, there were high-ranking navy men who were on strike because of substandard living conditions. In the meantime, they found out that RAF officers in Germany were being held in a castle as prisoners. And that's also true. They were lodged in a castle. And for that reason, the officers in the camp started a hunger strike. When I came to the camp, the hunger strike had just ended. And the camp had been moved to some place in Ontario. It was a school for unruly boys. According to what the people from the Red Cross said, it was the most beautiful prisoner-of-war camp in the world. We had an indoor swimming pool there that was made of stone with central heating and there were tennis courts.

Where was that exactly in Ontario?

In Oshawa. Oshawa near Lake Ontario. Near Ottawa. It was called Oshawa. And the small town was called Bowmanville. We were there for practically the entire war. We got our service pay in Canadian dollars. We were able to buy things from the cafeteria. We were able to buy beer if we wanted. The only thing that we weren't able to buy were weapons and radio equipment. We had catalogues that you can get here today – Eaton catalogues. And we were able to shop in the cafeteria using the catalogues. And we got rations from their army that were very good – I said before that I was a somewhat chubby, heavyset child. Every day in the camp I ran at least 3,000 or 5,000 metres so that my uniform still fit. That's how good the food was there.

Where did you work in the camp?

I wasn't allowed to work. According to our agreement, I received my service pay as an officer in Canadian dollars. Most of the regular soldiers were used for work. Back then in Canada, there wasn't a road that went right across the country. There were only two railway lines. From Halifax to Vancouver. No road. And our camp was located in the woods above the Great Lakes. Maybe the idea was to use German prisoners to build roads. But there were so many escape attempts that they soon gave up that idea.

What did you do the whole time in the camp?

I prepared for my medical studies. Our camp consisted of only officers, but we had about 150 men. It was on our own terms. Everyone wanted to come to the officers' camp because it was a beautiful camp. We had a small vegetable garden and grew tomatoes and everything possible. And, as I said, there was a course of study for law students, a course of study for technicians, and a course of study for medical students. There were also officers in the reserves along. In particular, transporters arrived from Africa in 1941 – from Rommel. There were a lot of officers in the reserves along. We had four or five doctors in our camp – and technicians, engineers, and chemists. And they held the lessons in these courses. Certification was awarded. I have a bunch of certificates on all classes I attended there. I had to hold lectures myself. Of course, we wanted to, you know. And afterwards, here in Bonn, they accepted one semester of transfer credit hours based on these certificates. I completed all the courses in Canada up to my preliminary examinations. But we didn't have any internships.

At the end of the war, the camp was disbanded, and we went to Edmonton near the Rocky Mountains. We performed dissections there. When the soldiers shot a deer or something like that, we brought it inside and dissected it. As a medical student, I was able to save one semester of study. Law students saved half of their studies. The credits were accepted, and then we went to Germany. I mentioned this before – as the war continued, officers came to our camp who didn't have an advanced high school degree. Those were Knight's Cross holders who received the Knight's Cross at the age of 18 or 20 – regardless of whether they had an advanced high school degree or not – and were promoted to the rank of lieutenant. And they received their advanced high school degree there. They wrote papers for the courses, and the teachers sent the grades to Germany, and the students were awarded their degrees.

How did the prisoners become so well organized and essentially establish their own university?

That was on their own initiative, I would say. There were sufficient officers in the reserves. We had the president of the Regional Court of Hamburg. He was an officer in the reserves and was in the air force in World War I. And he organized and taught the courses in law. And we had a doctor from Vienna who taught the medical courses. He had four or five medical students in the first camp and received a great deal of material from Germany. I was a prisoner of war for seven years during my studies. Twice I was enrolled in distance learning programmes: once at the University of Bonn as a medical student, and then at the University of Innsbruck in the medical faculty after it was centralized. I have the certificates at home. And the Canadians were happy that we were busy. If we hadn't had anything to do, maybe more men would have thought about escaping. And they would have built more tunnels. We had great operations to build tunnels. In the regular soldiers' camp, I saw that one tunnel was dug under the camp which was built on sand in the woods. And, in spite of that fact, we built a tunnel, and the floor boards were sawed out and frames put in place. The tunnel extended for about 70 metres past the fence. And twenty-nine men escaped. That was on 20 April 1941. That was supposed to be a gift to the Führer.

Where did they go then?

The camp was located in the woods, and there was only one stop for the railway. It was the railway line. None of the twenty-eight men who escaped made it. Three of them were shot. There was a long trial against the soldiers who shot them. They were charged. And they tried to find out whether it had been necessary to shoot the three men. Some of them shot randomly at soldiers who were lying on the ground. There was a big scandal even after the war.

Could you describe what the lessons were like?

In the camp, we had empty rooms that were used for the lessons. And someone stood in the front and held a lecture. In Bowmanville, where the camp was located, we had an academic library with 4,000 volumes. I personally helped to catalogue it. And there was a great deal of literature. We received everything that we needed for our studies.

The literature was in German because it was sent from Germany. As part of my enrolment at the University of Bonn, I was also sent medical books. They sent me books on physiognomy and anatomy. And I brought them back to Germany with me. After the war, each of us was allowed to send a box of books home – I don't know how many Canadian dollars that was – to an address in Germany. Most people were interested in doing that. I was able to send all my books – four boxes to people I knew – friends of mine whose addresses I still knew. The majority of the books that I needed here in Bonn I already had in Canada. And I sent them to Germany.

Camps in the UK

Walter Scharnagl was captured by British troops near the German-Dutch border in March 1945 during an Allied offensive to cross the Wesel River. He describes his capture, his transport across the Netherlands, and the prisoner-of-war camp in England.

Our next deployment was to the Lower Rhine near Rees where the English offensive to cross the Rhine took place on 25 March, pushing in the direction of the Ruhr District. And that was really horrible. We were poor souls. Somewhere in the background we heard a few German artillery guns – 8-centimetre guns – dangerous guns that were the best anti-aircraft guns – and somewhere there was an SS battery. And the English came with power – the 51st Highland Division – and crossed the Rhine. There were some incredible battles – really horrible battles. We retreated a little at a time. Near Wesel there was a major English air landing with 40,000 soldiers I believe. And we were caught in the middle. We retreated to Isselburg on the Dutch border. I was then deployed as a messenger for the regimental headquarters. I looked for the regimental headquarters that was supposed to be in a farmhouse, but they weren't there. I looked for them the whole day, but couldn't find anyone. At night, I went to sleep in a barn.

Early the next morning I went inside the farmhouse. I didn't have anything along to eat except for some lard. I gave the farmer's wife the can of lard and told her to make me a few fried potatoes. And she did it. I hadn't noticed anything during the night. I had slept in the hay in the barn – it was the first time in three or four days that I had slept. I hadn't notice that the Front had retreated during the night. On the farm, an artillery gun with 2-centimetre ammunition had been blown up. But I hadn't heard or noticed anything. And the farmer's wife didn't say anything. I was eating my fried potatoes when the door opened and three English officers came from a reconnaissance vehicle and entered and said: "Hello. Good morning. Hands up!" [laughs] My rifle was hanging on the wall. I said: "Hello! Good morning!" I ate fried potatoes together with the English soldiers. [laughs] They took me along in the armoured reconnaissance vehicle to the next post headquarters, and then I was off to the prisoner-of-war camp in Goch.

It was a difficult situation in the camp on the Lower Rhine which was filled with a few thousand men. We received corned beef and cakes for the first time. They were our rations for the period that followed. Then we were brought straight across Holland in the troop transporter of a freight train. It was horrible. The population stood there and threw stones at the train. They were really malicious. We arrived in Flanders somewhere between Ghent and Bruges. A large camp had been set up there, and the Allies had a lot of work with so many prisoners of war. At first, they weren't ready for so many people. Our camp allegedly had 20,000 prisoners.

There you were able to find anyone who was in the German Army. There were some from Hungary (from the Hungarian Honvédség), even some soldiers from an Indian division who had served in Germany in the army, and all European nationalities who had been called up for military service. They divided the men up to determine their nationalities. All the pure Germans and people under the jurisdiction of the German Reich remained there, and all the so-called foreigners, which began with Austrians, Sudeten Germans (we were actually Czechs: it was the end of April, and the Czechs had proclaimed their own sovereign state), citizens of Luxembourg, French, and anyone imaginable, were sent to England. We were brought to Ostend in a transporter and shipped to England in an American Liberty freighter – a massive freighter. It was horrible. They had brought tanks or something on board. And it stunk. It had been washed out with petroleum or something. We boarded the freighter, and it really stunk. The sea journey was wonderful. They told us that we had to travel in a zigzag to Tilbury in London through a canal into the mouth of the Thames. We were supposedly being chased by a German submarine. They travelled in a zigzag on the high seas to Tilbury. And I was so sick. The lard that I ate must have been bad. I had jaundice and was sick as a dog.

When we arrived in Tilbury in London, the first thing that we received was a beating. We got off the ship on a gangway with an iron fence, and English soldiers were standing around in uniform – who were really Poles – from the Polish Legion on the English side. They were standing around with sticks, and as we marched through, we got hit. But the English were always super correct – everywhere. We were then brought to a camp in a suburb of London called Kempton Park. Before the war, and probably afterwards as well, it was a racecourse. But for the invasion it was probably a camp for American troops. There were barracks and compounds surrounded by barbed wire housing various departments. We went inside and there was first a medical examination. And I'll never forget it: My Jewish doctor, Dr Cohen – I'm very grateful to him – he was such a short guy, but could jump onto a table. English and German medics were there, and he determined that I had jaundice. He looked at my eyes. There was a military hospital tent, and I was placed on a diet as was usual. I recovered, but after a few days I got a severe sinus infection and high fever because of the cold weather. This is an amazing story: One evening I started to have hallucinations – the war was over and Germany had surrendered in the meantime. It was already the beginning of May. We came to England on 25 April, the war was over, and there was a large celebration. It was a great relief. It was wonderful.

We heard about the German concentration camps and similar things while we were in England. We didn't know anything before that. No idea at all. My father had told me that there was a concentration camp in Dachau. We even had relatives there. But that was a re-education camp. Once you were released as a prisoner from there, you weren't allowed to talk about what you had seen. Near our hometown there was a concentration camp on the Bavarian-Czech border called Flossenbürg. It was said that the prisoners there made ammunition and things like that. We didn't know anything more than that. In England, we heard these stories for the first time and then at some later point. We saw films about the liberation of the concentration camps. It was unbelievable what had actually happened there. We always tried to be decent soldiers. How could that be true in Germany.

In any case, I fell ill, and in London there was a large victory celebration. The officers and my doctor, Dr Cohen, all travelled to London to the celebration. The German medics didn't know what to do.

I started to hallucinate. And an English medic got on his motorcycle and drove to London – we were in a suburb outside the city – he knew where Dr Cohen was in London. And the Jewish doctor, Dr Cohen, came back from the victory celebration in London to see the German prisoner of war to determine what he could do. And luckily, the first penicillin was available at that time, and I was treated. And the short Jewish doctor – I would like to know where his grave is – he probably died a long time ago – I would like to place flowers at his grave – is the one who saved my life. I'll never forget him.

When I was released, I came to a compound. It was a large collection camp which also had eight sections with barbed wire. Two or three officers received newspapers. And afterwards they even removed the barbed wire. I came to a camp that had men from the German Navy. Those were poor fellows. They had been stationed all over in their submarines: in France, and I think down in…I forget the name…south of Bordeaux, and abroad. They were told that they had to hand over their ships in England and travel home. They handed over their ships and remained there in England. And they were really strange. I came to these navy men as an air force paratrooper and didn't have any personal contact with them. I couldn't believe that it was possible. There shouldn't be any animosity among the various branches of the military. They wouldn't even look at me. No contact. After two or three days a petty officer 3rd class came to me and said: "Man, you were really lucky. We wanted to kill you". I asked: "Why?" He said: "We thought you were an English informer. And you wanted to find out whether we were Nazis or not". There was an English interrogating officer for the questionings, and he looked like me. It was first when this man was at the camp gate, and I was inside, that people realized that they had mistaken me for him. They really wanted to kill me. That often happened in prisoner-of-war camps. I heard from friends who later came from Canada that there were German prisoners of war who had been taken prisoner in the German Africa Corps in 1942 and 1943 and didn't have any idea about what it looked like in Germany after the bombings. And if any prisoner told them that the war was lost, Cologne had been destroyed, and Berlin looked so and so, they would have said that the soldier was a traitor and hung him at night. It happened.

In any case, since I knew English well and always received newspapers from the officers, I was first able to read the news about ethnic Germans being expelled from Czechoslovakia. I hadn't been aware about what was going on there. I received the last letter from home at Christmas 1944, and since then there was no more news. Well, they finally gathered us together and transported us a long way to the Midlands in England in the second-class compartment of a comfortable train and so on. Wonderful. We were supposed to be brought to a regular camp. The navy men went to the prisoner-of-war camp with two or three duffle bags filled with things. They had wonderful uniforms; fur-lined clothing, fur boots, two complete navy uniforms, several pairs of underwear, and so on. They weren't able to carry it all – that's how much stuff they had because they expected to go home. And on the road, the English told us that we were travelling in the direction of Manchester or near there, but that we had to march around 10 kilometres to the camp. Nobody believed it. But then they were forced to believe it, and the navy men started to throw things away. I didn't have anything. I only had a small bag with some shaving stuff. That was it. And when they threw things away, I collected them. Suddenly I had three pairs of underwear, a navy uniform, and fur boots. And we really had to march. The ones who didn't believe that we had to march so far had to throw away whole suitcases. First, I had a bag, then I had a duffle bag, then I had a duffle bag and a suitcase.

When we arrived at the camp, we went into the first barracks and there was a long table. The English soldier sitting there told us to put all the luggage on the table. One, two, three. It was gone. And because it was so hot while we were marching, I had changed my clothes during a break and put on the lightest uniform. I stood there and didn't have anything more. All my things were gone, and I had less to put on than before. In the mess hall next to our barracks, I was standing there with my silverware and wanted to get something to eat when someone said to me: "Hey, are you Walter? Are you from Tachov?" It was my uncle Theo who was four years older than me. And then we stayed together and went from there to the regular prisoner-of-war camp. I finally came to Camp Harpenden in Hertfordshire, north of London. This was a camp that was also probably used for the preparation of the invasion. The Americans and the English had previously stayed there and received training for the Normandy landing. And now it had been converted. We were supposed to work at that camp as prisoners of war in agriculture.

I received special treatment because I had somehow caught their attention. We were interviewed. The first camp was north near Manchester. There was a Czech military commission which questioned all former Sudeten Germans who were Czech citizens. They asked about our families, political affiliations, fathers' profession, and so on. They interrogated us. You had to have a good reputation and couldn't have had a Nazi past. And then they asked everyone: "Do you intend to return to Czechoslovakia?" "Yes, of course", I answered. "It's my home". "Then you have to prove your allegiance to the Czech state", they said. "What does that mean?" "You know that the war isn't over yet. The Czech Army is still fighting in Burma against Japan. Are you willing to join the army?" "No", I said. "For us the war is over even against the Japanese down there". Maybe it wasn't meant seriously. They wouldn't have allowed us to carry a rifle, of course.

And then we came to Hertfordshire to the camp. They immediately began to divide us up into A, B, and C groups. Nazis, followers, and democrats, or something like that. They conducted a lot of interviews. We established a parliament in the camp. I was young, but was elected deputy camp president. The first session was held and then parliament was dissolved. It wasn't needed. Then I was sent to the editorial staff. There was a prisoner-of-war newspaper. Until today, I don't know whether the newspaper was only meant for the prisoners in the camp or all of England. We had an editorial staff in our camp, and it became evident that those were all communists. They had changed sides or come from somewhere else and were sometimes used in the war propaganda against Germany at the BBC or somewhere else. And there was an editorial staff for the prisoner-of-war newspaper, and the English noticed that it couldn't go on like that – it was pure communist propaganda. And they sent me to the newspaper because I came from a politically correct family and had to work there to make corrections. I never took up this work because the newspaper was cancelled.

Hans Röttgen was born in Urbar near Koblenz in 1908. He served as a military mail carrier until he was taken prisoner of war by Canadian soldiers in Goes in the Netherlands. From there he was transported to a prisoner-of-war camp in England.

Approximately four weeks before Christmas – it must have been at the beginning of December [1944] – I was transferred to a small camp near Ascot [in Berkshire, England]. A winter quarter for a circus was there which they rebuilt with beds on two or three floors. It was a very nice accommodation. We received such good food there that we were ashamed because we thought that people in Germany were starving. In the mornings there was porridge, eggs – either scrambled eggs or boiled eggs – then white bread, and other bread, and cake, and so on. There was either coffee or tea or hot chocolate. And, in the afternoon, we had so much food that we couldn't believe it. We had an easy life.

And then they asked us who wanted to work. Work where? Renovate barracks and clean parks, etc. You know the way it is with the Germans. You can send them to the moon where there is nothing, and they will make something out of it. It was shortly before Christmas, and the prisoners in the camp were bored and started to make toys. They made a dachshund on a board, and when you pulled a string, the wheels moved back and forth and the tail wagged. And they made dolls from rags. The prisoners found leather and wire, etc. in the garbage. It wasn't allowed, but they did it anyway. They tolerated it in the camp. And what toys we made! You can't imagine. One prisoner built a train from a white tin cookie box that used to have cookies and waffles inside. On Christmas these toys were set up. The owner of a hotel and the managing director of an orphanage were invited to come and see them, and we showed everything that we had made. They enjoyed it. The toys were handed out as Christmas presents in the orphanage. That's the truth.

The English treated us very well. But we didn't understand why we were in such a small camp and received such luxurious food. We had so many different kinds of people in the camp from street cleaners and sewer workers to factory owners and professors and many other professions. There were Germans from the north and the west – a total mixture. The officers were separated from us and lived in lodgings made of sheet iron. There was a well-known music band in our camp. After the war they often played on the radio. And we also founded a group with about thirty-five singers. One morning at 6:00 am, they told us that the singers had to fall in immediately for roll call. They gave us English uniforms. We had to change clothes. And they drove us to the BBC in London, and we sang our Christmas songs there. It's unbelievable, but true. The show was broadcast on Christmas Eve in 1945: German prisoners of war in English camps singing German Christmas songs. Some of the German soldiers cried because we were doing so well, and people at home were still possibly living in basements, were ill, or even dead. At that time, we couldn't explain it. But, afterwards, we discovered that the English wanted to find out how the Germans would behave in a democracy. As far as I know, we were the first camp to be sent home on 26 February 1946. Those were my experiences in the English prisoner-of-war camp.

British Camps in North Africa

Bernd Hesslein was born in Berlin in 1921. He was taken prison of war in March 1943 in Ferrara on the Po River in Italy and was sent to a British camp on the Suez Canal until 1947 where he was transferred to Wilton Park, England for political re-education.

There were five large camps on the Suez Canal. Each of the camps had perhaps 10,000 to 12,000 men. Each of the camps was divided into so-called "cages". Those were individual divisions. And each of these had about 1,000 men. There were ten cages to one camp. There were five team camps ranging from simple soldiers to master sergeants. Those were the NCOs – the highest-ranking non-commissioned officers. Then there was the officers' camp ranging from lieutenants to generals. The officers' camp was centrally located and the other camps around it.

When I came to this camp on 8 May 1945 with some other soldiers who had been captured in Italy shortly after the surrender of Germany, we encountered a completely intact world. The so-called "Rommel soldiers" were well-nourished and in tip-top uniforms with all the awards and honours and marched into the C-block to the tune of the Horst Wessel Song – as a provocation – as if to say "here we are". They wanted to say that they were prisoners, but they hadn't been defeated. The English viewed it as a circus. They said: "The Germans are crazy, leave them alone". We played football with these soldiers, but that was all. An English sergeant came in the mornings and evenings to take roll call – there was an extra building where they had to march through. The camp commander – or camp spokesman – was always the person with the highest rank. He was always there with a camp interpreter and a deputy. The English never became involved in internal affairs. They said: "You take care of your business. The main thing is that you're all here. And we'll take roll call". The English weren't interested in what it looked like inside the individual camps. And we witnessed this completely intact group of men who were living with ideas from 1943.

We entered the camp, and they said: "You are amateurs. You lost the war". They believed that the English landing in France in 1944 was propaganda. It was pure propaganda. The English tried to give them a camp newspaper, but it was rejected. In the mornings, the sergeant came with a package of German flyers and gave them to the camp spokesman. He took them and threw them over the fence. The matter was then settled for them. The German soldiers received information about 8 May [1945] from the officers' camp through navy signalling and mirrors. They were completely uninformed and remained uniformed. Until the summer of 1945, the officers' camp shaped the opinions and ideas of all these Rommel soldiers. And there was a real battle between us and them. Of the 1,000 soldiers in our camp, there were three or four murders. Rommel soldiers murdered these men – which was later uncovered by the English – only because they said: "Thank God the war is over". And until August [1945] these Rommel soldiers marched into C-camp to the tune of the Horst Wessel Song with the swastika flag.

What happened to these Rommel soldiers?

There were so-called "screenings" to determine the level of political involvement. But these soldiers were later discharged like everyone else. That was a rather sad political story that showed the fanaticism or how well the propaganda worked, but the criminal activity came from the officers' camp. The worst part of the matter was that in the summer of 1944 there was a camp newspaper which was allowed. In one of the issues – which I have at home – it said that 10,000 German soldiers accepted democracy. And these guys marched to the Horst Wessel Song. They were the ones who mislead and abandoned the others.

What was asked at the screenings?

I can describe my own screening to you. My father emigrated from Germany. I joined the armed forces because my mother was alone at home with me. We had a difficult time. And so did I in particular because I went to war, although afterwards I recognized the truth of the matter. It is certainly true that I wasn't a deserter. It would have been the end of my mother if I had deserted. I went to the screening, and they asked: “Were you in the Hitler Youth?” I said: “No. I wasn’t in the Hitler Youth”. “Don’t lie”, they said. “You must have been in the Hitler Youth”. I said: “No. I wasn’t in the Hitler Youth because my father was politically persecuted. Therefore, I didn’t have to go”. “If that’s the truth”, they said, “why did you wage Hitler’s war?” It was a complicated discussion. The screening was carried out in the German language by German emigrants. They were mostly IOs – information officers. We got into a controversy. These questions touched me deeply. First of all, they told me not to lie and that my story wasn’t true and asked me why my father had emigrated and why I hadn’t deserted. I was in such a rage – utter fury. I left the room and did something that I normally would not have done. I went out and said: “Heil Hitler!”

It was an act of protest. I was 23 years old and enraged because of everything that I had experienced in the camp. I was then punished by being classified in the worst possible group – “C minus”. “A” were anti-fascists; “B” were followers; “C” were Nazis; and “C minus” were the worst Nazis that existed. I now regard the entire story as a blessing because I came together with real Nazis for the first time in my life. I was transferred to a dark camp and met the worst relentless Nazis I have to say. This was a misfortune that I caused myself. Actually, it brought me only good. I now know what Nazis are. I didn’t know before. During the war I was always with soldiers who said: “Let’s first win the war and then eliminate Hitler later”. That’s how simple the world was for us. One more thing that I should mention is that the soldiers in the camps talked about winning the next war. They said that we would win the next war together with American and English weapons. They didn’t know who would be fighting. But they talked about the next war. And the Nazis – they only talked about why the non-Nazis had lost the war.

The first time that I had ever heard about concentration camps in detail was in the spring of 1945 – I think in February or March – when prisoners of war came to us who had been guards in concentration camps that had been liberated. They must have been sent to the armed forces afterwards because suddenly we received two non-commissioned officers and a sergeant, and we asked them where they had served. And they casually said that they were guards in concentration camps. I don’t know whether they were telling the entire truth, but they claimed that they had been guards in concentration camps. They spoke more about political prisoners than about Jews. That was the first thing I want to say. Our simple solution was not to consider them as our fellow soldiers. They were outsiders for us. Ostracized. These are things that you're not allowed to do. They were not one of us. They were not our fellow soldiers.

Were you confronted with these topics during the screenings?

No. That's the second thing I want to tell you. They didn't ask about those things. The screenings were relatively early. But later there was a film that was on the German *Wochenschau* [Weekly Review] – it was the 5th *Wochenschau* called *The World in Pictures* produced by the Allies which consisted of scenes from various concentration camps – and which showed the liberation of Bergen Belsen by the English for example – as well as Buchenwald near Weimar – where German citizens from Weimar were led through the camp and were forced to watch with their handkerchiefs over their mouths. This film was shown to us in the middle of the desert on a screen that had been erected. And, of course, there was fierce debate. A large part of the soldiers – maybe the majority – then said: "That is pure propaganda. It never existed. We never would have done that. We've never heard about it. The Allies filmed that somewhere – probably in Hollywood – and want to depress us here". And, of course, there were enough soldiers among us who said that the protective custody internment camps [Schutzhaftlager] existed at a very early time – which the Nazis propagated themselves. At a very early stage there were thirty-four reports in the *Berliner Illustrierte Zeitung* [*Berlin Illustrated Newspaper*] for example. It was well known that Oranienburg [Sachsenhausen] existed. It was well known that Dachau existed. Each of us saw the signs: "Jews not wanted". Each of us saw the yellow benches in the parks where it said: "Only for Jews". And each of us saw at least once that fellow Jewish citizens were loaded onto trucks – also during the war – and transported away. No German of my generation can say that they didn't know that Jews were transported away.

Aloysius Rohfleisch was born in Guttstadt in East Prussia in the district of Heilsberg in 1922. He was taken prison of war on Crete in 1945 and was held in the British prisoner-of-war camp El Daba in North Africa until 1947.

We were brought to a troop transporter – we thought we were on our way home – and arrived in Alexandria. In Alexandria we had a short stop, and then travelled by railway during the day through the desert to the former combat area – El Alamein. This desert railway was used back then to take care of the political troops. We were then transported to our final destination, and suddenly we were in the middle of the desert. [laughs]

How many soldiers were transported?

There was a maximum of 2,000 men on our troop transporter. Not more than that. But the camp there held 60,000 men. I still wonder where they all came from. The campaign in Africa was long over – the troops had all been sent to the United States – and from there later to England and also France – but most of the troops there had been captured in the last days of the war in Italy – for example in Monte Cassino where there were a great number of paratroopers, and then, of course, the soldiers from the islands. There were three large camps, each of which held 20,000 men – with the numbers 381, 382, and 383. The camps were then divided into ten cages with a large camp road and were guarded by Basutos – Blacks from South Africa. They were peaceful people – not savages. We first had to get used to them. We left the train and had to walk with our bags – we were really loaded down – we had taken everything with us. The desert sand and the intense rays of the sun had a strong effect on us – we were really depressed. There was no town to be found, no buildings, no palm trees, no women, no camels – nothing, nothing at all. Only barbed wire and sun and sand. I have to say that really intimidated us. We thought that it was probably a punishment. They were trying to make an example of us – trying to show us who the victors were. But we didn't let them get us down. We did our work and that was the end of it.

At first it was difficult to get used to everything. We had ten men in one tent that was 4 x 4 metres in size. It was like being in a sardine can.

You couldn't stand up straight. Our daily routine was such that they woke us up in the morning, and everyone had to leave the tent. We were able to wash in a sink mounted on a slab of cement. We had to roll together our straw mats and pile them neatly in a row on the camp road in front of the tent. We had to fold our blanket and towels and organize our eating utensils and stand there while the camp commander walked past. He was a peaceful man – a colonel from South Africa – an elderly gentleman. [laughs] When he walked past, he looked at everyone to see if they were cleanly shaven. The camp discipline started to become more relaxed. We heard more about democracy. This camp commander from South Africa walked through the camp and looked for people for the camp police. Each of us was questioned about what we had done before. For example, the English were the only ones who believed that if someone had worked for the railway – and had joined the Party – that he had done so to find work and support his children.

And then I was questioned. The interviewers weren't anti-fascists because they were just as young as us. "Why weren't you in the Hitler Youth earlier?" I said, "I was in the Catholic youth and the boy scouts and wasn't interested. Afterwards, I moved to where I was working. And my boss didn't want me to go to the Hitler Youth in the evenings. But if he had allowed it, I would gladly have gone along". I was then immediately labelled a Nazi. [laughs] The people who spoke openly were brought to the Nazi camp. And there were a great number of non-commissioned officers and sergeants. The officers went to another camp and received different treatment than us – but they also had a small tent with three or four men. The highest-ranking officer was a colonel. And they sat together with the English and talked and drank a glass of whisky or whatever. And this colonel went through the camp where the Nazis were and said: "Cage seven is the best cage in the camp", and picked out the best people who were strongly built. [laughs] They received an olive-green coat with a white armband with the words "Camp Police" and a billy club as a weapon. They just walked around between the barbed wire fences for decorative purposes. There was still the barbed wire for the warning area that was three metres away from the fence. You weren't allowed to go over it; otherwise, they would have started to shoot. Nothing ever happened. In the evenings when it started to get dark, we spoke with one another over the fence. "Do you know this person? He's from there or there or there". And this is how we got information about everything.

Of the 104 men who were taken prisoner, how many do you imagine were still there [in our cage] after half a year? Two. It was as if they had a computer back then to move the people as much as possible. They didn't want the prisoners to form groups. But we had a lot of cultural activities. The rations were not that great. You can imagine what it's like to feed 60,000 men in the desert by means of railway supply lines. There was a large military bakery. They baked white English wheat bread for everyone – when you pressed it down it came back up again. Three men received one loaf of bread – it wasn't a lot but it was better than nothing. And then we got leeks from a ship in the Nile delta as a vegetable and lots of canned goods. It was a diet with little roughage. That means that we couldn't go to the bathroom. And Sundays there was a quarter pound of margarine. Mondays everyone went to the bathroom. Whoever didn't go to the bathroom had to go to the medic and get a liquid – it wasn't castor oil. We always said that it was "Polish milk". It came in a large bottle, and you had to drink two tablespoons full. And if it didn't work, then you got another dosage two or three hours later. If that didn't work, then you got an enema. Yeah, that's because we had so little roughage to eat. But nobody starved to death. We were all thin and lean and ran around a lot when we weren't working. We played sports such as football. Due to the food crisis worldwide, we received fewer rations. [laughs] We got less to eat. Those who worked got a little more.

The most interesting thing was that trained IOs came from England in 1945 and spoke German. They were supposed to show us – most of us didn't know about it because we were in other regions during the war – a film on the concentration camps. We had to watch. We had heard about them, but none of us knew exactly. They set up the screen outdoors. They showed us what had happened in Auschwitz and the other large camps – with the ovens and gassings and everything. The German soldiers thought: "That's crazy – that never took place". We didn't react to the film – nothing – nothing at all. At the end of the film, the officer said: "Go back to your tents and be ashamed". Of course, we went. They also knew who was responsible for the matter. But we had been labelled. During our time in the desert, we were able to write letters; we got pencils and wrote on the paper from cement bags. Many prisoners among us were instructors and professors and held lectures. There was also a library with books mostly on specialist topics – agriculture, gardening, developing fields in the colonies, and so on. The prisoners used these books. And, of course, there were sports. We also had a philharmonic orchestra – with fifty musicians. Whenever instruments or strings were missing – they were then ordered. The musicians were divided into five groups – as bands – that played for the English. We wore white shirts with shorts. We were supposed to play behind a curtain, but we said that we wouldn't play. And then in the end they had to open up the curtain. Whenever the English had a party, ten of our musicians were there. And they played everything they wanted. We got everything we wanted – a lot of sheet music. They ordered everything. It was a kind of swing music. What was his name? The famous American who died in a plane crash? He made wonderful music. Glenn Miller. The Germans didn't know him. And we played all that music. And they always wanted to hear "Lili Marlene". "Lili Marlene" was the most popular song in the entire Middle East. The radio station was in Belgrade in Yugoslavia and was a military station. Goebbels couldn't do anything about it. It was a strictly military station. They had such a powerful station which broadcast as far as Africa – on Crete we used to always listen to the news. At 9:45 pm they played "Lili Marlene", and we sang "Lili Marlene" on the troop transporters. There were a few soldiers with instruments who played along. That was the music of this time.[4]

Mass services were also offered. On Sundays there were mass services, and we went along. Cage seven had to go with cage nine through the camp road with a certain number of men. Most of them went to chat with the others on Sundays. Once a bishop with the Red Cross came in white vestments and asked us how we were doing. He wished us all the best and left again. He was Catholic. All the Catholic military clergymen were medics – normal men. Each division had a priest with a rank of a major or a lieutenant and a cross that was half covered. This only existed in the army and the navy. It didn't exist in the air force and not at all in the SS. And these others were simply medics as non-commissioned officers – also sergeants – and they had military training as medics. They were clergymen and came to us in the camp. We talked with them and sang. We were happy that these things were available –

whereas in the Third Reich they weren't offered. On Crete, there weren't any SS men. In Africa, there also weren't any SS.

We also played a lot of football in the English camp. First, among ourselves – air force against the navy and the navy against the army and so on. The East zone against the West zone. A few of us painted ourselves black so that the guards thought we were the Basutos – their colleagues. We played football in the sand and always beat the English. We had our own football strategy on the field. The first time we beat the English 9:1. The second time 6:1. The third time they pooled together all the men they had in the Middle East – from Malta, Palestine, everywhere. There was only one grass field – Queen Victoria Field – it was irrigated in the Suez Canal region – the players couldn't stay on their feet and continuously fell down. The halftime score was 0:0. The final score was 1:0 for us shortly before the end of the game. The English commander said: "My German boys will win". He won fifty English pounds – one English pound was worth twelve marks back then.

French Camps in North Africa

Hans Füssenich was born in Cologne in 1920. He served as a medic in the Hermann Göring Air Force battalion in France, Sicily, and North Africa. He was taken prison of war by French forces in Tunisia in May 1945 and held until 1947.

On 11 May 1945, we were all taken prisoner of war in Tunisia right before Zaghouan. We couldn't get any more supplies – we couldn't defend ourselves – and the English came with their big tanks, and we couldn't shoot back. [laughs] Then we were French prisoners of war and were divided up. But we didn't want to go to a French prisoner-of-war camp, but rather to an American camp. At that time, the Americans were the most well liked. But I went to a French camp in May 1945 and did relatively well, except for malaria, amoebiasis, and other diseases. I had paludism – the first stage of malaria – until 1945, and then I went to a few health resorts with German doctors who told me to do this, or that, or another thing. I was as yellow as a lemon – even my eyes, but the malaria went away.

I was a French prisoner of war from May 1945 until 1947. I was first brought to the camp in Tunis and became the secretary for the French doctor in the camp with the help of a friend of mine who was working in the office of Head Physician Mundier. My friend Ernst Proctor arranged for me to get my job with Doctor Mundier as a secretary. I had to escort the ill patients into the office. I was in charge of the pharmacy, and so on. Those are the things that I did in Camp Tunis. Of course, all of us wanted to return home. In Camp Tunis, there were 5,000 prisoners of war, all of whom were Germans as far as I know. At first, the conditions were very bad because the French initially didn't even have drinking water. It was all delivered in tankers, and that's the reason why I contracted amoebiasis. It wasn't hygienic. I was in the military hospital for a long time. We were deathly afraid because many people died of the illness.

In the beginning, the French didn't have anything themselves. There was only de Gaulle who survived with his people. And they had only those things that they got from the Americans because the Germans were still in France. For this reason, we got American bread – an eighth of a pound – and it was full of mould. It was a loaf of round white bread that was old, and full of mould, and bad. And in the pot of soup there was one broad bean – one. [laughs] That's what I remember. In the evenings we got a bit of bread. I have to say that was only in the first six weeks. It became better once the camp in Tunis was organized. They received somewhat more rations from the Americans and then it got better. The French organized the camp themselves, but received more and more rations – probably from America. It was mostly food in cans. Later, the French had strange little houses scattered throughout the town. In each house, different types of food were stored. It went to the German prisoners of war and to the French soldiers. No one was tortured or harmed in any way. However, I have to say that prisoners were told that they had to join the French Foreign Legion or else. I knew that from stories and from people who were suddenly gone. Many people joined the French Foreign Legion in the hope of getting home faster, but I don't know if that happened because I never saw one of them again.

I forgot to mention that I was temporarily in a supply camp for fencing material, etc. for one month. Three of us there joined together: a staff sergeant, a non-commissioned officer (that was me), and a private, and we tried to escape. We got as far as the Algerian border and were caught. Arabs were paid to help catch us – they were Jewish Arabs. I can't say it in any other way. They were paid if they saw anybody. We managed to make it that far, and in the morning the Arabs went to the market. I never knew any English – just a few words. I tried to explain myself, and they died laughing. [laughs] But the Arabs didn't know any English themselves. They knew French – that was clear. They turned us in. We sat down and drank tea with them, and then the French came and said "hello". [laughs] Then I was brought back to Camp Tunis – maybe it was for the best – because none of us wanted to be in the other commando. They shaved our heads and put us in a hole in the ground for fourteen days as punishment. It was a hole in the ground about a half metre deep. I stood or sat in there the entire time with a shaved head. They gave us rations and water on a regular basis.

French Camps in France

Father Wendelin (Reich) was born in Fronhofen near Ravensburg in Baden-Württemberg in 1926. After a short stay in an American prisoner-of-war camp near Heilbronn at the end of the war, he was transported to France where he worked as a forced labourer in the farming and coal mining industry. After the war he became a Franciscan priest.

I was in an artillery unit for six weeks before I was transferred to the Black Forest. And then the Front came nearer, and we marched from the Black Forest eastwards. The Americans and the French were coming – at that time it was primarily the Americans who were coming from the direction of the Black Forest – the French came afterwards. At the beginning of May, I became a prisoner of war. We were in a bunker and our sergeant told us that the situation was hopeless and that we should leave everything behind and walk towards the Americans. And we walked towards them with our hands in the air, and they took us along with them. And we had to give them everything that we had with us: our mess kits, spoons and forks, and maybe our coats. And they repeatedly said: "Guys, give us everything, give us everything. You'll get new ones". [laughs] But we didn't get new ones.

And then I was brought to Neu-Ulm for two or three days to the same barracks where I did my training as a soldier. From there we were transported for three days and then we were brought to a large camp near Heilbronn. It was being filled up at that time. We weren't the first or the last prisoners being brought there. The camp, which was on the side of a hill, is said to have had 500,000 prisoners of war in total. After the first three or four days we got something to eat, but nothing to drink. After four days, we finally got something to drink. I still remember that they drove in with a barrel of water, and then everyone stood in line in order to get maybe a half pint of water. In the meantime, several thousand soldiers were fenced in a square area the whole time. I brought along a square camping tarp. Then, four of us lay down under this camping tarp and tried to gather sticks – four shorter sticks on the ends and a long stick in the middle – in order to protect ourselves from the rain which had just begun. Around the outside of this tarp, we dug a small ditch for the water to drain. But, of course, the next person to join us always shouted when he got wet. But we helped each another. It was a difficult time there.

After six weeks we heard, or it was announced, that all the soldiers who lived 70 kilometres from this camp could be released. I lived 300 kilometres away, but I didn't care and reported immediately and stood in line. And then something interesting happened. There was a soldier from Laubheim together with me under this tarp. Laubheim is 40 or 50 kilometres away from my hometown. And the two of us reported and went to the so-called "discharge camp" – it was a huge area that was about a kilometre in size. And we went there, and there were four or five posts that you had to go through. There was always an American soldier in a small guard house, and he wrote down your personal information. We were waiting in a long queue in front of it, and on the other side people were coming out again and going back to the camp. I also got into this queue and went to the American soldier, and he only asked me how many brothers and sisters I had. And then I said "seven". "That's fine", he said. And then I was able to go. And on the other side, the man from Laubheim also passed through, and I caught up with him because I was directly behind him. I later realized that the American soldier had written an even number on the piece of paper for the man, and obviously it was a secret number. Prisoners with one number were sent to France and with the other number they were released to go home. The even numbers went home and the odd numbers were transported to France. And the man in front of me from Laubheim had an even number. He then went to the discharge camp. I followed him and also went to the discharge camp. But my papers weren't there because I had an odd number. And, so, he was released the following day, and I had to stay there because my papers weren't there. That was a Friday. On Saturday and Sunday nothing happened. And on Monday they started processing the soldiers again. I had to go back to the camp where the processing began. Again, I went to an officer and received a piece of paper and the number – in the meantime I knew that it meant I would be transported to France. The first time I went through I was able to just walk away because no one was standing guard. But the second time that I went through, someone was standing on the other side of the guard house who asked about the number. And then he said "left" or "right". And you had no other choice. And then I knew that I wouldn't be sent home. I would have tried it again, but I couldn't because someone was standing there who said: "No, you have to go here". And that's why I knew that I wouldn't be sent home.

Three or four days later we were transported from Heilbronn to France – first to northern France – I think that I was there for four or five weeks. There was a large camp there which had very bad food. All the prisoners thought that it was just the opposite of the American camp where the food was relatively good and in the French camp the food was bad – but they didn't have anything themselves. There were carrots which they sometimes cooked and things like that. I still remember that in the large camp where I was for four, five, or six weeks, we had to empty out the toilet bucket and carry it to the front of the camp. And, by the way, we had nothing to do. And the prisoners were lying along the barracks practically dying. They didn't have any help and most of them had diarrhoea and no chance of survival. I wasn't suffering from this. And then we were transported again and travelled across France in cattle cars. We always had little holes in the cattle cars – on the top there were little holes – so that the cattle didn't suffocate. You were able to look outside. I still remember how we travelled across the plains – plains after plains for kilometres – and there were ditches lined with poplar trees. We travelled to Lyon – no it was further – to Saint-Étienne where we were unloaded and brought to a camp. And it was there that I was sent to the coal mines.

Near Saint-Étienne there was a huge coal mine, and I worked there for fourteen months on the afternoon shift. In the morning, the coal was taken out, and the empty holes had to be filled again in the afternoon. There were different kinds of fillers. Sometimes it was filled with the dirt and stones that were removed and which were normally saturated with water. It was basically the hardest work that you had. There were also fillers that came from the coke ovens above. That was light coke and easy to shovel. It was transported in coal cars that were emptied out and had to be carried 4 or 5 metres with a shovel. The first time that I went down there – it was 700 metres underground – everything was lit up. And then when you entered the actual tunnels, there wasn't any light being produced from the compressors. And you only had a lamp. You got a lamp from above that you came down with. And then it got hotter and hotter so that you worked without any clothing on at all. We only had a belt on in order to hang the lamp on it. Not only was it hotter and hotter when you entered the actual tunnels, but they were supported by timber beams that were cut in the middle. They were removed so that you could come through with the coal cars. And I still remember that the first time I went down there, the tunnels got lower and lower so that I could hardly stand upright. I bent over and looked up to see if anything was falling down. It was all very ominous, but afterwards you got used to it. Today, I understand that when a tunnel collapses that you're lost down there. But I don't think that they fill [the holes] by hand today. But back then that was the case. There was a foreman, or an assistant foreman, who was a black man. And in every coal car there was a nail that you had to take out and hang on to. And there was a daily quota that we had to complete. That was about ten or fifteen coal cars which we were supposed to fill. But that depended on whether you filled the coal cars with the heavy debris and stones and such things – then it was hardly possible. But if you had ash then it was easy.

As prisoners we received money for this work. That was something special because we hadn't received any before. And with this money you could afford to buy small things. We were even able to send packages home from the things that we were able to buy in the camp and the canteen. But the camp itself was horrible, I have to say. The guys didn't normally have to work on Saturdays and Sundays. They got money for their work, and alcohol became their comfort. On Saturday and Sunday evenings it was so loud in the barracks that you could hardly stand it. There was a short guy from East Friesland whom I'll never forget. He said: "I have two cows at home. I would give up both of them if I could get out of here". That's how oppressive it was.

Hermann Niemann was born in 1927 in Neustadt-Glewe in Mecklenburg. In 1945, his signal maintenance company was transferred from Pomerania in north-eastern Germany to Saxony, and finally to the Allgäu region in Bavaria. He was taken prisoner of war on 5 May 1945 by French soldiers.

At the beginning of May – on 4 or 5 May – our senior officers got together and said: "We are going to disband. You can go home". This was before the end of the war. The end wasn't far away. But I found out everything later. I didn't know that the war was just about to end and about the location of the enemies, and so on. We didn't know any of that. Along with some of my fellow soldiers from northern Germany, I decided to go back home on foot. Since we didn't know our way around the region, we moved south instead of north and went into the mountains. And there was high snow there. Then we threw our weapons away – some of the rifles we smashed to pieces. We wanted to enter a village and ask where we could get civilian clothing, so that we would not be recognized as soldiers, and work. The people in the village were all under pressure by the French who were already there. They told us that they couldn't help us because they would be punished themselves. They said that the French were paying close attention to what they were doing, and so on. It didn't take much longer – one or two days later – and the French captured us.

Twenty of us were put in a barn in the village – a French soldier stood guard – and the people in the village had to feed us. They didn't have much themselves. They had plenty of milk and cheese from the cows. And they brought us cheese every day. In the evenings in the barn, we lit candles and placed them around us in order to produce some heat. We didn't have anything else on besides our uniforms. We didn't have anything: no blankets, nothing. We stayed there for two or three days, and we found out that the war was over. The French started shooting into the air. Then we knew the war was over. And from there we were brought to the island of Lindau – that's where I experienced the shooting celebrations by the French. They brought us together onto the island. We had enough to drink because they made sure that there was a water line so that we had enough to drink. But there wasn't any food. A few days later, they brought us from Lindau to Tuttlingen. That was the first of the large camps where 10,000 or 20,000 German soldiers were gathered together. I don't know where it was exactly. I didn't know the region anyway. And on 12 or 15 May, it was later and somewhat warmer down there so that we were no longer freezing, they brought us to Kehl on the Rhine. And from Kehl, we were brought to Strasbourg and loaded onto freight trains.

We travelled in open freight trains with forty or fifty men – we couldn't lie down and relax. The transporter left and we asked ourselves: "Where are we going?" We travelled straight through France. And on the bridges, where the trains travelled 80 to 100 kilometres per hour through France, there were the French who hated us. They threw stones onto the open cars of the trains or urinated on us. Rightfully so. The French really hated us. I can only remember a few large cities such as Portier and Orleans – I only knew these places from my atlas. And from there the journey continued further south. Suddenly we were in Bordeaux. And then we travelled to Bayonne – that is present-day Basque country. And there was a large prisoner-of-war camp there. The French had built it. And we were brought there. At first, they took a count of us. By the way, there was a roll call every morning, and they counted to see if everyone was there. There were barracks, but without any glass windows inside. The French didn't have anything either. They were even poorer than us. They used a light-coloured paper – a yellow paper – in front of the windows. In the back of the barracks were three-tier bunk beds with straw mattresses. And that was our lodging for the time being. In the mornings, there was one loaf of bread for seven men. And we had to divide it up ourselves. [laughs] It was divided up more or less equally. They somehow noticed that I had a good sense of measurement, and I had to divide it up. I managed to make sure that we had equal portions, but we didn't have a scale or anything. And it had to be divided up. For lunch, we received a half litre of broth. If we were lucky, we had two beans or peas on the top – or a few drops of grease. Otherwise, we had only water or cabbage leaves, depending on what they had just cooked. Well, that was our daily routine.

Slowly the lice came – at least we had something to do – we sat outside because it was very hot. Afterwards, we were busy catching and cracking the lice. You know? It wasn't unusual to catch one hundred of them per day. For a toilet we had a large slab with a roof over it. It was very common for the French to have a slab on the floor with a hole in it. That's what I remember from back then. And they had it with ten or twenty holes, and you squatted down over them. At some point it had to be hosed down, and then it wasn't a problem. And for bodily hygiene, they had a floor with a fence around it and open on the top. And there were showers – one after the other – you could turn them on and wash yourself with cold water. That was our daily routine. You know? In the evenings, they had roll call again. Everyone went back into the barracks, and they were locked. In the first few weeks we didn't have to work. That came later. The French first had to organize the camp. They were surprised by the large number of prisoners. Instead of twenty prisoners that were easy to take care of, there were 10,000 or 20,000. I heard that in Reims in central France the Americans had a camp with 30,000 or 40,000 prisoners. And here near Remagen it must have been a similar situation. I first found out about these things when I was back home. They often reported about it in the newspapers.

And then gradually during roll call, certain men were chosen and allowed to go along. We heard that they were going to a work camp. You had to work on roads, or some others went to the arsenal in the barracks and had to clean up there or sort goods. Of course, it was a change of pace from the dreary life in the camp. And sometimes you had the chance to have an additional job. That took half a year, and people were needed for "déminage" – clearing the mines. Bayonne is not far from Biarritz – maybe you know it. It was and still is an important seaside resort. And that's where the Americans settled in because it was a well-known seaside resort. There were beach homes and hotels, and the Americans were there. And the entire beach had been mined by the Germans. In the front part of the beaches, there were posts made of tree trunks that had been planted during low tide – approximately 20 or 30 centimetres wide and 4 or 5 metres long – and German military engineers flushed them into the sand with jets of water. They were high enough so that they couldn't be seen at high tide. They were used against the landing boats which were expected during an invasion. And the French needed volunteers for the work to remove them. We had an engineering officer with us, and he showed us precisely what we had to do – which kind of mines were there – how they had been planted – how dangerous they were. Before the war, the engineers had diagrams of the exact locations of the mines. But in the final year of the war, they didn't keep such exact records which meant the mines could have been anywhere.

The most dangerous mines at that time were the so-called "bounding mines". Today they call them "bouncing Bettys" because they explode in the air with pieces of shrapnel. They were the most dangerous at that time. The officer also told us about "glass mines" in which the igniters were made of glass and therefore could not be located with a metal detector. And I did this work. We were dispatched to a group. First, there was better food. The mine clearers also received a quarter litre of red wine from the French. That was common practice. So, there were certain material advantages. Perhaps we didn't think enough about the dangers. Fortunately, I didn't experience any of the mines going off. We always had one Frenchman who supervised us and who was also trained as a mine clearer. We had to bring the mines that we found to a pile in a field. One time, I saw how a Frenchman went over there and sorted the mines. There were tank mines and various kinds of other mines. And he sorted them. As long as they didn't have an igniter – no problem – you could do with them whatever you wanted. You could hit them with a hammer. And while he was sorting them, he missed one of the mines that had an igniter. When it exploded, he was completely torn to pieces. That was the only thing that I experienced. Otherwise, I was lucky. That's also true for the other men who were together with me. We worked on the beach in Biarritz, and then we had to go to San Sebastián near the Spanish border. We worked all along the border, and every day we were brought to a new place. And all of the minefields were searched three times by different people with detectors – there were iron pokers that you can use to find them. These areas were checked three times, and beaches with a lot of bushes were set on fire. In this way you were able to look under the bushes because they had grown during the years if the mines had been there for a long time.

And then after a year we were transferred to the mouth of the Gironde River near Soulac-sur-Mer. We were in the small town of Montalivet. They built a camp for us in the woods. I don't know whether they had also built it for other purposes. There were a lot of burned pine trees there. Everything was bare. That also happens today – which means that it doesn't have to be the result of war. We also had somewhat better lodgings. And the food was better too. So, you couldn't say that we were starving. Some of us were allowed to work in the kitchen and came across valuable goods. At night, we crawled under the fence and went into the neighbouring areas and got additional supplies. Montalivet is now a camp ground. My daughter was there twice. She came home and said: "We were camping in France in Montalivet". I told her: "That's where I was during the war". What a coincidence! Well, gradually two years passed. By the way, my mother hadn't known where I was since Christmas 1945. I was drafted in January, transferred twice, and, if I was able to write, it never said where the letter had come from. You know? This means that she received mail from me during the last part of the war, but once the war was over, and everyone had been gathered together, she no longer knew where I was. She didn't have any idea where I was or how I was doing. We were first allowed to send mail from the prisoner-of-war camp beginning in the autumn of 1945. Before that, there were forms that we could fill out and submit, and she received the first letter at Christmas 1945. I had been a prisoner of war for considerably longer than I had been a soldier. If I count the time that I was in the Reich Labour Service [Reichsarbeitsdienst], then I was a soldier for approximately half a year. I was a prisoner of war for two and a half years.

As I said, we were transferred after two years from the mouth of the Gironde River where we had finished searching for mines and came to Alsace near Haguenau. It's located south of Pirmasens in present-day France. Before the end of the war, Alsace and Lorraine were German territory. I was then transferred from there and had to work along the German border. Every day we had work to do and were sent here or there. They never told us in advance. And I met a friend there who was from my hometown. He had been there from the very beginning. And he knew his way around this region well. Once when I was talking to him, he said that he sometimes wondered how he would get home. No one ever told us how long we had to stay or when we would be released and so on. There were a lot of rumours, but no one knew what was going on exactly. They could also give us another job after the mine clearing work had been finished. After we had devised an escape plan, he said: "I cannot go along because I was an SS soldier, and the Russians will seize me immediately". And, besides, he had somehow found a girlfriend in Alsace and wanted to stay. He gave me tips and provided me with some food and told me how I could try to make it through. He said that I had to go through three valleys, up and down the mountain, and after a certain distance there was the border. Once I had crossed the border, I was still not home because the region was occupied by the French. If they caught me, they would bring me back. I had to try to cross over the Rhine. That's where the Americans were. They probably would take me prisoner, but at some time would send me home. That's the way I planned it.

We had been working a great deal in the woods, and at noon there was a lunch break. We all sat together and ate our sandwiches. And I told them that I had to go to the bathroom and never came back again. We always had two guards along, and I knew that at that moment in which they noticed that someone was gone, they could not follow me. They weren't allowed to leave the other ten or twenty men alone. This meant that they would first have to bring the prisoners to the camp and then sound the alarm. There were no cell phones back then. [laughs] From there, they had to sound the alarm and take up the chase. I figured that I would have a head start. I went over mountains and valleys, and even more mountains and valleys. But it became dark, and I still wasn't at the border. I lay down in a hole and covered myself with leaves and slept there. The next morning, I continued. The woods were empty, and I didn't come across anyone. After the third day, the border was on the top of a hill. And I climbed up there. My friend had explained the border to me exactly because he knew the way it was. But it was dark again. At night everything looks the same. I actually didn't know where I was or where I had to go. I lay down in the woods until the next morning and then I knew where I was. At least I was in German territory. And supposedly there was a village behind the border. There was allegedly a pastor who helped prisoners. He gave them some food and clothes to take along. He always helped the prisoners when they came.

When I entered this village, a woman happened to come by, and I asked her where the pastor was. She said: "I know what you want, but that doesn't work anymore". He had come under suspicion, and the French were watching him to see who entered and left his house. This meant that prisoners put themselves and the pastor in danger. He would also be punished. This meant that I could forget him. So, I had to continue on my way. And then I came to a remote road or path through fields and continued in an easterly direction. And suddenly a farmer on a bicycle stopped and said: “You’re really brave”. “Why?” I asked. I had a jacket on with the large letters “PW” on the back – prisoner of war. [laughs] He said: “If the patrols come by, then they’ll know exactly who you are”. I had to take off my coat so that they wouldn’t notice from the distance that I was a prisoner. I was in Germany, but I certainly wasn’t the only one walking around like that during the day. There were certainly more people. You know? So, I continued walking until I came to Wörth on the Rhine. I somehow had to cross over. I wasn’t able to swim with my clothes. A railway official happened to come by. I asked him: “What is the best way to cross the Rhine?” He said: “Take the freight train. It’s leaving in half an hour to Karlsruhe. Climb in the brakesman’s cabin”. Years ago, all the freight trains used to have brakesman’s cabins. If the train was parked somewhere, someone had to climb inside and pull the brake manually. He said: “Hide so that no one sees you. And when you’re on the other side in Karlsruhe, you can get out”. And that worked. I had a lot of luck on all of my adventures.

The Russian Gulags

Bernd Steinlein was born in Trier in 1926. After training as a mountain infantryman, he was sent to Upper Silesia in early 1945 as an infantry replacement against the advancing Russian forces. He was taken prisoner of war in April and released from the Caucasus in 1949.

On 1 April 1945 on Easter Sunday – if I remember correctly – I was taken prisoner of war. Two days before, we were getting a great deal of pressure from the Soviet Army – we had to constantly retreat – and during the night leading up to 1 April we retreated to a temporary line of battle – which were small ditches that probably came from Home Guard units – I don't know. On that day we dug the trenches deeper, and the Russians slowly came closer to us. In the evening, they bombarded our position, but we didn't have any major losses. But on the next day, on Easter Sunday at noon, the Russians suddenly reached our trenches on the right or left – I don't remember anymore – I believe it was on the right. There was a street, and we couldn't see over it. And they were lying there with their rifles ready to fire. That was clear. And I was standing in my hole and had a machine gun and wanted to shoot. But once I saw their faces it was over. That's clear because there were more of them. I didn't have any choice and had to get out of the trench. The Russians waved me on. And I went back with the Russians on my belly to their front line. I don't know how far that was – 200, 300, 400, or 500 metres. I can't tell you.

We came to a village, and, as far as I can remember, it was a village with small wide houses which were apparently small farms. Naturally, the village was empty and there were only Russians – Russian soldiers. They lived in the houses or – how should I say it – they probably came with the front that was passing through, slept there, and then moved on the next day. That's what was going on. I was taken prisoner of war.

The Russians first conducted an interrogation. And now is the funny part. There were two of us. The other person next to me was a private 1st class from Austria. Basically, there were three of us: one was left behind – probably dead. And they asked us questions – of course we didn't understand anything. The Austrian was an old infantryman as a private 1st class. These were men who were never promoted to non-commissioned officers and were the backbone of the army. He had experienced everything. He also survived the war. He believed that the Russians wanted to know where we were from. He told them very coldly: "Austria". And then I became alert and thought that I had to be careful. And then they pointed to me, and I said: "Aus Trier" [from the city of Trier in Germany]. And I wasn't lying because I was from Trier. That was the funny part. And then they locked us up and beat me that night because I didn't tell them everything that they wanted to hear during the interrogation. They had other information to work with because there were other prisoners who had made statements. They wanted to know where the replacements were from – how many men had been transported in the railroad cars, and so on and so forth – everything that was important for the Russian advance.

Did they hit you with their fists or with a stick?

With their fists. They didn't have a board or a stick. They brought me into a cellar and started hitting me. These were the instructions of an officer – probably a German Communist Party officer – he gave them instructions to beat me and make me submissive. After this scuffle, I sat in the courtyard. It was cold at night, but I was warm because I had just been beaten. And in the morning – it was still dark – the Russian officer interrogated me again and was entirely different. He was accommodating. He asked me political questions which I answered. For instance, he wanted to know where I was from and about my family. I told him that I had five brothers who were in the war. And then he pointed out that we were all traitors and my brothers, too, because our war was unjust. He said that to me as a 19-year-old. Was a 19-year-old able to judge that? I never thought about the fact that I was serving such a person [as Hitler]. These were things that we had done, but you can't say this to a 19-year-old because he has no perspective. In any case, he was much nicer and even offered for me to join the National Committee of Free Germany – which was a group of prisoners – German officers who were under the Russian Army and made propaganda against the Nazis. He made me this offer, but I thought that it was all deception. He was a political officer and got this assignment because he spoke German well. He was a young man and could have been a Jew – which I don't mean negatively – but where did the Russians get such good interpreters?

Well, that went on until daybreak and then the two of us – the Austrian and I – were told to march off with two Russian soldiers who were guarding us. But we didn't know where to. That was a dangerous situation because you might have thought that they would go with us 300 metres or 500 metres and shoot us from behind. But this didn't happen. We walked quickly for about three hours and arrived at a large farm where there were a lot of Germans. We first came to a house, and the German prisoners were sleeping next to one another in a room like this one. And from there we arrived at a farm and lived in the barn. And then there is a small break in the story because I don't remember how we left there. I only know that in Krakow there was a small concentration camp that had been destroyed – probably by German troops – I don't know – and there was a camp or barracks that belonged to it for the guard detachment of the SS. And we prisoners were locked up in this camp. The SS was no longer there.

And not too far from there at the train station about 500 metres away, we unloaded goods from railway cars on the Russian tracks to the German tracks. The Russian railway tracks are somewhat wider, and we reloaded the cars. It was predominantly grain – wheat that came from Russia to the West – and the other way around. From the West there were packages that were nicely wrapped and sewed together which Russian soldiers probably wanted to send home. This was now after the war. I am telling you that I became a prisoner of war on 1 April and on 8 April the war was over. During that period, we were in Krakow. But the time extended beyond the end of the war until the beginning of the time of peace – if you could call it that – and we were in Krakow. We stayed there until August or September and were loaded onto trains from open platforms. And then they told us that we were going home: "Скоро домой!" [soon home!] We were convinced that we were on our way home. But no way. We landed in Auschwitz. Yes, yes. In the camp in Auschwitz – in the large camp that you can still see today with barracks.

What did Auschwitz look like in 1945?

I could see the large barracks that were made of red brick – we were able to see them. They were built right next to one another. I can't remember eating there. We were probably there for several days – I guess around three or four days – and I can't remember where we slept. It was probably in these buildings. I don't know. In any case, the Russians came very quickly and divided us up – the healthy men from the others. The Russians were so fair. They asked: "Don't you feel well? Are you ill?" and so on. They didn't just examine us, but rather asked first. And these men remained in the camp in Auschwitz, while we marched off to the train station and were loaded onto railway cars. We didn't leave immediately, but instead remained standing there. It was a kind of quarantine. They wanted to wait and see if anyone had diarrhoea because it could turn into typhoid the next day. So, we got into the railway cars and drove off after four or five days. The others who were ill remained in Auschwitz. I don't know what happened to them. Except for the large buildings that I told you about, I didn't see anything – no barbed wire, nothing. That must have been in another part of the camp. We rode on the train for a while and stopped in a valley and were unloaded from the train. And about 300 metres away we went into a railway car – a passenger train – that was equipped with a bathroom for showering and washing and being deloused. We were full of lice. That's clear. There was a railway car with a basin on the wall with water in it, a bit of soap, and that stuff – what's it called again – that makes your hair fall out everywhere when you lather with it, let it dry, and rinse it out. From there we got back onto the cattle cars and travelled for three or four weeks until we were in the Caucasus.

How was the general treatment during this time?

Except for the first few months, the treatment in Russia was fine. The Russian soldiers weren't unpleasant – they also weren't pleasant –

but they behaved properly. They didn't hurt anyone. They were hungry themselves – not just us – they were also in this bad situation. They were outside in the Steppe and bought and ate melons from the Nomads who passed by. They cut the melons open and ate them. And, of course, the skin was left over with a bit of the white part and the rest of the red. That's what we ate. That was for us – the part that remained. But, as I said, the Russians were just as bad off as us. A great disadvantage in the first camp – in the summer camp – was that the water was full of oil. You could hardly drink it, but we didn't have anything else. This is why people died. I can't verify the number because I only heard it from a fellow soldier – I don't know where he got his information from – he believed that 70 per cent of us died in the first year. Those were people between 20 and 35 years old, whereby the "older" soldiers were worse off than us. Our bodies adjusted better to the hunger and the strain. From those who survived the second and third year, only a few died – not like at first.

When you were awoken in the morning it was still dark – that was three in the morning in the Caucasus – and it wasn't uncommon for some of the men to remain lying. We already had on our shoes if we had any. The men remained lying on the ground in the hay. They were dead. They fell asleep at night. I remember that a fellow soldier, who was working together with me gathering hay, took a short break when the Russians told him to do so. After ten minutes we tried to continue and someone was missing. We found him in the hay stack. He was dead. The men died from exhaustion and naturally from diseases such as dysentery and typhoid. That was in the first year. But otherwise, the Russians behaved correctly. I remember in the winter of 1946 – from 1945 to 1946 – the Russians examined us and discovered that some of the men had dystrophy. We were held the same way as the Jews were held in Auschwitz. They brought the extremely weak and sick men to a special camp. That was a small camp that was fenced off in a village. I was there for four weeks. We lived there and got food, but we didn't have to work. Many of the men recovered so that they could work again. The Russians themselves did that. Of course, they didn't bandage and feed us like at home – this wasn't the case – but they didn't behave incorrectly.

What did the rooms look like where you slept and how were the rations?

In the first camp, there weren't any rooms at all – but the camps varied completely. The first camp was nothing more than poles and tree branches that were placed next to one another and connected by a wire. On the outside they were covered with loose hay. We lay below in two rows – if I remember correctly – in the middle there was a ditch for our shoes. And we lay with our heads towards the outside. I don't know how many could fit into one tent – maybe thirty. That was the worst time. I survived it, but it was horrible. We were in the second camp in 1945, 1946, and 1947 – I guess – and then we went to Yerevan in Armenia and built houses for the Red Army. And we slept in a camp hall that was made of concrete or mortar. We built bunks to sleep on. There were no floors in the building, and everyone was in one large room. I don't know how many people were there – maybe 200 in this camp. The rations were really awful in the first year because all the garbage was used. I'm thinking of pigs – I don't know about other animals – their entrails, the intestines and that stuff, were preserved with salt water. And that's what we got to eat. We got 600 grams of brown bread which was heavy because it was wet. The officers got 500 grams of bread – sometimes white bread and sometimes brown bread. We got 17 grams of sugar which was a level tablespoon. We got tobacco – and if I remember correctly, it was 5 grams per day – but I don't know anymore. It was a rather coarsely cut tobacco. And what else? We had soup in the morning – a watery soup – and the same thing at noon – with some vegetables in it and two spoons of kasha. This was pearl barley porridge – two spoons of it – which many men couldn't eat anymore because it made them nauseous. And in the evenings, we got a third of a herring. That was part of the protein ration. Each prisoner either got a piece from the head, the middle, or the tail. We always swapped pieces. The bread was first divided up by the people in charge of the rations in the camps. Of course, there were always great disappointments. The bread was distributed to the barracks. There were people in each of the barracks who weighed the bread. We normally received 600 grams each for nine men. The bread was distributed for nine men. It could have been more or less – but it was mostly less. But we wanted to be just. Each person was supposed to get the same amount in terms of weight. Therefore, we had to cut it up and needed a scale for it. That was easily done. The old Jewish traders had a scale that was held on the top, and down here you had a wire and a small dish. And the bread was placed inside, and the other piece was weighed against it. We cut the bread until each person had the same amount.

Did you have the chance to have a bath or to wash?

In the first camp, it wasn't possible to wash at all. But in 1947 – I believe – they gave us the chance to wash every night. There was a small basin with water in it, and you could use it if you were in the camp early enough. There were different work groups that gathered in the evenings, and when they were dismissed, some men ran there immediately. And they had water and the others didn't. We fought the lice in the first few years by breaking their shells the way that the soldiers typically did. And then we realized that you could kill them quickly with heat. There were two possibilities. You built a concrete bunker that was heated from the inside and clothes were hung in it. They just had to be off to the side so that they didn't burn. And when they were taken out after an hour there wasn't anything anymore – no eggs, nothing, everything was dead. This didn't mean that we didn't soon have lice again because they came from all sides. But there was nothing in these clothes. The second possibility was to place the clothes on a hanger and hang it from a shaft that was heated from below. It once happened that the shaft broke out in flames – my clothes were also there – and we didn't have anything to wear for weeks. Yes, that's the way it was. And then the fleas came. In 1947 we almost died from fleas. There were billions of insects that jumped all over – it was horrible. That was just an epidemic. They came and were with us a few weeks, died off, and nothing followed them. The lice remained loyal. And then we had bedbugs which were the most disgusting insects because you could only get hold of them when they were big. Then you could feel them and crush them. But when they were small, they were evasive and gone before you could get hold of them.

Karl Belling was born in Beuern in Hesse in 1926. He served in a communications unit and was taken prisoner of war near Prague by the Russian Army. After being forced to march across Czechoslovakia on foot, he was then transported to the Donetsk region in the Ukraine to Gorlovka near Stalino. Upon returning home in 1947, he was questioned by American military authorities about the location of the prisoner-of-war camp and the extent of the armaments industry in the Ukraine.

When we were brought to this camp, we discovered that it must have existed for two or three years. There were "военнопленные" [prisoners of war] – the designation for soldiers who had been captured by the Russians during the war. Barbed wire fencing ran through the camp, and we weren't immediately allowed to mix with these earlier German prisoners of war. We had to wait and go through a period of adjustment. We were very surprised – shocked – when we saw and talked to our fellow soldiers who had been prisoners of war in Russia for at least one or two years. They looked off sadly into the distance and walked over the grounds very slowly. They were rather emaciated. Afterwards, we noticed that this was due to the fact that we received very little food so that we became very thin and were sent to so-called "dystrophy groups" for examination. If you were extremely thin and ill and so on, then you were sent to a sick ward where I had been several times. I was put to work in an iron ore plant in a blast furnace in Stalino, and in Gorlovka near Stalino, and in the summer and winter on a collective farm. I have very little memory of this because of the language barrier, but I had conversations with Russians who were very gracious and accommodating although we were the ones who invaded their country. I remember a lot of these experiences. Fellow soldiers told similar stories. And this helped us to rid ourselves of the concept of the enemy. I have to add one thing: In the first period – during the first few years – when we came to this camp, there was a bulletin board hanging on the camp wall with grotesque pictures of well-known Nazi personalities to be jeered at. We still believed in this system and didn't want to allow ourselves to be influenced. This required a certain rethinking process which lasted almost until the time that we returned so that we realized what we really thought of this thousand-year period.[5] These were amazing human experiences, and we noticed that we would have been able to establish a friendly relationship with the Russians if we had had the possibility.

Edmund Janik was born in Opole in Silesia in 1926. He was drafted at the age of 16 and first saw action near Breslau at the end of 1944 against the advancing Russian Army. After retreating to Prague and attempting to surrender to the Americans, he was captured and beaten by the Czechs. He describes events leading up to being handed over to the Russian Army as a prisoner of war.

It was somewhat better for us when we were handed over to the Russians because we weren't murdered in some corner like with the Czechs. They were unbelievable. The Russians were drunk. They got a bottle of vodka, drank it down like water, vandalized, and didn't know what they were doing. The Czechs were less drunk. This means that they all acted in a state that wasn't humane. We were afraid, of course. I saw them standing on the streets, digging up large cobble stones, and throwing them at columns of prisoners. And if you got hit on the head, then you fell down. And they didn't tire of it. They then jumped on your head with their boots and trampled it until your head was mush. This happened mostly to older, perhaps ill prisoners. At that time, I was young, 18, and as agile as a cat. We had to walk at least 18 kilometres. We did this in a continuous march. Out of fear.

Why were the Czechs so enraged with the Germans?

That's a good question. Some claimed that the SS had humiliated them in Prague or Czechoslovakia during the war. I don't know because I didn't experience it myself. I only heard from acquaintances that when the Germans went through a village, a German soldier would suddenly go missing. They either beat him to death or stabbed him and then buried him in a pile of manure. I can only imagine what the SS did to the village. That's what I heard. I didn't experience it myself. They were angry with each other, and the Czechs reacted to the SS.

What did the Russians do when they came?

At first, it was bad. I'd say that they weren't much better than the Czechs. Once in a while you meet sensible Russians – which was rare. The Russian NKVD[6] and the German Gestapo were both bad. Sometimes it was better when you met some Russians who spoke a bit of German because they had been prisoners of war in Germany. It was only when they drank that the 15- and 16-year-olds shot at everything they saw. It didn't matter whether they hit each other – then they were simply dead.

I stayed in Czechoslovakia for about two weeks in the camp, and we were packed into cattle cars and sent East. We landed in Austria, and we noticed that we weren't on our way home. Suddenly we were in Constanta in Romania on the Black Sea. We thought: "Why are we here? This isn't the right way home". From there we were shipped in cattle cars and ended up on the Crimea. There were over forty of us in each car. Ninety in the big ones. Like mice. Like rats. You know? If someone died while we were travelling through Romania, he was thrown out and a civilian came inside. The number had to be correct. When they counted in the evening, there had to be ninety inside. It didn't matter to them whether it was someone from the railway or a Hungarian. He could scream as much as he wanted. He was brought inside and couldn't get out again. And then we were in Sevastopol. The rations were really bad. For three or four days we didn't get anything. Even today I can live for three or four days without food. I could live off grass for a week in the forest. We didn't get anything at all. And then the epidemics came such as diarrhoea, jaundice, and malaria, and half of the camp died after one week. There wasn't any medication, and many went insane. I myself had jaundice, malaria, and diarrhoea three times. These were fatal for the most part. I was one of the few that made it, but most people didn't survive it.

I was on the Crimea, and many said: "Be happy that you were on the Crimea. In Siberia, they had it worse". On the Crimea, it was hot – terribly hot. And in Siberia, it was cold. One was as bad as the other.

I must have learned twenty different jobs there. None of them correctly. But you signed up for whatever they had so that you had the chance to get some food. I'll tell you very frankly, and you can say that I'm crazy. I would have eaten dead bodies. Hunger is the worst thing there is. If you don't get anything to eat for five days, and you're hungry, you will devour someone. You will eat grass or a flower. I know. You can't compare it with today. No, you can't compare it at all.

Joachim Schmidt was born in Rostock in 1924. He was drafted in 1942 as a radio operator and taken prisoner in Czechoslovakia in 1945. He was then transported to prisoner-of-war camps in Sevastopol, Theodosia, and Simferopol on the Crimea and was released in 1949.

Germany surrendered on 8 May, and I managed to reach Písek on the other side of the Vltava River because the Americans were there. I wanted to reach them. But I never made it. We were then rounded up and sent to Brno with 10,000 men. From Brno we were transported to Odessa, and from there by ship to Sevastopol. In Sevastopol, we heard that the Russians had driven German soldiers into an area that was mined, and men were blown up. The minefields had to be cleared. And then I came to Theodosia and experienced numerous things. I would like to tell you just one episode. I worked there in a lumber yard, and the wood was delivered to a hospital and there were doctors from the camp. The coal wasn't delivered in small pieces as we know it today, but rather in large pieces. As the head of the detachment, I was in charge of a group of four men. When the hospital personnel wanted to have proper coal, they came to me. When the commander noticed that I had given them good pieces of coal, he cancelled the orders and gave them the slack. [long break] I could tell you things.

I learned how to repair watches. People started telling one another that I was a German watchmaker. And the first thing that the Russians asked when they took someone prisoner was: "Do you have a watch?" They rolled up our sleeves and looked. And, so, the Russians had German watches. I didn't have any idea about watches, but I imagined that a watch had worked at one time, and I took it apart one piece at a time to find out how it worked. One day the camp commander came to me. He said: "This doesn't work. Fix it". It was a very cheap Kienzle watch that didn't have any jewel bearings, only imitations. And, of course, it didn't work. He picked it up after two days, and I knew that it didn't work. It wouldn't work for a long time. I gave it to him, and, of course, he came back a short time later and said that it didn't work and that I had to repair it again. After two days he returned. Sometimes the watch worked and sometimes it didn't. And then he got angry and said: "You don't have any strength to repair a watch. Come along. We'll go to the kitchen". He placed a large bowl of kasha in front of me which I was supposed to eat along with one and a half pounds of bread. It was a porridge that was boiled, and salt was added to it. He remained standing there until I finished eating everything. I couldn't eat all of it. I saved some of the bread by hiding it under the table one piece at a time. He didn't bother me for a while, but, ultimately, I couldn't repair the watch.

Then I was brought to Sevastopol. I was so sick that I couldn't walk anymore. I could only move about on all fours. They declared that I was unfit to work. One day, a truck arrived carrying prisoners that were extremely emaciated – I had never seen anything like it before. They were also unfit to work, and we were all transported to Simferopol. There was a death camp there for the men who were brought there. There were twelve of us on the truck, and four had died on the way from Theodosia to Sevastopol. The camp was previously a horse stall, and there were still harnesses and some hay on the concrete. And everyone was assigned a spot. [emotionally shaken, interrupts the interview, begins again after ten minutes]

Where are you now chronologically?

I have to make a correction. While we were staying at the death camp in Sevastopol, we weren't able to work. We were totally without work. However, we became acquainted with the people who had to dissect the dead. There was a room like a wash room where the dead soldiers were lined up in rows. Their hearts, lungs, and liver had to be removed, placed in a bag, and were then picked up by a courier from the University of

Sevastopol. They were delivered there and used for research purposes. And I thought to myself that I would never make it home again because of these dissections. I knew too much. I had dissected so many prisoners that the Russians would never let me leave. In any case, I recovered and was sent to another camp where they had dystrophy and no hope of working again. And that was where I met the camp commander with the watch. And then I came to the camp with the horse stall. It was there that the medic went from one row to the next and kicked the leg of each prisoner lying down, and if he didn't move, he was pulled outside. I saw how the dead, naked prisoners of war were thrown onto a truck in the morning and then buried somewhere in a mass grave. That was Sevastopol.

Then I developed my skill – so to speak – to fix watches. There was a clockmaker. He left, but he first gave me some tips. I followed in his footsteps and continued his work. The camp doctor first brought me his watch, and the glass was broken. I thought: "Oh my God, how am I going to fix it?" In the camp there was an automobile workshop and they got new glass. I then made a device with a flame whereby I was able to bend the glass. I sanded the bent piece of glass so that it fit perfectly into the watch casing. By then I was already well known. Once I repaired the watch of a doctor's assistant, and then at night she helped me onto my feet. And I thought: "What's going on here?" She had half a bottle of Crimean wine hidden under her work coat. Red wine from the Crimea. Nobody was allowed to see it or know about it. And I enjoyed it by the spoonful. By the spoonful. And I repaired the watches of staff members, and word got around up to the commander. One day I was officially designated as the watchmaker in the camp. I needn't work. I had my own room where I could repair watches, and sometimes I had twenty or thirty watches to repair. If they had three watches that didn't work, I could turn them into one watch that worked properly. And then I went to the wood shop and had a clock mounted on a pole. It didn't take very long before the watchmaker came to the camp commander with a delegation and complained that he didn't have any work anymore. He said that I had taken work away from him. But I still got watches to work on, and it was a good business. I didn't care how much the other watchmaker made. In the end, I had the most money in the camp.

When 1949 arrived, I had already bought cigarettes with the money. The Russians set up a table in the camp. At the end of the table there was a Russian officer who called our names. We had to place all our things on the table, and they examined whether these things were okay or not. And things were confiscated such as knives. I found an old potato sack and put my cigarettes inside. The Russians said that you could recognize the cultivation of a person based on the length of his cigarette holder. And we hadn't any holders on our cigarettes. And, therefore, we didn't have any culture. I placed my potato sack with the cigarettes onto the table, and he looked at it and said: "You, speculator. You, speculator. You want to make money?" But he let me go. These weren't criminal activities. And I managed to make it through with my potato sack filled with cigarettes all the way home.

Friedrich Jansen was born in Leverkusen in 1927. At the age of 18 he was taken prisoner near Küstrin and transported to a series of military hospitals and prisoner-of-war-camps including Yelets and Tula. After two and a half years as a prisoner of war, he was released and returned to Germany in 1948.

Where was your first prison-of-war camp?

It was near Küstrin in a place called Neudamm [Dębno]. There were row houses that were empty, and the inhabitants had all fled. In these row houses, there was a makeshift but still relatively intact military hospital (a prisoner-of-war hospital later). There were also German doctors and the food was quite good, and we were also treated well. We hardly noticed that we were prisoners at all. We barely saw any Russians. Well, I was there until I had regained some of my strength and from there was transported to Poland, namely to Posen. There was also a large prisoner hospital in that place, and I was admitted to it and it was a bit harsher. The food was worse, the guards were a bit rougher, and occasionally someone was shot if he got too close to the fence. At some point, I recovered and was sent to a work detachment on an estate near Poznan, which used to be owned or administered by an important Nazi and which housed a Russian city administrator of the city of Poznan during my imprisonment. Due to the events of the war, all the agricultural work that was supposed to be done at that time was left undone, and we were put to work, for example, chopping weeds that were a metre high.

As forced labourers?

Yes, exactly, as forced labourers, but in itself still relatively free. For example, I was later appointed stable commander. So, I had the task of keeping the stables in order and grooming the horses, feeding them, and harnessing them in the morning. You didn't notice any supervision there either. I always had to get up early in the morning before everyone else, but when the horses were gone, I had the day to myself. Then I went swimming in the lake, which was all relatively nice.

Was that all still in March 1945?

No, that was in April and May 1945, or June I think, but I don't know exactly. Well, at some point the work on this estate came to an end, and we returned to the prisoner-of-war camp (no longer at this military hospital, but to a normal prisoner-of-war camp). I have relatively few memories of what everyday life was like there. But I do have one very bad memory ... I'll tell you about it. The whole camp was rounded up, assembled into companies, and then many soldiers were released, placed into cattle cars, and these cattle cars were attached to normal Polish trains and then sent to Frankfurt on the Oder. In the camp itself, the camp orchestra (there was such a thing) played upbeat melodies.[7] And one company after the other went in the direction of the train station. At some point, they packed up their musical instruments and left. A Russian crew suddenly came by and frisked us roughly. We also went to the train station, not to go home, but to be transported to Russia. You have to imagine, so close to returning home, and then suddenly this disappointment.

And how was the selection made? Why were some people allowed to go to the West?

I still don't know to this day. I suppose it was all about what people looked like. I'll get to that. There were several levels of nutrition and malnutrition, and the people who were obviously not able to do heavy work were dismissed earlier at that time. This happened later in Russia in a similar way. Well, then we travelled in this cattle car for three or four weeks, and we were transported to Russia in that way. First to a camp in the city of Yelets where we were housed in a former academy or university. The roof was gone, and there was only a makeshift roof (with boards, etc.). We lived there, and this camp belonged to the Russian railway. So, we were also given orders that had something to do with the railway (emptying wagons, laying tracks, etc.). Yes, we were still relatively free there. We were allowed to leave the camp occasionally. We couldn't go anywhere anyway, and the Russians knew that.

Did the Russians have people who spoke German?

Very few. It would have been a very big exception.

So, they spoke to you in Russian?

Yes, practically in every camp there were one or more interpreters. These were mostly prisoners from the eastern part of Germany who had already had contact with Slavic languages and who then acted as interpreters. In the course of time, of course, we learned a few Russian words, so we were already able to communicate reasonably well. I then also taught myself Cyrillic writing. I can explain it to you briefly. In the camp, where I was a horse driver, I saw a map of Germany with Cyrillic writing. I knew what the cities were called in German and where they were located, so that I was able to learn Cyrillic writing in this way. Not completely, but well enough so that I can still decipher it today.

Let's get back to Yelets. Then we stayed there for about half a year. In terms of nutrition, the winter was already very hard, and many froze to death during that time. Out of the 900 prisoners from the first transport from Poznan, several hundred died in that first winter (I don't know the exact number). Yes, and then everything is blurred in my memory. I was in a total of four or five different camps. I spent most of the winter in a kind of military hospital because the health examination showed that I was undernourished.

The degree of malnutrition was usually determined by pulling down one's pants and the doctor grabbing one's rear end and feeling how much flesh was left. Then either class 1, 2, or 3 of malnutrition or dystrophy was diagnosed. I always managed to end up as a dystrophic patient in the military hospital over the winter. But then we were in the new camps, where we had to do road construction work. The road from Moscow to the Crimea was redone. It was a dirt road. The road was widened, ditches had to be dug out on the left and right, and then the road was asphalted. That was a terrible job when you had to break stones. It was very bad because you were weak, and then imagine you had a huge stone lying in front of you and you had to make gravel out of it with a hammer. That was pretty bad in the heat in a part of Russia with no shade. There was no food or drink. It was a very, very terrible time.

How many hours per day did you have to work?

Oh, I don't remember exactly. I think it would have been ten hours, and before that we had to walk 3 kilometres to the construction site and back again in the evenings. If we were lucky, we were driven by truck.

What did the rations look like?

The rations looked quite good on paper. A prisoner was entitled to hot food three times a day and 600 grams of bread. That sounds great, of course, but not if these three times a day with hot food consisted of hot water (there was hardly anything in it, no meat in any case) and 600 grams of Russian bread that was very heavy. I assume that the actual rations were sold by the Russian officers. They had nothing themselves.

You said you were in four different camps. Can you describe each of these camps?

Today, I can practically only give the names of the main ones. As I said, I was in Yelets, from there I came to Tula, from there we were transported further because it was a transit camp and from there I have practically only the names [phon.] Sergokov, Chern, and Termoskia, but I no longer know what happened in the individual camps. We sometimes lived in barracks, sometimes in tents, but that was more than half a century ago.

Heinz Poll was born in Keldenich near Cologne in 1923. He was taken prisoner of war in Romania in 1944 after having served on the Eastern Front and was held in the Russian camp Ulyanovsk on the Volga until his release in 1949.

We were transported from Galatz [Romania] towards the Ural Mountains in freight cars. We were crammed into one railway car with 110 men. Inside the railway car, a piece of board was set up so that you could do your bathroom business. It was scorching hot that summer; it was terrible. Every two days, we received a handful of dried potatoes and small, salty fish. Every few days the train would stop at a station with a water pump. One person from each railway car was let out with buckets, and when he returned, everyone eagerly rushed to get the water, so there was hardly anything left afterwards. We had to throw out people every day who had died of thirst.

Then we arrived in the camp, that is, in the city of Ulyanovsk on the Volga River. This was the birthplace of Lenin, and the people there hadn't experienced war at all. We were greeted with heavy stones and clubs, which was terrifying and horrible; it was a miracle that we survived at all. Then we were transported by truck to the camp on the other side, where we entered the camp through a factory building. In the evening, a truck came into the camp with loads of white cabbage, which was dumped, and the whole group of men surged towards this white cabbage. The next day we asked: "What's going on, we haven't had anything to eat today", and the answer was: "Yes, you got your food last night. Nothing more". That's how it was. In winter, we had to build our own bunks. We built three-level bunks with a flat surface on the top, middle, and bottom, where four men lay on both sides.

It was not uncommon when the winter came (yes, it was cold) that we had no blankets, nothing. One person warmed the other. It was agreed that whoever lay on the outside would stay there for a certain time, and then we switched the person in the middle to the outside, and so we constantly rotated. It was not unusual to see dead bodies lying next to you in the morning, those who had died during the night. Outside, there was a latrine, where the Russians had placed a large beam, and behind it was a trench, where you sat down to relieve yourself. And the bastards placed the beam too high, so that you had no contact to the ground at all, and whoever lost his balance, would then end up in the trench. It was disastrous.

I was not a specialist; there were others who were specialists. There was a work detachment that took the specialists to work in the city in factories. And I had to work in the summer with a pick and shovel because I wasn't a specialist, and in the winter, I worked with a hammer and chisel. I had to dig trenches for the big pipes leading to Samara, where there was a large plant. In any case, it was a difficult job. In winter, they did mason work and made concrete ceilings. A supervisor always came and checked the temperature, and then we had to push wheelbarrows with concrete up and down. It was backbreaking work. From November to February, practically three months, 1,400 of the 2,400 prisoners were 2 metres under the ground after the winter. It was catastrophic. Then came Christmas 1944: there was a primitive dining hall where the food was served. The prisoners put together a tree themselves with scrawny branches, and there was an Austrian who sang songs. I was really tough, but at this Christmas celebration, a colleague of mine came and said that fifty men had died again that night. That brought tears to my eyes for the first time in my life.

In all these five years, we were led to the work site and back with rifles aimed at us, like hardened criminals. That was a Mongolian unit. One day, as we were about to be led to work, a long line of prisoners arrived with a lot of noise and baggage, without being checked. Nobody had taken anything away from them. Those were the troops that had surrendered and were transported there. They were gathered outside the camp on a large meadow, and we were then led into the camp. Our lieutenant colonel in the camp was a Jew, the head of distributing the bread was a Jew, and the Jews had all the major positions there. When the "Bread-Jew" went to the bread factory to get bread, he always needed people, so I always volunteered. I always broke off the crust of the bread when loading it. Then the "Bread-Jew" said to me: "Comrade, make it snappy!" The crust of the bread always made me full: That's why I always volunteered.

That evening, when the surrendering troops arrived, I paid close attention to the food that was being prepared for them: It was a simple cabbage soup with nothing in it. When the food was being served, I volunteered. Then I said to them: "Listen, they'll take everything away from you and strip you naked." Suddenly, in the darkness, I stepped on something, bent over to pick it up, and I had a Wehrmacht wristwatch in my hand. Yes, later on, they had taken practically everything away from them. They were a distance away from us outside our camp and had to set up a new camp, and with this wristwatch I got lots of rations for myself. There was a guy from Cologne, Mattis, as we called him, who lived in Siegburger Street in Cologne Deutz, and was a former boxer. The guys from the Rhineland tended to stick together. Then I talked to Mattis. He was responsible for distributing the food. He had a large chart with the individual groups on it that were divided into companies. This was German militarism at its best. I told Mattis: "I have a new wristwatch, a Wehrmacht wristwatch, it's great and works perfectly. In return I get double rations". "Yes, fine, you'll get that." In the morning, I had already had my food, when he called out: "Hey! You haven't had your food yet", but I had already received it. That's how it went in the morning, at noon, and in the evening. That's how I kept my head above water, with the wristwatch. And then when clothing arrived, he always took care of me.

It then happened that we moved to the new camp, which had already been built, and which is recorded in books and by people who were there, for example, by a man who was the company commander and was to become a well-known man in the Ministry of Defence in Bonn before we returned home. People worked together in this way and handed out jobs among themselves: kitchen jobs, leadership jobs, and so on. In any case, a colleague of mine, who was with the city detachment, said to me: "Listen, Heinz, come along to the plant". We were building a new factory in which tanks were to be manufactured. "I need drills and can sell them here in the city." I said: "How should I do that?" My colleague replied: "I'll give you a crowbar, you lever them out and bring them to me." "Okay," I said. "Will I get something for it?" He replied: "Of course, I'll give you bread and tobacco". In any case, in the morning when we were led to the workplace, which was fenced in and had watchtowers and guards, I first ran into the production hall where the big machines were, the drills. Then I quickly removed some drills with the crowbar and took them with me. In the last winter of 1948 to 1949, an engineer came to us in the camp: "I'm looking for specialists in structural steel engineering". "Man", I thought to myself, "you've been too stupid up to now. Sign up as a specialist too". Then I volunteered and was taken there. We had a certain advantage that winter. The Russians had received instructions that we could go into the warm-up room without asking any questions. We could go in at any time.

The Russians were so sloppy when they built the foundations, the raw steel construction halls; one hole never fit on the other afterwards. You had to drill new holes with a hand drill. We could see the whole area from the steel structure on the top. It was very high up, and many people had already fallen down from there. They already had the safety belts, but some of us had fallen from that height. But we had an overview. At noon the Russians knocked on a piece of metal, which meant lunch break. The Russians then dropped everything and quickly hid their tools under the boards, and we saw that. Then we waited a short time and stole their saws and other tools. I had never taken anything from a person in my life, but as a prisoner of war I stole like a thief. In any case, we then hid these things again, and the Russian civilians were keen on such things. We said, for example (in Russian): "Saw?" "Yes, yes, yes." "Drill, how much?" "Bread." "I'll bring it tomorrow."

There was an officers' kitchen, and I went there with my friend for lunch. We met at the gate, and everything was strictly controlled. Before that, on the way there, I saw that the door was open to the room where the officers had brought their things. I said to my colleague: "Come, Leo, in here". It smelled so good, and behind the officers' room they had put the ready-made meals. There was such a tall pot filled with meatballs. I said: "Oh, Leo, it smells so good in here, we have to take a chance". There were storage rooms for potatoes and many other things. I said to him: "Come on, grab the pot of cabbage". That was in the winter, and we had these quilted trousers that we filled with meatballs. We emptied out the pot. Afterwards, we quickly left the pot where it was and rushed to the gate. The guards were standing there and wacked us on our behinds. Then we stowed all the meat behind our bunk beds. I said to my colleague: "Hey, get the food, you can have some of it", but we didn't say that we had the meatballs. Then we had to fall in for roll call for the guards. The NKVD guards came and apparently thieves had stolen these meatballs and were supposed to be reported. We were careful to stand in the back of the line, and nothing came of it. But we had the meatballs in our possession.

How was it decided that you were allowed to go home?

One day we were at work and all of a sudden in the morning we were told to round up everything and march off to the camp. We thought: "What's going on?" Then we were led into a large room, which was the dining hall. It was a primitive hall and there stood the lieutenant colonel, suddenly addressing the crowd as "comrades": "You can now go home. You are leaving tomorrow", he said. This was conveyed to us through an interpreter. "And if you feel like it, you can go anywhere you want today and do sightseeing", the lieutenant then said. Up to this point, we were under constant surveillance, and, for this reason, I told my colleagues that we would not take one step off the camp; otherwise, the Russian would beat us to death. The next morning, we had to line up, and the Russians separated some of the prisoners. The ones on the left were transported to Stalingrad. But this was only for half a year, then they also came home.

Back to our journey home: We travelled through Poland in the direction of home in freight cars with Russian guards, and I had a folding cigarette box, which had been made for me by a Russian. At the train stations, there were Poles who wanted to barter, and we wanted to get something to eat. So, I wanted to exchange my box with a Pole for a bit of food. So, I gave the box to the Pole and then he tried to run away. We then jumped out with a few men and caught him and blackened his eyes. And the Russians were very happy about it. They said in Russian: "Poles are dogs". He wanted to cheat us, this Pole.

Hans Nahr was born in Aschersleben in Saxony-Anhalt in 1918. He describes how he was taken prisoner of war in Belarus in 1945.

I jumped up and raised both my hands, and two soldiers, two Russians, approached. One of them was 17 or 18 years old, and they all stood in front of me with submachine guns. When they saw that I had no weapon, they didn't shoot. They asked me for my pocket watch and inspected the watch. Finally, they took the watch and quickly pulled down my pants to my knees. Now, this one young guy was supposed to take me to the nearest village. He had a submachine gun and hit me with the butt of it. Someone waved at him to stop. And then, suddenly, one of my fellow soldiers, the ration master, came over and said: "Why did you let him capture you?" I said: "Be quiet, man!" The young soldier didn't know what to do and shot at him, and he tried to shoot back. I hoped he would run away. So, I stood there with them and was relieved that I didn't have to shoot. I wouldn't have made it out alive.

We were then taken to the next village. Oh, there were vehicles and trucks everywhere, and the drivers lay slaughtered in their own blood. And then we continued with five or six men. Civilians came along, and suddenly, a horse-drawn carriage came directly towards me. I tried to ask what they intended to do with us. Two were wounded, and they gave them milk so that they had something to drink. Then they said we were supposed to be brought to the next village. I had to hand it to this young soldier on his own. Our men were all so stubborn, and some were from the punishment company. I rolled up my sleeves because it was so warm, and we reached the next location. In the next village, there was a commissar, and he didn't like that I had rolled up my sleeves. He came right up to me and laughed: "You German swine. How many comrades have you killed?" He spoke perfect German. I didn't say anything, and he slapped my face. I went flying. And the young soldier who was escorting me, I have to give him credit, said that this wasn't permitted. He believed that it was his job to hand me over. Then we continued until it was turning dark. There was a big slope, and it was full of soldiers and prisoners.

They threw away my badges and everything. We entered a large room, and we couldn't lie down anywhere, and we were kicked and pushed. During the night, I had to pee urgently. Oh, I thought, I need to go out. And as I went out the door, the guard caught me. I had a pair of wonderful Italian boots on that I had managed to acquire, and I had them on. Oh, when he saw the shoes. Oh. He said: "Take them off". I pretended to be stupid for a long time. Then he started hitting me. "Take them off!" He also had a pair of shoes. I asked him to give me his shoes. "No!" And then I lost my shoes. I thought: "That's the last thing I need!" And at night, everyone was brought out onto a large field, and it was terribly hot. Then we were counted. They beat us all night. That's the way it started. And they had an old shovel, a rusty thing, and they started digging. And I thought: "What are they doing?" If you didn't work, you couldn't drink. It was a brown liquid. I also got a sunburn. That's when it started. I took a handkerchief, tied four knots in it, and pulled it over my head. When I woke up the next morning, my handkerchief had also been stolen. That was gone, too. Then they said: "Everyone, go and get water for yourselves at the water pump". We went with them, and I pushed to make sure I could go. We went down to the Dnieper, which was the nearest big river. There was a dead horse in the water down there, where we were scooping the water.

We were there for two more days. It was scorching hot, and we were hoping for rain. Suddenly, they called out: "Everyone, fall in!" We had to march from that place to Borisov, which was 80 kilometres east of Minsk. Then we crisscrossed through Minsk. It was filmed for the German news, Wochenschau [Weekly Review], and broadcast. We walked to Borisov for two more days, and I was in pain. My feet were a mess. I thought: "What are they doing?" I couldn't walk anymore, and I had to go barefoot. There were sharp pieces of glass on the road, and everything was broken. I remember being on the march – it was miserable. There were people lying there, naked and bleeding, with various injuries. And I had a stroke of bad luck, too. There were people in front of me, and, on the other side, the Russian supply troops were coming. They were all drunk on the vehicles and intentionally drove into the prisoners in front of us. They were all killed. They simply killed them and laughed while doing it.

My hand was injured and hung at my side. I didn't know if it was broken, but I couldn't move it for a long time. I thought, "You really have bad luck". We lay there all together without blankets. The next morning, we continued walking. The man next to me said: "You can't go on any further". He told me: "You know what we should do? We should just fall to the ground". Someone else overheard this and said: "Hey, don't be foolish. I've been observing this. I can't go on, either. Anyone who can't go on will get shot. They'll just shoot you. You won't make it this way".

Then I did something you wouldn't normally do. A soldier went past me, also barefoot, holding a pair of shoes in his hand. They were small shoes, two sizes smaller than mine. I said to him: "Why are you stealing my shoes?" He said: "Can't you see? They are too small and won't fit you". I said: "Those are mine. Hand them over". I hit him as hard as I could. He had the shoes in his hand when the guard intervened. The guard hit him because he thought he was trying to take my shoes. That was my lucky break! I took the shoes from him. I thought: "This is my salvation". I took them and ran. I couldn't walk well in them because they hurt. They had taken everything from us, and we didn't have a knife or a pair of scissors. I thought: "I have to cut a hole in them so that I can at least stand on the soles". Then I found someone who still had a razor blade. I told him that I had found the shoes and had to cut them to make them fit. I was so happy that I could stand again, but I couldn't walk well.

Endnotes

Chapter I: The Eastern Front

1. The Nazis held annual Reich Party Rallies from 1933 to 1938 in which they reinforced party support and made a showcase of National Socialism. Leni Riefenstahl captured the atmosphere of the Reich Party Rally from 1934 in her film *Triumph of the Will* which was heavily criticised after the war.
2. The Molotov-Ribbentrop Pact, also known as the Nazi-Soviet Pact, was a non-aggression treaty signed between Nazi Germany and the Soviet Union on 23 August 1939, just before the outbreak of World War II. Bessarabia was occupied by the Soviet Union as the result of this Pact.
3. Bessarabia historically refers to a region that includes parts of present-day Moldova and Ukraine. The Prut River forms part of the border between Moldova and Ukraine.
4. Crimea Shield: This badge was awarded to German military personnel who fought in the Crimean region. It was instituted on 25 July 1942. To be eligible, soldiers had to have participated in the battles for the Crimea region for a specific period. The badge featured an image of the Crimean Peninsula with a swastika in the centre.
5. Field Marshal Ferdinand Schörner was head of the Army Group South and later Army Group North in 1944. While commanding the Army Group Centre in 1945, he was captured by Soviet forces and released ten years later. He was said to be Hitler's favourite general.
6. The Russian Army used the Dukla Pass from 1944–45 to cross the Carpathian Mountains from Poland to Slovakia on their way to Hungary.

7. The Battle of the Seelow Heights marked one of the last assaults by the Red Army in World War II, fought over three days, from 16–19 April 1945. It was followed by the Battle of the Oder-Neisse which was the opening phase of the Battle of Berlin.
8. The "Hetzer" or "tank hunter" was a fast light-weight tank manufactured by Skoda in Czechoslovakia and introduced to the Eastern Front in 1944.

Chapter II: The Navy

1. Captain Hans Langsdorff is a controversial figure in German naval history for having scuttled his own ship and having taken his own life three days later.
2. The *Atlantis* initially pretended to be the Soviet vessel *Crimea* by flying the Soviet naval flag and displaying a hammer and sickle on the bridge. After crossing the equator in April 1940, it assumed the identity of the Japanese vessel *Kasii Maru*. The *Atlantis* was capable of taking on twenty-six different appearances.
3. General Andrey Andreyevich Vlasov played a notable role in the defence of Kiev against the Germans in 1941. However, he was eventually captured by the Germans in 1942. While in German captivity, the Nazis allowed him to form the "Committee for the Liberation of the Russian Peoples" in 1944, with the objective of overthrowing Joseph Stalin and establishing a collaborationist government.
4. Erich Raeder was promoted to the position of Grand Admiral by Hitler in 1939. Later that year, he suggested "Operation Weserübung" [Operation Weser Manoeuvre] in order to secure docks in Denmark and Norway and to provide access to the North Sea. He resigned in 1943 after a series of failed operations.
5. Karl Dönitz served as commander-in-chief of the German Navy from 1943 to 1945. In his last testament, Hitler designated Dönitz as his successor as head of state. On 7 May 1945, Dönitz authorized the surrender of all German forces to the Allies.

Chapter III: Western and Southern Campaigns

1. The Moresnet Viaduct, constructed in 1915, is the longest metal railway structure in Europe, providing passage from southern Germany to Antwerp. It was partly destroyed by resistance fighters in May 1940 to slow down the advance of the German Army. The bridge was rebuilt by German forces in December 1940, but later destroyed by them during their retreat from Allied forces in September 1944.

Chapter IV: The Fall of the Reich

1. Karl Friedrich Goerdeler was mayor of Leipzig from 1930 until 1937 when the Nazis forced him to leave office. Shortly afterward he began his involvement in the resistance movement and established ties with Western Allies. After the failed assassination attempt on Hitler on 20 July 1944, Goerdeler went into hiding and was arrested in Poland on 12 August 1944. He was hanged five months later.
2. The "People's Militia" [Volkssturm] was established during the final months of the war by the Nazi party on the orders of Adolf Hitler on 18 October 1944. It conscripted German males between the ages of 16 and 60 for the German Home Guard who were not already serving in the military.
3. Franz Ritter von Epp served as the Reichsstatthalter [Reich Governor] of Bavaria from 1933 to 1945. This position made him the highest-ranking official in the state of Bavaria under the Nazi government. Von Epp's role involved implementing Nazi policies in the region and maintaining control over the local government.
4. In April 1945, American and French troops were on the outskirts of Munich. The Freedom Action of Bavaria attempted to end the war by organising the immediate surrender to the Allies to avoid further bloodshed. Initiated by Rupprecht Gerngroß, the resistance movement took control of radio stations in Schwabing-Freimann and Erding on 28 April 1945 and called upon the general population to

overthrow the Nazi regime. The rebellion was brutally crushed and numerous freedom fighters were executed

5. Two of the Nazis' eight military prisons were located in Torgau: Fort Zinna and Brückenkopf. Torgau held prisoners who had been convicted by German military courts of having expressed anti-military spirit which included draft resistance, insubordination, desertion, and espionage. In 1943, the Reichskriegsgericht, Germany's supreme military tribunal, was relocated to the town of Torgau and issued nearly 1,400 death sentences, many of which were carried out in the Torgau prisons themselves.
6. In 1936, the "Gestapo" [Secret State Police] was merged with the "Kriminalpolizei" [Criminal Police] under the umbrella of a new organization, the "Sicherheitspolizei" [Security Police].
7. The Slovak National Uprising began on 29 August 1944, aiming to liberate the country from Nazi control. The plans for the revolt rested on the hope that Russian forces would soon cross the border and involve the Germans in a battle on two fronts. After crushing the partisan Slovak forces, the Nazis rounded up approximately 13,000 Jews for deportation to Auschwitz and Theresienstadt.

Chapter V: Allied Prisoner-of-War Camps

1. Camp Algona was located in northern Iowa and held more than 10,000 German prisoners between April 1944 and February 1946. The first prisoners were captured in the North Africa campaign, with many more arriving as the result of the Normandy invasion.
2. Paul Brägelmann. Auf den Rheinwiesen 1945: 101 Tage Kriegsgefangenschaft. Günther Runge; Cloppenburg, 1992.
3. The C-ration was issued to American troops during World War II and consisted of individually canned, pre-cooked food. It was used when A-ration [fresh, unprepared food] or B-ration [mess hall or field-kitchen food] was not available.
4. This song was popular during World War II with both the Axis and Allied soldiers. It quickly became a hit on Radio Belgrade following the Nazi invasion of Yugoslavia in 1941 and was heard by German soldiers throughout the Mediterranean and North Africa. Propaganda

Minister Joseph Goebbels attempted to ban this song, originally performed by Lale Anderson, but Radio Belgrade received so many letters from German soldiers that Goebbels reluctantly changed his mind. Marlene Dietrich later recorded a rendition of the song in 1944 to lift the morale of American troops.

5. The Holy Roman Empire of the German Nation.
6. The NKVD [People's Commissariat for Internal Affairs] was a law enforcement agency of the Soviet Union under the leadership of the Communist party which was often used during World War II to prevent Russian soldiers from deserting from the Front in battles such as Stalingrad and the Crimea.
7. A camp orchestra played music in prisoner-of-war or concentration camps to provide a moment of pleasure or a flight from reality in spite of the horrific conditions.

Index